BEST
BEHAVIOUR

BEST
BEHAVIOUR

Empowering managers and
HR leaders to coach and
align employee behaviours
to supercharge growth

TONY HOLMWOOD

ABOUT THE AUTHOR

Tony is passionate about human behaviour and development. A commercially focused chartered accountant with substantial business performance experience in large global organisations, his recent career has provided deep insights into business transformation and change management. He is also a qualified motivational, behavioural and emotional practitioner with the solid understanding that people drive business, and without people there is no profit.

A lifetime of coming to terms with and overcoming his own social anxiety disorder has provided Tony with a unique appreciation of behaviour. His methods are uncomplicated and intuitive, with the objective of reducing organisational complexity so strategy can evolve and adjust to community needs and market forces. Compliance and strategy need to be in balance. A culture of reactively fighting fires may mask a proactive search for solutions. This is the power of Tony's Balanced Behavioural Development Model (BBDM) when all employees are aligned and directed for purpose, and balance is managed.

The BBDM was developed in response to a perceived injustice following Tony's involvement with an HR insourcing start-up some 15 years ago, where he witnessed first-hand how employee development was being devalued in many sectors through HR outsourcing, and how HR professionals were largely relegated to a compliance role.

Today, when human potential is again being realised, with market leaders such as Apple, Google and Netflix showing the way, the BBDM presents a credible solution.

Having undertaken successful change and business transformation programs for Fonterra, Oracle, Downer and the Victorian Government, Tony has developed an appreciation for strategy that enables HR departments, managers and leaders to lead proactive, forward-focused organisations. Wisdom may not feature in productivity calculations, but it does count in strategy and innovation.

Tony's wealth of experience and significant professional success underpin his belief that emotional intelligence (Ei) in leaders and managers is a strong indicator of success because they enable a big-picture, future-directed cultural competence. Ei accounts for nearly 90 per cent of what moves people up the ladder when IQ and technical skills are roughly similar.[1] The symmetry of the BBDM also supports this. Intellectual, emotional and cultural development expand at similar rates when all behaviours are aligned.

For you courage & compassion

Tony Holmwood

(168/200)

---

1   'What Makes a Leader?', Daniel Goleman, *Harvard Business Review*, January 2004.

ACKNOWLEDGEMENTS

I find myself writing this one week after the Christchurch mosque shootings, and my heart goes out to the victims' families and to my fellow countrymen, knowing the spirit of a nation has been rocked to its core by a senseless act. Humanitarian compassion, kindness and love will always prevail over hate.

Hate comes from unresolved childhood insecurities. As agents in life, we fail to appreciate life's bountiful pleasures and rewards if we seek to blame others for our failings and shortcomings. Our environment can guide and make us aware, but in the end, it's our decision and personal responsibility to develop and challenge ourselves to grow. I do feel we are at a turning point, and I do know we are finally becoming an enlightened species. I have huge faith in humanity and know that love and commonsense will prevail.

Through such tragedy, we have been witness to the kind, compassionate, secure characteristics of Jacinda Ardern, a true cultural leader and a rare find in this day. We must support these leadership characteristics and such people who can secure our futures and express hope. My hope is Jacinda will give courage and pave the way for other cultural leaders who shy away from the adversarial nature of our outdated political systems and bureaucratic institutions. I hope this book encourages the true leaders of this world who are inspired to follow her example and influence positive change.

In memory of my grandmother, who through her actions and compassion taught me about cultural leadership and guardianship. Her life and work ethic expressed her voracious energy and strength dedicated to sustaining and promoting life's bounty. Not a sociable or religious person, her deep-felt connection was with life's beauty and all its sensory pleasures.

To my birth mother and adopted mother who both went through significant hardship to bring me into this world and to raise me. I really value our relationships and cherish our time together.

And to the rest of my family and friends who have persisted with me over a period of 15 years, the time it took to conceptualise and reason my findings and to bring this book to fruition.

I also thank my editor Michael Hanrahan who has done a stellar job in representing my deep understanding and compassion.

First published in 2019 by Tony Holmwood

A catalogue entry for this book is available from the National Library of Australia.

ISBN: 978-1-925648-98-0

Printed in Australia by McPherson's Printing Group
Project management and text design by Michael Hanrahan Publishing
Cover design by Simone Frances Geary and Peter Reardon

The Myers & Briggs Foundation, Myers-Briggs Type Indicator, Myers-Briggs, MBTI, and the MBTI logo are trademarks or registered trademarks of The Myers & Briggs Foundation in the United States and other countries.

The paper this book is printed on is certified as environmentally friendly.

Disclaimer
The material in this publication is of the nature of general comment only, and does not represent professional advice. It is not intended to provide specific guidance for particular circumstances and it should not be relied on as the basis for any decision to take action or not take action on any matter which it covers. Readers should obtain professional advice where appropriate, before making any such decision. To the maximum extent permitted by law, the author and publisher disclaim all responsibility and liability to any person, arising directly or indirectly from any person taking or not taking action based on the information in this publication.

CONTENTS

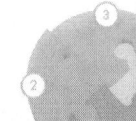

Contents

PREFACE

As a **human resources (HR) professional**, are you struggling under the burden of regulatory compliance with only limited time, resources and support to influence your organisation's profitability?

As a **manager**, are you finding it difficult to keep your employees motivated and engaged? Do you feel the need to help them realise a better quality of life without necessarily knowing where to start? Would you rather be developing employee potential to increase strategic value and innovation?

As a **leader,** would you like to be respected for your strength of character, resilience, strategic awareness, empowerment of others, strong sense of purpose and your contribution? Would you like to inspire others to grow and fulfil their dreams, to make a difference, and experience improved wellbeing, connection, and longevity?

Imagine your workplace in a future where every employee has complete clarity about their development objectives and is stimulated to grow, knowing how the organisation's goals positively influence future security and community. *Best Behaviour* presents a strategy that will change the face of HR and managers by elevating their profile to a transformational coaching capability. It puts the HR professional back in the primary role of a trusted, independent confidant whom employees respect and are willing to engage with as they aspire to grow, rather than just being an administrative or compliance functionary who manages staff issues. The greater critical reasoning and Ei skills outlined in this book will help HR leaders and managers achieve this.

THE BALANCED BEHAVIOURAL DEVELOPMENT MODEL

The Balanced Behavioural Development Model (BBDM) outlined in this book is completely balanced and symmetrical, and therefore provides a mathematical basis to behavioural learning. This framework can be used by HR and managers to positively change people's lives with targeted employee development, to rapidly transform a business's culture and supercharge growth.

Starting with the individual …

Knowing how change, growth and leadership start with the individual, this book works from the inside out, and also provides strategies for HR professionals and managers to become transformational coaches, to exhibit and engender trust, and to inspire employees. To know yourself inside-out is to know who you are unequivocally. The power of knowing yourself is to understand how to purposely change behaviours and rewire your capability. From an independent, secure, holistic view of the world, the confident leader can firmly place themselves at the core of every experience and respond authentically and automatically. Your perception is fully evolved when driven by opportunity, not inhibitions or limitations.

It can take a lifetime to achieve this adult perspective. This enables a 'one-to-many' perspective where the self-aware leader can operate at the centre of every interaction.

… to transform the business

This book also represents a business transformation approach that will supercharge business performance. Some of the content around protectionist 'boss' styles of governance (command–control) and the need to develop self-awareness is confronting, but necessary in an age where human potential, behaviours and imbalance are often neither recognised nor respected.

The book includes a number of firsts, including:

- introducing a method where all behaviours can be learnt for a fully adaptive, cultural competence

- establishing the importance of identity and intuition in human development, allowing a spontaneous, multidimensional intellect

- representing how experiences, actions, associations and a lifetime of learning support leadership spatial awareness and a strategic, big-picture capability to leverage executive functions.

When our environment is not constrained by limitations and problems, our world becomes more about opportunity and we can better focus on delivering solutions. Our focus switches from selfish endeavours to manage our esteem to unselfish objectives for the betterment of the collective.

Self-assurance and cooperation are essential for constructing effective strategy. At this level of developmental maturity we recognise the sum of the parts is more powerful than individual contributions. HR are well placed to identify these opposing traits in leaders and to direct them purposefully to ensure leaders are working strategically and to the benefit of the company.

THE PAST	OUR FUTURE
My pay cheque	My purpose
My satisfaction	My development
My boss	My coach
My annual review	My ongoing conversations
My weaknesses	My strengths
My job	My life

How millennials want to work and live[2]

---

2   Gallup, Inc. Research, 2016.

My objective with *Best Behaviour* is to encourage professional development and help HR executives regain their authority, to elevate them to transformational coaching and leadership roles. This book sets out a framework for HR professionals to identify incompatible or ineffective leadership attributes so people can be coached and their skills enhanced. The performance benefits will be substantial when behaviours are aligned purposefully and proactively.

With this book, I'm hoping my actions will dawn a new era of collaboration and cooperation. Too often, our industrial-age bureaucratic systems can promote the most insecure, transactional 'boss' styles fixated on competition, problems, regulations and control to limit growth. Here in Australia, we still have leaders who are climate deniers. Their refusal to acknowledge science and the mounting environmental impacts displays limited awareness and only promotes insecurity. The reasons for their narrow perspectives are laid bare in this book. One of our biggest challenges in life is to overcome our insecurities. Our insecurities influence our work choices, which help us to balance them. Many employees have yet to feel this level of security. Secure, collaborative leadership styles that can express hope, visions and strategy are a requirement for transformational change.

This book is structured so chapters can be read as standalones and to reinforce the concepts. Some parts are exploratory and not a quick read, and you may have to return to chapters or sections to fully connect the concepts.

MY DIFFICULT JOURNEY

During my youth and well into my professional career I struggled with social anxiety disorder, the fear of interacting, assuming other people thought I was boring, inept or timid. I strongly disliked who I was. My long journey to self-discovery has provided valuable insights into behaviour and emotions and how they influence every aspect of our development. I'm passionate about learning and development, knowing how it transformed my life.

In over 30 years working for major companies in business performance and change projects, I have seen the best and the worst of corporate cultures. **I have come to appreciate how leadership behaviour influences a proactive or reactive culture**, and this will usually significantly impact business results. The major factor inhibiting employee change and growth is the failure of leaders and managers to exhibit trust, inspiration and purposeful objectives. This book sets out an emotional development program focused on positively transforming people's lives, one individual at a time. Leaders and managers equipped with this Ei are more effective at implementing visionary strategy and motivating employees to change and grow accordingly, resulting in huge benefits for the business.

The importance – and opportunity – of HR

By respecting the essential role HR plays in developing employee potential, I came to believe there needs to be a balance between HR compliance and employee development to realise growth opportunities. I also recognised the past damage the big accounting firms inflicted on the HR profession with the wholesale outsourcing of HR capability in some sectors purely for profit. Many HR professionals were relegated to an employee watchdog role, which reduced their authority and was also a massive wasted opportunity. A flow on from this was employees became disillusioned with HR as their personal development took a back seat.

Realisation of this wasted potential drove me to conceive the Balanced Behavioural Development Model, which is about defining and promoting HR functions and behaviours in organisations. HR are assigned relationship roles where personal one-to-one attention is preferred, such as:

- learning and development
- coaching
- innovation
- planning
- aligning roles to capability
- Ei
- social engagement, and
- change.

These social qualities are underappreciated today, especially in government. Government needs to act as a social development or HR department to its citizens.

The BBDM framework also provides an optimal pathway to develop all behaviours, both from a personal perspective and organisation perspective. The framework works for both. Opposing behaviours are aligned in a way that is both balanced and mathematically symmetrical, to remove complexity and provide a pathway for continual growth. Some understanding of the Myers–Briggs personality types (MBTi – chapter 12) is important to understanding this symmetry.

A competent leader can draw on all behaviours to unlock the full capability of the mind for a powerful, inside-out, past–present–future, 360-degree awareness of the world. They can maximise their executive functions to realise opportunities and execute strategic visions. It just takes the right environment to develop this capability, which then provides substantially more than a base unit of labour. Command–control or 'boss' styles use a limited set of learnt behaviours, and will typically inadvertently limit growth by focusing on problems and compliance rather than solutions and opportunities.

SO, WHAT'S IN THIS BOOK?

This book is about professional development – change, growth and leadership start with the individual – and people strategies, and I make hypothetical arguments and assumptions about behaviour and prove them. As well as life experience, research is added to support arguments with the premise that healthy, well-adjusted people are being targeted. This book is as much about bad behaviour as it is good. The mind is perfectly balanced to recognise both. Positive growth approaches are offered, while negative content is added to support arguments where necessary.

I make some bold statements on the future of people strategy and human development, and predict that organisations that adopt the Balanced Behavioural Development Model will prosper in the future as employees seek greater meaning from their employers. These employers will grow to appreciate the importance of community, cultural identity, emotional development, diversity, sustainability, and how humanitarian causes and representing secure pathways are essential to employee wellbeing and performance.

Many of my theories are provocative. As a strategist, I make some overarching, big, bold statements. Academic and research communities are invited to prove or challenge the observations and theories put forward. This is pure strategy, and will be of tremendous value to a world obsessed with searching for obscure remedies to behavioural imbalances. These constructive arguments are vital. Too many people are not developing awareness, are dependent, and can be too easily taken advantage of.

Appreciation of big-picture future awareness is fully dependent on how much we empathise and engage with all aspects of life. The humanitarian brain must be respected before self-awareness for emotional and social intelligence can flourish. To establish a cultural competence we must respect our custodian duty to sustain, diversify and secure our environment.

This book is also about self-awareness, and indicates the depth of understanding required to question who you are so as to develop the multidimensional, transcendent capability of our right brain hemisphere. It may be a difficult read for some, but the questions raised must be addressed for people to progress. Everybody needs to analyse these arguments, especially those concerning identity. Behaviour plays an essential role in defining who we are.

Twenty-five per cent of the proceeds from this book will be used to promote the following strategic objectives:

1   To raise funding and promote community development projects and research studies to allow children the freedom to safely roam, experience, associate and identify in their communities.

2   To design emotional and social development programs, which will be offered free to high schools to help adolescents to raise awareness, mature, discover their independence and make their own decisions.

3   To lobby governments on the crucial need to offer emotional development programs that educate and protect their citizens

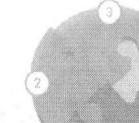

when they are most vulnerable to external influences. These programs need to be accredited to reputable coaching organisations.

4   To lobby governments for change in constitutions and parliamentary systems for a balance of all behaviours in a constructive and non-adversarial environment so that people can be adults, and hope and future security can be represented more readily.

My hope is that humanity be allowed the freedom to expand and secure our environment. We all need to collaborate to achieve this aim. The rewards will be substantial.

PART I

UNDERSTANDING THE BALANCED BEHAVIOURAL DEVELOPMENT MODEL

1. Introducing the Balanced Behavioural Development Model

Up to now, little respect has been demonstrated in business for how the environment defines us or how the simple laws of nature have given humanity the powerful ability to create and diversify life through husbandry and science. On Earth, and indeed in business, life creates and sustains opportunity. Leaders need to appreciate this.

This is essentially a professional development book to enable leadership capabilities, and to encourage human resource (HR) professionals to appreciate and capitalise on their powerful role. I present an evolutionary model for behavioural development – conceived when I worked in an HR insourcing start-up – to protect divergent capabilities in organisations. (Targeted small-to-medium businesses seldom had their own HR presence.)

The Balanced Behavioural Development Model is based on mathematical symmetry and brings together behavioural research dating back to Sigmund Freud. Freud's school of thought emphasised the influence of the unconscious mind. The power of the unconscious mind is our awareness and our growing ability to process an increasing array of environmental data. Our conscious mind only employs a fraction of our capacity at any given time. Unconscious biases and living in our comfort zones can limit what we associate and process.[3]

---

3   'Unbiasing', re:Work, https://rework.withgoogle.com/subjects/unbiasing/

THE ORIGIN OF THE BALANCED BEHAVIOURAL DEVELOPMENT MODEL

My design of the BBDM is an innovative response to a deeply felt problem. In 2002, I resigned as Finance Director of a software company, disillusioned with its toxic culture driven top-down by the founder who had reasserted control after stepping out of the business for a period. The resultant authoritarian, reactive culture drained my energy. I had managed Sales Planning and Compensation for Asia Pacific during a time when the visionary Chief Operating Officer led the company. I was responsible for sales strategy and targeting incentives to drive sales, and we consistently met our revenue growth targets of around 35 to 40 per cent per annum across the Asia-Pacific region.

Compensation schemes were generous, but did not always promote the desired behaviours from the sales teams. We experimented with team-based bonus schemes and management by objectives, but almost always settled for individual commission-based incentives. It was a constant battle to meet sales targets and to rein in the egos of high-flying sales executives.

I came to appreciate how promoting the right behaviours – including through compensation – supported strategy in organisations, and how toxic environments grew out of authoritarian control where egotism and selfish intentions prevailed. These are learnings most well-healed professionals would accept, and many are coming to terms with how reactive, toxic cultures do not prevail in the longer term.

It wasn't all bad though. The major benefit of working in a large international company was the exceptional cross-cultural experience and professional development offered. In the Asia-Pacific region, a great HR team ensured personal and management development were at the core of development programs, and in those six years I learned to know myself and to understand the positive influence that professional development had on my work performance.

I decided to turn my back on corporate life and – with my lifetime of knowledge and experience – pursue a business start-up in HR insourcing, aimed at leveraging HR development, incentives and processes into small to medium businesses. The concept of introducing the benefits of HR to businesses that could not afford a full HR department was innovative when HR outsourcing was only just gaining traction. I understood how employee development underscored strategic success, and that this would allow small to medium businesses to take on major rivals by offering employees industry-leading HR development, incentives and processes.

The HR solution was to be best practice and industry-aligned to increase effectiveness, with industry-leading processes to automate transactions, and with a targeted industry-knowledge base for employee skills and knowledge development.

HR outsourcing in the US was initially dominated by the big accounting firms. I felt these firms were driven purely by the numbers, with no wish to promote or develop employee potential, which can greatly boost profits. By outsourcing HR transactions and much of their capability, many organisations chose to either eliminate an HR presence or reduce it to a decentralised HR business partner role. Many HR professionals took a back seat, reduced to simply enforcing regulatory compliance and management policy. The wholesale outsourcing of HR in certain sectors meant HR lost its independence, strategic responsibility and power. It also lost the trust of employees and became largely ineffective. Staff had no sense of what HR stood for – or at least the message was mixed.

How governance and compliance became the new norm

To help build the business, I joined the Australian Human Resources Institute (AHRI), which was unwilling to take on the accounting firms. In 1999, following financial difficulties, AHRI was purchased by Deakin University and lost its professional independence and authority. At one conference I attended, there was little awareness of the need to protect the profession from accounting firms and respond with an alternative strategy. The automation of transactions meant many HR transactional processes were an easy target for accounting firms, which effectively took ownership or outsourced many HR processes and responsibilities. This pushed HR professionals to focus on compliance, as strategic development took a back seat. Even company boards

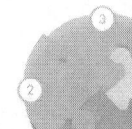

became dominated by accountants and lawyers, while the creative professions of Marketing, Communications, Human Resources and Innovation were noticeably absent.

As I explain in this book, to run an effective HR strategy you need a deep understanding and control of every aspect of employee performance and development programs, as well as payroll, compliance and employee incentives. Throughout this book, I build a case for HR professionals to learn a holistic set of capabilities for a leadership competence. By selectively outsourcing HR capability, the levers and tools to build a comprehensive, integrated, end-to-end employee development strategy can be disrupted. Employees can learn any number of skills, and – for those wanting to progress into management and leadership roles – exposure across the organisation is important. With outsourced functions, a complete capability profile may be difficult to obtain.

This potential must be retained within the organisation, developed, and made accountable and strategically aligned. If an organisation respects any intrinsic capability so little as to outsource it then it fails to understand how capability supports strategic growth and how the sum of its parts can vastly exceed individual input. In addition, capability development is a gradual process when part of a longer-term strategy, which goes to the very core of how organisations treat capability. If capability is valued as a productive unit of measure then you will probably only appreciate incremental returns from your employees. To apply visionary strategy is to invest in the longer-term capability.

EFFECTIVE STRATEGY REQUIRES LOCAL MEANING

For a strategy to be effective, both strategy and culture should have local meaning and be tied to the local community. For employees, meaning seldom extends beyond the community they live in, where they learn their skills and seek out a new niche. What incentive does the outsourced subsidiary have to increase capability and deliver on strategy when the message is purely cost savings? How does a graduate program work effectively if some of the key capabilities have been sent offshore? Graduates need to develop left-brain preferences to build up their self-confidence. These are best learnt on the job, appreciating cause-and-effect relationships and critical problem-solving. The left-brain programming of skills and memory function ultimately supports the strategic right-brain application of social engagement and creative attributes: reasoning, independent thought and self-awareness. This underappreciation is having an adverse impact on our millennial generation. Many of their career options have been outsourced or are being replaced by artificial intelligence (AI), roles so important to building a strong identity.

MANAGERS AND HR CAN BE VITAL IN DEVELOPING CAPABILITY TO ACHIEVE STRATEGIC INITIATIVES

I came to appreciate that managers with the support of HR are best placed to enable and be accountable for soft skills in organisations. Soft skills include the right-brained, one-to-one supportive attributes of emotional intelligence (Ei) to build resilience, strengthen self-awareness and leverage the power of relationships in support of strategy. This may not have been understood in the past because throughout its brief professional history HR has been effectively controlled, and lacked the independence, authority and trust needed for employees to respect the promotion of soft skills. Once HR is transformed into an emotionally intelligent strategic team, all the benefits of Ei are on display. Calm, positive, engaged, mature, selfless, energised coaches who understand an employee's aptitudes and will challenge them. Performance is optimised when employees are empowered to challenge their understanding and skillsets.

Effective communication, inclusion, openness, relationship management and social connection need to be at the core of implementing a visionary strategy. I found HR professionals generally lack an appreciation of their Ei responsibility and how to promote these characteristics within organisations. HR professionals have a good sense of their strategic development responsibility, without necessarily understanding their role in promoting emotional maturity for management development, including compassion, individual thought, creativity and networking employee growth with corporate strategy.

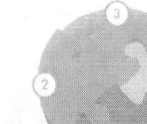

If I sensed that HR was being marginalised in Australia, what I witnessed in the United States completely floored me. The HR outsourcing conference I attended in New York was headlined by the accounting majors. I witnessed the wholesale outsourcing of corporate HR processes and capabilities by the accounting majors on a massive scale purely for profit. When I questioned the integrity and motives of some of the executives of the big firms, I was met with blank stares and evasive responses. They must have known there was real conflict in what they were doing. The common thread throughout these conferences appeared to be that HR was a cost that could be reduced.

On returning to Australia, I felt a strong ethical responsibility to show leadership, and to ensure that Ei attributes and development were both promoted and protected. Learning to overcome social anxiety disorder gave me a powerful sense of how important emotional development is to human capability and wellbeing.

What appeared obvious in relation to the general direction of the corporate world at the time was that emotional development and social capital were being sidelined by instant gratification and the never-ending short-term pursuit of increased productivity, profits and shareholder value. As a chartered accountant, I can say that these fundamentals were promoted by my profession as the main levers available to deliver growth. Innovation was a buzzword confused with incremental or continuous improvement. There was no sense of how real innovation could deliver superior profits to companies. Behaviours were little understood, and the need to promote and protect a diversity of capabilities and the attributes of Ei is only now starting to feature in professional accounting magazines.

INTRODUCING THE BBDM

My response to all of this was to create a framework that recognised the significance of which characteristics and capabilities each function promoted in an organisation, and what attributes each function could be responsible for developing.

1. Introducing the Balanced Behavioural Development Model

The model represents a very simple construct, coordinating functional responsibilities around two axes, providing a completely holistic perspective:

- Past to Future (Knowing to Doing) along the X axis
- Inside to Outside (Person to Collective) along the Y axis.

Whereas Sales and Service, and HR, are focused on the person (one), Systems, Operations and Administration, and Marketing and Public Relations (PR) are focused on the organisation or collective (many). Looking at the horizontal hemispheres, the Systems and Administration functions focus on present to past events while HR, Marketing and PR are more focused on the present to future events. The whole premise of defining organisational functions in this way was to represent the very different objectives of each quadrant and the divergent responsibilities of each role. To remove a functional responsibility was to leave a company exposed.

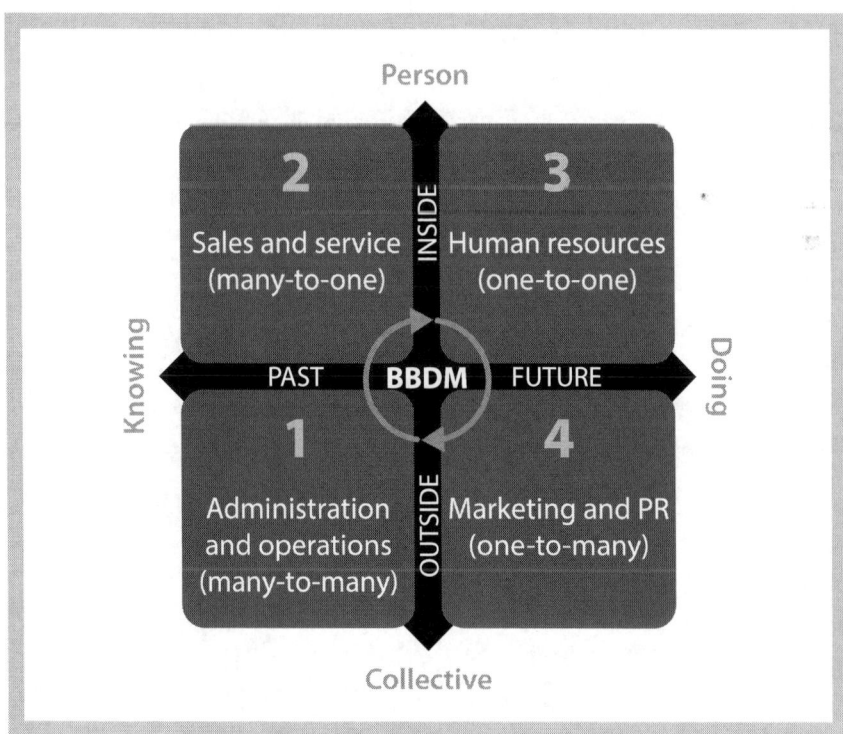

The BBDM: functional associations

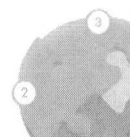

In the BBDM the organisation's functions are aligned based on parent–child relationship associations used in information technology (IT):

1   many-to-many

2   many-to-one

3   one-to-one

4   one-to-many.

These are used in both mathematics and IT to define data relationships and how data is organised. This also holds true for people, and their mastery of each of the four ways we associate data and events influences our functional preference at any given point in our development. At the most granular level, we process and recall data, actions, experiences and events through emotional associations. HR professionals tend to place themselves at the centre of their interactions and associate their understanding from a very personal, one-to-one aspect. Technical and Finance functions straddle the boxes on the left (many-to-many, many-to-one).

My mathematical and IT expertise played a big part in creating the framework, although the symmetry of opposites was also important to assign the functions to the boxes. The framework took about five minutes to outline on paper despite my getting stuck defining the many-to-one functional capabilities. However, when discussing them with a colleague, the Sales and Customer Service streams jumped out at me, as these functions are heavily dependent on internalised or personal knowledge, processes and skills (knowing). Any one employee can handle multiple customer interactions (many-to-one). Decision-making is best learnt in a team.

Unlike the opposing more macro, solutions-focused, one-to-many Marketing and PR capabilities, many-to-one interactions are specific and geared to defining personal problems. HR capabilities were missing in many organisations when I developed this model, and there was a need to promote one-to-one attributes and purposeful relationships to connect strategy and supercharge organisational growth. The HR functional characteristics of development assessments, coaching, change and innovation that involve critical reasoning are focused on personal attributes, and are best applied one-on-one.

At first I thought they were purely relationship-based, but over many years of developing this model I have come to realise they are far more than relationship associations: they represent how we connect with our world. I have spoken to hundreds of people to hone my understanding of how they associate themselves in their environment. Like Maslow's (chapter 19) simple test of happiness to show where people were positioned in his hierarchy, the test I use to position people is to ask them *to describe themselves.* **Many HR professionals would have used this statement in job interviews but few may realise the power of the statement.** Self-aware respondents who are centred with a strong sense of self will know themselves unequivocally. They may define themselves with personal attributes such as honest, truthful, driven, or being a community person – one-to-one or one-to-many. There is a maturity in the way they experience the world and they place themselves firmly at the centre of everything they do. They search for a deeper meaning in life's relationships and view the world from a personal bias, adding their values and personal interpretation to every interaction and personal story.

In the absence of self-awareness, people with an undeveloped identity who are purely externally focused will view the world at face value and describe how other people view them – hence the many-to-many, many-to-one identities. Many-to-one people who appear confident may be self-absorbed, always switching the conversation to their own perspective, but this may also indicate a need to self-reflect and mature. Recognising its essential contribution to behavioural development, our locus of control or how we identify in our environment is covered in the early chapters of this book.

What was very evident was the framework also represented a pathway to maturity – a development approach. I define these levels of association as:

1   Trainee (many-to-many)

2   Team member (many-to-one)

3   Manager (one-to-one)

4   Leader (one-to-many).

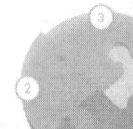

The functional attributes of Administration and Operations (Admin & Ops), Sales and Service, HR, and Marketing and PR then become development attributes available for every employee to learn; that is, a manager should be familiar with HR relationship capabilities. A well-developed leader would be across the future outward-focused Marketing and PR capabilities. Whether in HR or a management role, a left-brain capability to support right-brained capabilities needs to be developed for self-confidence.

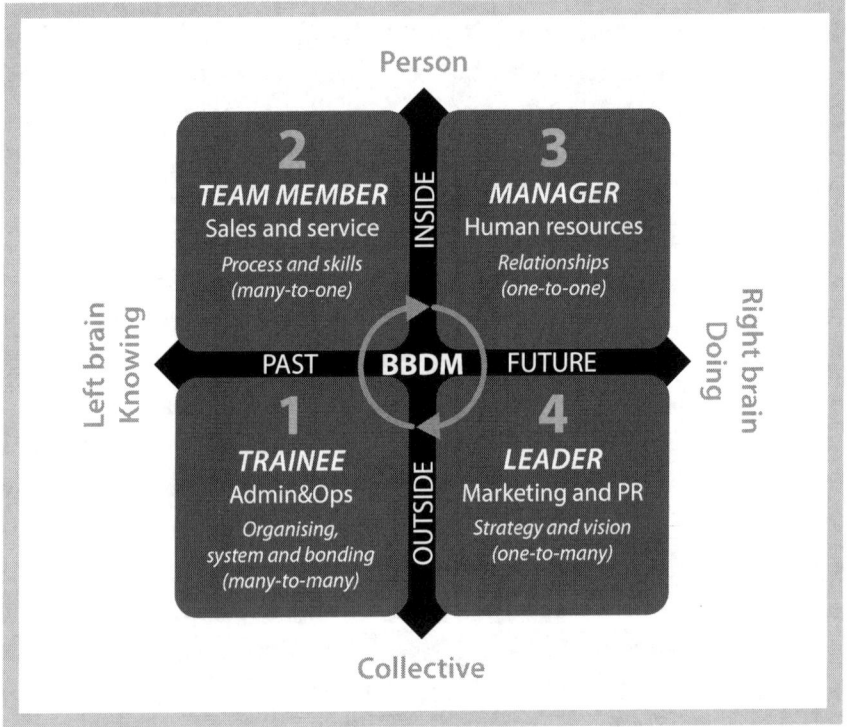

The BBDM as a development pathway

In the BBDM above, employees tend to find comfort in one of the functional quadrants dependent on their level of development. In later chapters I show how individuals can grow and improve their well-being through all quadrants. Inasmuch as development is a measured, gradual process, each step must be completed before moving on to the next. Financial accountants who may have broadened their skills and understanding in the second quadrant will only learn to apply those skills with deeper meaning by learning the managerial attributes of relationships in stage 3 and leadership skills in stage 4. When I say 'leadership skills', I mean employing the executive brain function for heightened perception to implement purposeful future-focused strategy, and a powerful radar to connect the strategic dots.

After setting out the framework, I concluded the divergent learnings of the left quadrants encourage self-confidence. New employees inducted into an organisation may have developed stage characteristics elsewhere, but when we join a new organisation that we must identify with and relate to, it's important to go back and learn the associations and particular ways of doing things. We must learn the culture by revisiting and re-asserting our relationships and emotional associations. Employees who don't have a good understanding of their left-hemisphere attributes and strengths may lack confidence.

DEFINING A HOLISTIC, INCLUSIVE FRAMEWORK OF BEHAVIOURAL ATTRIBUTES

It's important to note that the model represents a helicopter view of divergent development attributes. The beauty of the model is that every organisation can define the development characteristics around each quadrant to promote their own specific values and objectives. I purposely leave the classifications broad so HR representatives can workshop the required capabilities to determine their organisation's distinct characteristics and identify powerful community stories to support them. My main objective was to identify, align, develop and make accountable a broader suite of characteristics in any organisation or community, especially the undervalued behaviours supporting the right-hemisphere characteristics of HR, Marketing and PR.

An evolutionary pathway

In developing this model in later chapters, I show that stages 1 to 4 are in fact an evolutionary pathway available to everyone for developing a leadership capability. I demonstrate the model in several different

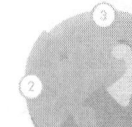

ways, including adding the Myers–Briggs 16 personality types (chapter 12) to define an optimal succession of behavioural development; Personality Profiling, to identify which stage people are at in their growth cycle; and aligning Kolb's Learning Cycle (chapter 26) to determine the most effective way to develop each quadrant.

To better comprehend the model, at a macro level the classifications of the BBDM's X and Y axes can be interchanged with any combination of the following associations:

X AXIS (LEFT TO RIGHT)	Y AXIS (TOP TO BOTTOM)
Past to (present to) future	Personal to collective
Knowing to doing	Individual to organisation
Left-brained to right-brained	Self to community
Reflective to big picture	Internal to external
Support to challenge	Inside to outside
Competitive to collaborative	Reserved to outgoing
Questioning to accepting	Cautious to fast paced

The various classification alternatives when defining the BBDM development cycle

All the combinations in the table achieve the same objective of recognising the divergence of opposing attributes and associations in the person and also in the organisation. The model remains inclusive, holistic, symmetrical and balanced with all combinations. The intention is to remove the complexity and provide a generalist framework for a holistic perspective. I apply the 80:20 rule when analysing behaviours – there will always be exceptions to the general rule. Many of these distinctions are represented in personality profiles.

By providing a balanced, all-inclusive development framework, companies can attend to the growth needs of each individual in their organisation according to their level of advancement. This is pure strategy – an inside-out approach to developing potential from the ground up; an open-source change approach that acknowledges the individual and their wellbeing.

What grew out of a sense of unethical practices by some of the major accounting firms outsourcing HR capability and disrupting a company's ability to develop its employees was an innovative response to protecting and promoting behaviours in the workplace.

To be effective, HR leaders require the autonomy and independence to be trusted advisors in the workplace. To be seen to be strategic, the representation of an independent HR leader on the board is advisable.

This BBDM framework is a powerful tool for HR leaders to guide employee development and managerial effectiveness. It is also a basic guide for individuals in pursuit of meaning and happiness in a world that offers few insights to behavioural development. In fact, the HR insourcing venture did not get off the ground. We were trying to sell a vision of valuing and respecting employee capability at a time when the HR brand was being devalued.

Appreciation for Ei and cultural awareness is fast becoming a strategic advantage and will in the future be more of a market disrupter than robots and digital technologies. There is a strong correlation between developing employees, improved employee productivity and wellbeing, and organisational performance. Our transcendent right-hemisphere attributes represent innovation in support of life's ultimate goals: to increase diversity and secure the future. These objectives are at the core of our development capability, and proactively support our wellbeing. Our creative right-brained capability is only available to those who respect the power of the mind and the environment in which it excels. These are our cultural guardianship attributes and a measure of our development success.

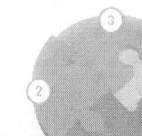

2. THE NEW WORLD OF HR AND MANAGEMENT

THE MANY BENEFITS OF ENABLING HR LEADERS TO COACH, CHALLENGE AND MOTIVATE EMPLOYEES

It's time to get on board with Ei. Realisation of all the life benefits, growth opportunities and rewards of the positive social mind and HR will play a vital role in leading organisations through the transition.

Today's most progressive organisations are already on board – and this book will make complete sense to them. HR managers can use this model to develop and increase the competence of their teams, and therefore the businesses they work in.

Capturing the collective spirit

Fifteen years ago, when I first worked in an HR insourcing venture, there was limited interest in optimising the value of HR services to support, coordinate and capture the collective spirit. This book is intended to show a belief in collaboration and strategy to restore the fundamental human need for a purposeful life, and to welcome in a new era of truth and growth.

HR cannot succeed in overtly competitive environments built on the protection of knowledge, supremacy of thought and formality. This is where HR has failed in the past to build credibility and trust. These industrial-era hierarchical organisational structures dominated the past. Collaborative, inclusive, organic environments challenged to share knowledge and skills transfer will dominate the future.[4] But the development must be organic, not a quick fix from a one-day course. It must permeate the organisation, from the board and CEO right through to the customer/client interface and supporting roles.

Equality and respect for liberated intelligence define today's successful organisations. Representing these at a community level will define the success of future organisations. This is where meaning starts and finishes for the individual – it's their playground to grow.

The reactive nature of seeking value through structural change by diverting resources to achieve cost efficiencies, or in the aftermath of downsizing, has an impact on employee security as well as cultural implications for the business. In a rigid market preoccupied with cost control and risk prevention, senior management may inadvertently represent insecurity to the workforce, inhibiting future growth opportunities.

But it doesn't have to happen that way.

The role of HR

Organisations that adopt open-source change techniques avoid the destructive nature of top-down, authoritarian change. Numerous studies[5] have confirmed that effective human capital practices drive superior business performance, underlying the trend to make HR strategically accountable. Fundamental to the success of the transition is matching or adapting skills in support of the business role. By elevating HR to the board, senior management recognises the essential role it

4   'The Five Trademarks of Agile Organisations', Wouter Aghina, Aaron De Smet, Gerald Lackey, Michael Lurie and Monica Murarka, McKinsey, January 2018.

5   *The ROI of Human Capital*, Jac Fitz-enz. 'Strategic Human Resources Management Effectiveness as Determinants of Firm Performance', Mark A. Huselid, Susan E. Jackson and Randall S. Schuler.

plays in establishing a business environment to motivate and support business strategy.

The role of HR needs to be valued within the organisation, the community, the government. Without people there is no profit. In companies that respect HR and employee development, revenue growth strategies work. Companies that do *not* appreciate the worth of human development inevitably destroy value by focusing on cost reduction and outsourcing. Expansion tends to be by acquisition. In government, the focus is on productivity and cost containment, and there is little appreciation of what capability is required for revenue recovery. Lack of respect for HR and how leadership can influence emotional growth and a balanced, successful lifestyle is what in many ways is wrong with today's society. The inability to use our creative mind for balance and understanding and to provide inspiration and passion to define future security is, among other things, characterised by stress, fear, depression, dependence, drug and alcohol abuse, and crime.

Managing business transformation

HR executives are best placed to develop employee trust and manage strategic alignment and business transformation, but often lack specialist expertise. *Best Behaviour* introduces a transformational approach to turn HR into a strategic, right-brained, Ei coaching role. The approach is repeated to ensure the management team has the selfless, empathetic skill to recognise strengths and vulnerabilities, realign roles and responsibilities and support a proactive, development-centric growth culture for the benefit of all employees. An inclusive environment ensures success for organisations in promoting strategic initiatives and to better represent future job security.

By empowering employees to contribute to continuous improvement and innovate in support of their core competence, a well-executed underpinning strategy can achieve superior business performance. A reactive, problem-focused culture can be rapidly transformed to create a positive or proactive strengths-based, solutions-enabled environment built on a foundation of technology and knowledge, increasing awareness of opportunities and a belief in the future.

By collaborating in accomplishment and intelligence, employees are more inclined to identify with, and develop to respond to, strategic initiatives. Top quartile companies are starting to appreciate the benefits of successful cultural transformations – not just one transformation, multiple transformations. These cultures are proactive and adaptive.

Technology companies are leading the way with transformation. GE Digital's country manager for Australia and New Zealand, Belinda Vassallo, believes getting transformation right is about embracing and empowering people. Salesforce's Asia Pacific Senior Vice President, Eileen O'Mara, said great leaders tend to share a number of characteristics, and a key one (especially in a period of transformation) is transparency.[6]

Values-based organisations help employees embrace change. With inclusive, respectful organisations, employees appreciate how and why their contributions enhance their organisation's success.

A global level of mistrust

The current global level of mistrust is plainly due to our creative right mind being the sole guardian of trust. **Trust cannot be fabricated. It is inherent in the individual and is our social reward for respecting humanity and life's diversity.** Without respect, life's purpose and our passion are concealed. Once you respect the strength of your deeper feelings, you unlock the ability to innovate and adapt to most opportunities and environments.

For agile, change-ready organisations in search of value and sensitive to employee needs, there is substantial opportunity in creating dynamic, employee-centric cultures. *Best Behaviour* introduces an innovative approach to organisational development with a cultural difference. By objectively revisiting core skills and realigning roles in a balanced, objective model, responsibilities are delineated and

---

6   'Successful Leaders Change Culture to Drive Transformation', Mark Eggleton, *AFR*,
     31 July 2017.

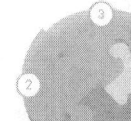

leadership can focus on networking talent to create opportunities and strategy. HR are very well placed to lead this workplace transformation.

Development happens organically when employees are encouraged to get involved and to apply their strengths. Development and growth are second nature, an intuitive endeavour for people who respect them. Employees only need to know what objectives they must meet at any given stage. It's up to them to accept the challenge, but they need to feel respected as individuals and know we all have what it takes to grow and contribute. They simply need to be given direction and opportunity.

Developing one's self

Learning need not always be structured. Encouraging self-development ensures employees can make good and well-informed career decisions and plan their future. In the workplace, employees can be challenged to communicate openly and in innovative ways, and can enhance valuable skills by contributing to strengths-based agile teams and innovation groups to define business strategy and solve problems. Welcome to the new world of business ideology, driven by learning and knowledge, where development is targeted to a need and users collaborate to objectively create value within a defined strategic framework.

Development is fundamental to helping people understand the power of the right mind for extended happiness, shared prosperity, health and wellbeing.

Online learning and development, collaboration technology and knowledge hubs meet most employees' requirements, allowing them to develop at their own pace with external encouragement. Kolb's learning styles (chapter 26) provide insights to differing learning preferences. HR companies and education providers are well positioned to create community-aligned development portals targeting business and the community for greater meaning. Intuitive solutions guide the learner to the most appropriate solution to their problems. By canvassing feedback and targeting projects to organisation and community needs, knowledge and skills portals evolve.

Knowledge should be community-specific and meaningful to the individual. **Every community needs its own online knowledge base or Wikipedia, and Meetup groups to connect them. Communities that respect this will prosper.** Communities made to compete against each other to improve lifestyle choices and liveability for all their citizens will flourish. Working in the community should be viewed as a privilege, not a right. Communities will power the future.

Meaning, fairness, equality, balanced governance and ethics together with risk-and-reward objectives must be inherent in any HR solution. HR, government and leadership need only lead, coach and observe to build trust and security to support organisations and communities. It is a fundamental right to choose one's level of participation in the community. Governments must stop overregulating so people can make their own choices, learn from their mistakes, and progress. Behaviour, competence and intelligence only need to be respected and liberated for us to lead meaningful lives. Therein lies our power, and our minds are engineered to sustain world prosperity. Balance and reason allow us the freedom to create and support a new world of cooperation and respect for diversifying ability.

HR AT THE CENTRE OF STRATEGY

For HR to be effective, personal development and growth must be central to an organisation's strategy. A trusted and effective HR department of the future will promote and deliver:

- independent, employee-centric knowledge and communications
- one-on-one coaching
- innovation groups and strengths-based teams
- Ei expertise
- diversity of decisions
- choice
- exemplary HR leadership practices.

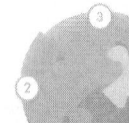

Development can be delivered in agile environments as and when required, in an intuitive, personalised, self-service environment with the option to engage with instructors, coaches and providers. Development portals should encourage community development and coordinate dynamic skills networks founded on shared value preferences to open up opportunities and raise awareness.

Focusing on employees' behavioural needs to motivate superior performance and reward desirable characteristics to provide opportunity is rare, but most progressive organisations now see the benefits flowing from networking employees in dynamic strengths-based teams and inclusive work environments, and encouraging strategic input at the individual level.

Employees secure in their roles and respectful of an organisation's direction will collectively develop or combine skills, knowing they will share in the rewards of strategic success.

Recognising individual value and contribution also helps to identify future opportunities. To understand why an employee selects a certain role in a sought-after corporation or within a particular industry in a given community, organisations can draw on a wealth of experience to develop valuable insights as to the future needs and desires of customers and communities. By understanding an employee's lifestyle choices and social needs, it can also profile prospective customers and encourage employees to network to develop an awareness of opportunities.

* * *

Open, responsive environments will define the organisations of the future that will effect change and growth strategies. Creating an environment of trust will underpin this, and the one-to-one qualities and powers of HR are well placed to assume accountability for their coaching role. First and foremost, senior management and leadership must accept the responsibility required to implement emotional development programs. Successful Ei requires the transformation of an employee's maturity and aptitude. The coach must selflessly understand employee needs, independent of external priorities. Rather than support, the coach must inform and challenge an employee to grow.

3. START WITH WHO

BELIEVE IN YOURSELF TO ENABLE YOUR GROWTH AND THE GROWTH OF OTHERS

My interest in human behaviour began early on, as my own difficult childhood made me a shy, reclusive boy, fearful of people and what they thought of me. I completely failed to connect with the outside world, finding comfort on my own and in the environment where I grew up and was free to explore. At home I had a rebellious older adopted brother and a strict mother who had adopted me just before her husband died, and then struggled with single motherhood in an age when it was frowned upon. My first three years, while my brain was forming, were difficult, and it was a long, hard road to make up for them.

Communication and reading did not come easily. I had difficulty recognising patterns externally and was mildly dyslexic, evidenced by my distortion of words and sentences. Speech therapy, listening tests and the removal of my adenoids exacerbated my prolonged isolation. When I was old enough to find serenity and freedom beyond the four walls of my home I fared much better at individual pursuits, building up strengths and interacting. Thought processes and skills seemed to come a lot easier than communication in my youth, and mathematics made sense. I internalised well, but was completely disconnected externally, trapped in my mind from my earliest memories. I was a loner.

Team sports were difficult. I was forever playing catch-up with language and bonding – the external-facing capabilities – but although I failed in fundamental early development, I excelled and found comfort as I grew up independent, always feeling the need to fend for myself and deal with my own problems. Diagnosed as a social phobic much later in life, my fear of how people perceived me was acute, and I developed a strongly analytical mind. My interest in behaviour was for all the wrong reasons: fear people might think I was either inept because I couldn't communicate or was too passive.

What dominates our thoughts as children tends to determine our behaviours and career later. Our main fears and insecurities preoccupy us as we grow up and we inadvertently develop life skills – sometimes known as coping mechanisms – around these vulnerabilities. For example, if we were never tall enough, we somehow learnt associated skills to cope with this perceived disadvantage. These coping mechanisms are often supported by unrealistic belief systems. Our self-confidence is dependent on understanding and accepting how these vulnerabilities defined us. If we don't face up to them, we may not mature. We may also fail to recognise our true self and our best career purpose. I now appreciate the complete balance in the human psyche. We are able to resolve our environmental fears and insecurities we harbour in our youth when as adults we find security and balance in addressing them. This natural balance is a survival mechanism and has helped us to excel in our physical environment.

Once aware of my social anxiety disorder, I addressed my personal and professional limiting beliefs, learning the tools and principles fundamental to the objectives of this book. I would like to share them with you, to guide you – and indeed organisations – to challenge understanding, open minds to new behaviours, and to show how we can all readily adapt and evolve with awareness and the right environment, and value the many rewards that come from such growth.

INSIGHTS FROM MY DEVELOPMENT EXPERIENCE

When we are born, we are delivered into life totally dependent on our external environment. A newborn is as one with its environment, without identity and completely extroverted, dependent on parents for food, nurture and love despite all dysfunctions. Lights, colours and objects stimulate sight, thought and muscular movement. We need instructions for living in a world of unknowns. We assimilate these instructions and learn confidence.

In our adolescence, we discover a sense of self and learn about trust and independence. We find out we are capable, we are strong, we are intelligent, and we can take care of ourselves. We fight to establish our uniqueness and to be an individual. The fight occurs as we try to establish our bearings. By furthering our quest for understanding, and in questioning our power, we continue to learn about independence while developing respect for the opinions, approval and needs of others. We learn our success is influenced by our connections.

Start With Why, Simon Sinek's inspirational book (a must-read for learning and development enthusiasts), puts 'why' at the centre of how we behave and react: 'If we're starting with the wrong questions, if we don't understand the cause, then even the right answers will always steer us wrong.' How can we lead authentic, fulfilling lives if we have yet to understand who we are? One of my most important conclusions is how our motivations and what we love to do express our Why, and how the layering and programming of thoughts, emotions, behaviours, skills and capability over our lifetime are represented by our singular identity, our Who.

Our identity or Who is essentially a blank canvas at birth, and over our lifetime we develop the Where, the What, the How, the Who, the When, and the Why through an evolving cycle of perspectives. If we do not understand who we are then we will fail to make an informed career choice and lead genuinely fulfilling lives. Identity is to a person as culture is to a collective: intrinsic to everything we do. It represents all the norms, values, stories and behaviours specific to a community and an environment.

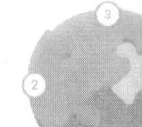

Starting with 'Who questions' further develops Simon Sinek's theory that great leaders inspire. If we have a strong sense of identity, of who we are, and are provided with purposeful objectives (the Why), everything should fall into place.

HOW OUR IDENTITY EVOLVED AND LEARNINGS FOR OUR DEVELOPMENT

Throughout this book, I explore the very different perspectives of internal/external, inside/outside, self/community. Our behaviours exist in polarities and opposites, and there is little understanding of how important these perspectives are in allowing us to lead a balanced, holistic life. For every right, there is a wrong; for something we fear, we can learn to trust; a childhood belief can be exposed as fantasy when we discover the truth in adulthood. These polarities of opposites can be applied to our development – from fear to trust being our biological to emotional development, from insecurity to security being our physiological development. Again these expressions may appear simplistic. However, as we further develop the classifications around the opposing quadrants, the attributes when grouped in each quadrant support each other and begin to make complete sense.

When I say 'identity', I'm not talking about the outside, nationalistic view of identity which has been hijacked throughout history to control the thoughts and beliefs of the masses. I mean the very personal, internal expressions that define who we are. Identity is everything, and knowing who you are is powerful. Identity is crucial to childhood development. It establishes our niche and our role in life. Our identity establishes our environmental positioning or locus of control.

Culture

The collective view of these expressions, if left to evolve freely, is called a culture when shared with many people. Culture represents our truth as we identify externally or in our environment. Our identity is the software that brings the hardware to life. It is the program that brings meaning to the physical form, and the physical form which distinguishes culture from emotion. Culture is an expression of who we are as a collective and why.

Anyone who has studied biology will appreciate our primary development functions, being biological and physiological. Whereas emotion represents the growth objective of our biological form, culture represents the growth objective or expression of our physical form. Our growth is defined by two distinct development polarities: emotional from our biological beginnings and cultural from our physical beginnings. These very distinct objectives are expressed in four stages, where one objective takes precedence over another. All stages become deeply interwoven, although the primary development objectives are clear – and developed throughout this book.

Primary growth objectives

While our biological-to-emotional and physiological-to-cultural developments are intertwined, there are primary objectives at each stage. This pattern of primary growth objectives is true across all our development, including behavioural. What is most evident is the development stages encompass the following primary objectives:

1   infant = brain expansion (biological)

2   childhood = body expansion (physiological)

3   adolescence = relationship expansion (emotional)

4   adulthood = work expansion (cultural).

We can find comfort in any one of the stages, and the interrelationships between the stage characteristics may inhibit us from moving to the next stage unless we challenge ourselves to grow. But why classify growth from an infant, child, adolescent and adult perspective? The reason I make this distinction becomes obvious when we broaden the development framework into instincts, moods, personality, learning and intelligence. Our progression through these four distinct development stages also replicates our biological to physiological to emotional to cultural evolution. What I want to drive home is each of these stages should preferably be developed in succession and mastered before

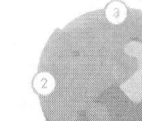

moving onto the next. If you skip a stage then your development is incomplete. This can be expressed in many different ways, including a lack of confidence or – at the opposite extreme – an over-inflated ego.

Identity is at the core of our development. As we progress, we appreciate our environment in the evolving context explained in this book. This model may appear oversimplified, but that is my intention. My objective is to represent a holistic framework to ensure we cater for all behaviours in an organisation or a community. The simple laws of nature seem to have been lost – the biological and the physiological forms, and the distinct development objectives. What we learn in our youth, we apply in adulthood – and this is our opposing duality of perspectives. The complexity is in the detail and how our development objectives evolve and loop back on themselves, from learning to doing. My intention is to outline the framework so that organisations and communities can fill in the gaps and define the detail, the detail that distinguishes their own purpose and cultural identity.

The following diagram sets out the opposing stage objectives from a biological (stage 1 to stage 3) and a physiological (stage 2 to stage 4) context.

This diagram introduces these overarching principles, which are further developed throughout this section. What is important is to appreciate how the primary characteristics and objectives of each development stage help to support the successful stage completion and allow us to move onto the next. The frameworks throughout this section are presented as a lifecycle, starting from the bottom left (stage 1), and progressing clockwise to the bottom right (stage 4). As the framework is developed, classifications and definitions are added and substituted, however each of the four stages of the framework are distinct and related. The learnings are layered on each stage (quadrant) of the framework.

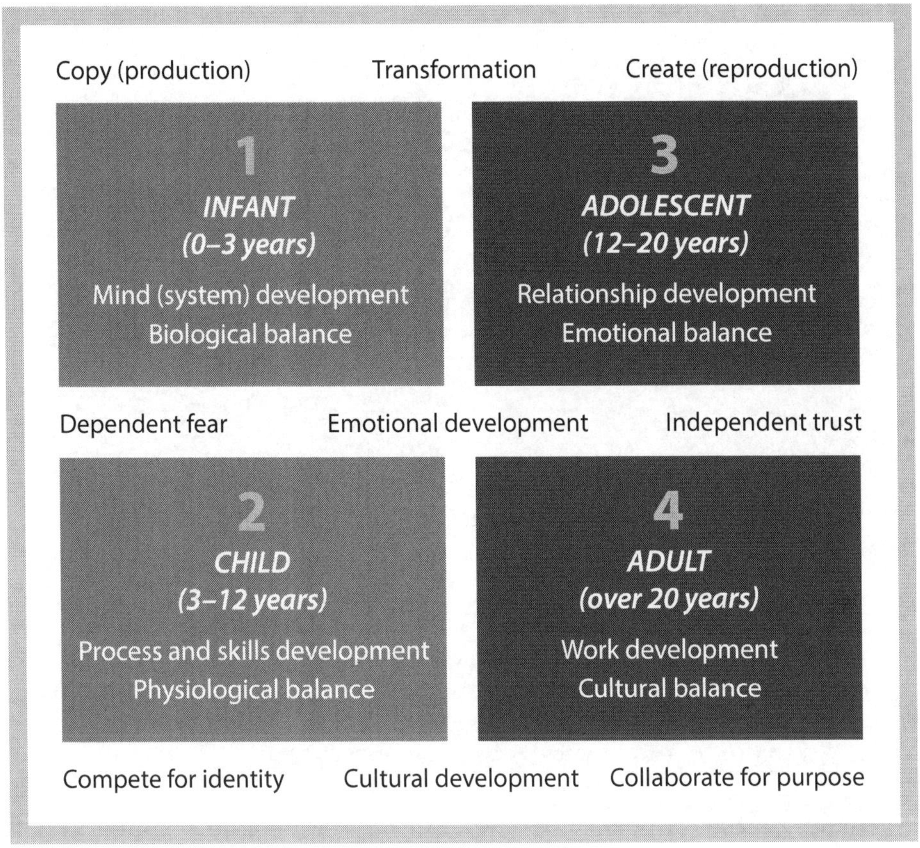

Copy (production)　　　Transformation　　　Create (reproduction)

1
INFANT
(0–3 years)

Mind (system) development
Biological balance

3
ADOLESCENT
(12–20 years)

Relationship development
Emotional balance

Dependent fear　　　Emotional development　　　Independent trust

2
CHILD
(3–12 years)

Process and skills development
Physiological balance

4
ADULT
(over 20 years)

Work development
Cultural balance

Compete for identity　　　Cultural development　　　Collaborate for purpose

Primary development priorities throughout a lifecycle

4. WHY IDENTITY AND BEHAVIOUR DEFINE US

HOW OUR EARLY YEARS IMPACT OUR DEVELOPMENT

To me, change was an aspiration from early in life. I avoided the mundane and craved new things, having grown up in a modest Anglo-Saxon household in Auckland, a small city with a population of around 800,000. On the whole, New Zealand is an inclusive society, and culture is respected. People have a strong connection to the land. Living in a middle-class suburb on the outskirts of the CBD was almost like growing up in a small town: everybody knew everybody and life was normal.

However, this wasn't true for our family. Before I was born, my mother lost her first adopted daughter to heart disease, but instead of my mother getting support and time to grieve, the government offered me as restitution. My adopted father then died of lymph node cancer when I was 11 months old. At this stage my mother must have been completely broken; I don't doubt that she disconnected from me, as anyone would without proper support. So the first six years of my life were a struggle for my mother as well as for me. I feel no resentment, and realise she was only human. The skills I developed to overcome my drawbacks have provided me with excellent foresight. Money did not come easy, and I remember helping with her sewing work when I could. It was hard being a single mother in the 1960s. She was strict, and my brother and I were taught to be seen and not heard. No wonder I had a speech impediment and struggled with learning. While my brother simply rebelled, I was very shy. Life was nondescript, and I yearned for the things other children had.

How differing characteristics influence our impressions

My grandmother was my saviour through those years. She taught me about life's abundance and how to trust, and helped to sow the seeds of inspiration. I always looked forward to the school holidays and escaping to my grandparents' hobby farm, where my brother and I had complete freedom to explore, fantasise, and enjoy the garden and cooking. I learnt early about prevailing temperaments, and how to tiptoe around my mother's mood swings – and how much more freely I could communicate with my grandmother, who had a positive, accepting outlook. My memories of my grandfather are of a stern, serious character, and we knew to give him his space. I recall my grandmother telling him off on occasion for his grumpy demeanour towards us children. Fortunately there were so many things to discover and do on the farm that there were few reasons to be in the house.

When I was eight, my grandfather's health began to fail and my grandparents sold the farm and moved to South Auckland. My grandfather died a few years later, leaving my grandmother on her own, but I still loved to visit her – especially to escape my strict stepfather. I felt accepted and free to be myself with my grandmother.

I'm not surprised that my grandmother outlived my grandfather by 40 years. Attitude, gratitude, a positive outlook and being a guardian of life can make a substantial difference to wellbeing and longevity. I noticed the strong contrast between the behaviours of the most influential people in my life at an early age. Happily, times and attitudes have changed, and now most parents would agree that treating

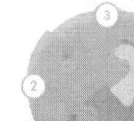

children like this would not be conducive to their development. But have parents in this day gone too far and become overprotective?

It's no wonder I had such low self-esteem and identified as being inept, believing the world thought the worst of me. Shyness and timidness affected me greatly, and communication was difficult as I was required to engage with people I feared. Reading was hard, but I needed to read and to engage with my mother. When I had to communicate, my heart would sink – I would focus on the other person's face, searching for negative feedback, and my barely audible, meek voice defined my communication style. But I did appreciate people who were compassionate and caring, and I learnt to read Ei characteristics early on.

Cognitive dissonance

Much later I realised my failed first stage of learning was all about belonging, basic language and bonding externally. I was trapped in my own world. Reuven Feuerstein's work on adjustment problems found that cognitive deficits of poor learners centre on their inability to identify with their environment. This results in impulsivity and failure to identify problems, or even to appreciate important discrepancies and analyse balanced comparisons in the environment. His cognitive dissonance theory relates the effects of perceived inconsistencies between left-brain beliefs and feelings or actions. Our world is largely of our own choosing and of our own construct. When impressions or mental constructs do not correspond to our mental models, the human tendency to deny their reality is known as 'cognitive dissonance'.

Social psychologist Leon Festinger's 1957 book *A Theory of Cognitive Dissonance* suggests we tend to reconstruct knowledge of our actions, beliefs and feelings in order to balance them with each other. In balancing our physiology, we prefer a predictable world and a positive self-image. If we hear one thing and see another, we feel uneasy, guilty or insecure, and in denying our thoughts, feelings or actions we unconsciously reconstruct reality. Cognitive dissonance acts as a motivated state. When making a decision, if we sense an inconsistency between our behaviour and our attitude, we consciously deny the conflict. A common consequence is to produce an excuse for making a wrong decision to counteract post-decisional depression.

Understanding behavioural attributes – successes and failures

I always found mathematics rewarding, and my analytical mind helped me to read people. I had good judgement in problem-solving. I could analyse and calculate in my head without having to engage other people. Although I failed in the external-facing competencies of bonding and language, and struggled with reading, I excelled at stage 2 mathematics, thought processes and skills.

When I started my professional career, I had to resolve language and communication. I had managed to get through university, and my writing improved well before my speaking, but the process of writing and structuring language in my head helped me to converse better. This was more of a process than a sensory skill. I learnt to confront my communication fears when I started my professional accounting career. The interesting thing was that many of us accountants were in the same boat, so we learnt to converse from a very low base. Being an accountant was perfect for me at the time. It helped me to deal with the insecurities of never having money and to relearn communication from scratch. Language, bonding and learning to communicate are our stage 1 objectives. They are outward focused and structure our foundation or system.

The biggest contribution and purpose in my life is the subject of this book: *behaviour*. Once I had mastered communication and knew how to make money, I played to my strengths, learnt self-confidence and grasped my left-brain attributes. My next objective was to overcome what I had despised as a child – my identity – and to learn to love my internal self, and my capability. I needed to study my elevated right-brained attributes of self-awareness and Ei. Self-awareness, self-love, and self-trust can all be used interchangeably, as they essentially achieve the same aim: to be your authentic self and know your capability inside out. That objective has been a much bigger journey and a lot more rewarding. Rewarding, because it has provided rare insights, and fulfilling because, by respecting my intuition, my decisions are my own and spontaneous: I have a complete mind/body connection and have mastered my feelings; I have inside-out awareness and can define my own destiny. I have a multidimensional capability and can call on all my behaviours and intellectual capabilities to support myself.

Establishing independence is an essential objective of emotional maturity. I developed a strong sense of self and independence very early in life through having to fend for myself financially. I started a paper round when I was 10, so never had to ask for what little money my parents had.

The following BBDM model sets out the steps to the mastering of our stage objectives but also the evolving context of how we develop our self-image from external, external to internal, internal, internal to external (or inside out).

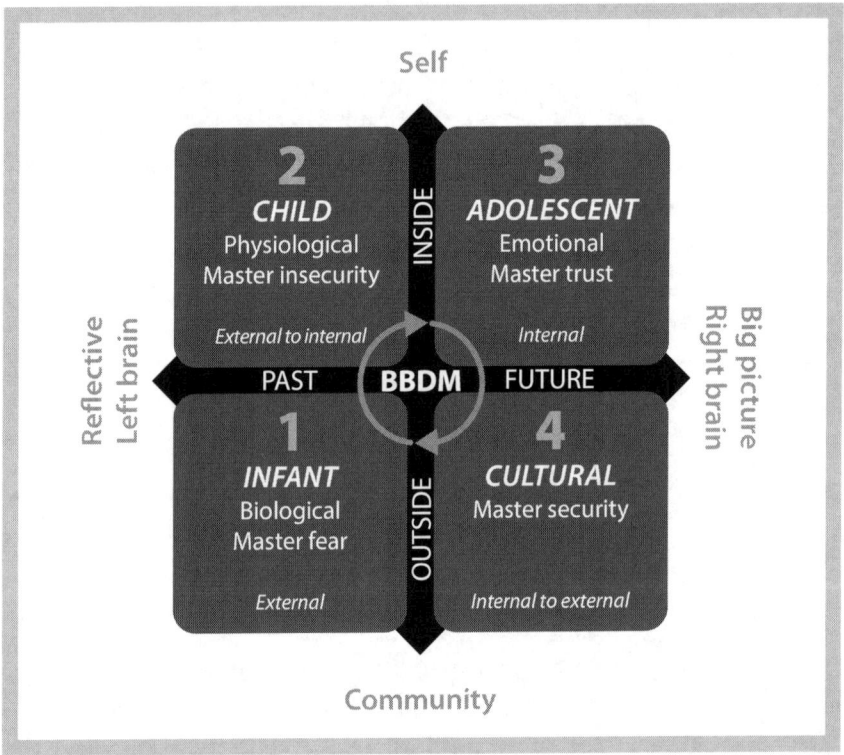

Our identity develops by mastering a succession of instincts

Trusting my own ability was another objective of emotional maturity: trust builds as we learn to override our fears. I became acutely aware of people's behaviour because I studied every interaction. The lead-up was about dispelling fear during the interaction, the search for any form of negative response, and then overanalysing to understand how the other person confirmed my own fears and low self-belief. Quite often I was so wound up that I would completely miss what the other person was saying. To this day, I have a problem remembering people's names within seconds of their being introduced. Overcoming my fears took time, but what evolved was an acute sense of self-trust. What life may serve up as a deep biological fear is learnt as strong emotional trust at the opposite polarity of behaviour, as we seek to imagine or look beyond the fear. We just need to learn to be aware of this ability.

I was too timid to challenge situations, seek attention or to react, so I always knew how to avoid situations and where I could find solace and calm. What distracted me from the negatives in my life was going out and enjoying the freedom to roam and explore. This provided me with the balance and calm to move forward. On the other hand, my brother, whom I feel for, coped very differently, rebelling against our parents. He still struggles with life and relationships, but has a huge heart, and was named New Zealander of the Year in 2009 by the readers of the *New Zealand Herald* for his role in rescuing two police officers from a gunman during the Napier Siege.

OUR IDENTITY IS A PRODUCT OF KNOWING WHO WE ARE

A central part of our development lifecycle that is both undervalued and misunderstood is our identity or strengths. Our role in life, or identity, is extremely important. If you don't know your identity then how can you recognise your cultural identity or community purpose? Identity encompasses everything that defines you in your environment:

- your locus of control

- your capability and strengths

- your self-confidence

- your strength of character

- how you see yourself relating to other people.

43

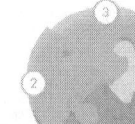

How can you be a good judge of character if you don't know yourself? If you establish a strong identity in childhood, your judgements and logical mind will evolve accordingly. Your judgements and comparisons help to mould your identity.

Childhood is all about mastering our body physiology in our environment, and our developing identity helps us to confront our environmental anxieties. Regulating our environment, wrapping us in cotton wool and being overprotective may prevent us from learning valuable life skills. The processing of skills, procedures and associated knowledge programmed in our brain while we are children supports acute, future-focused, data-gathering, external awareness in adulthood. This external awareness is distinct to a person's role and aligns their abilities to gather information for cultural or work purposes. This cultural competence is our most powerful form of capability and enables our executive brain function.

Our reward for understanding childhood environmental insecurities is developing security in adulthood. Our creative ability and self-awareness can be used to balance our shortcomings and vulnerabilities. Recognising the enlightened, radiant, charismatic characteristics of a fully developed adult or leadership cultural competence shows **there are entire populations who fail to develop awareness, and are thus unable to represent the future or realise the associated security of being able to define one's destiny**. This may be due to being 'treated as a number', or disrespect for humanity or life or overpopulation. (On visiting populous cities, I would invariably connect with locals originally from the country or smaller towns. Do people who live in densely populated cities divert their perception to protecting their limited personal space?)

A secure, centred identity frees our external strategic awareness

People who have the deepest sense of self and can describe themselves unequivocally also have a greater sense of cultural awareness or forward-focused perception. This was a major revelation for me. **Protectionist or insecure instincts inhibit the development of our**

big-picture awareness and creativity. Once you know this, you can understand the power of cultural identity and the Why, and why there is so little appreciation of the power of collective purpose and future-focused, big-picture strategy. When we can leverage this power, how different the world will be.

The equilibrium of care and nurturing required is represented in the following balanced support model to align responsibility for development. This represents an evolutionary model of how the individual can best be supported to balance fear, self-belief, self-trust, and seeking out our truth or purpose in an evolving context. These interactive learnings align to our advancing level of security but with added risk for each stage helping to move us forward. Infants will find comfort in family, children with friends, adolescents with a prospective partner, and adults with colleagues or community representatives.

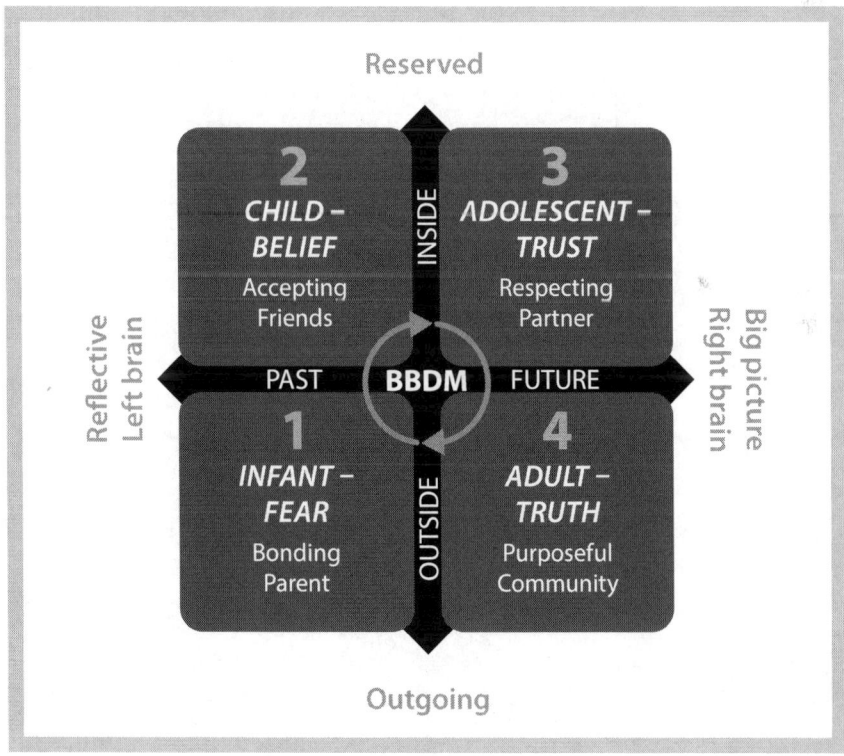

A balanced cycle of shared support

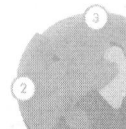

Identity and behaviour are central to how to develop fully. To achieve growth, both must be respected in organisations and in functioning communities.

5. THE INDIVIDUAL AND CULTURAL IDENTITIES

PEOPLE NEED RESPECT, ACCEPTANCE AND DIRECTION TO GROW

When defining the cultural identity of an organisation or community, the vision should embody purpose and a growth pathway. There is an undefined behavioural balance, which is not fully appreciated or understood: what develops in the individual, and expresses everything about their identity, is also conveyed in the community as purposeful interactions or our cultural identity. If cultural identity could develop freely, it would probably demonstrate the purpose of the community. It would have a meaning closely associated with the habitat we occupy, and encourage diverse niches and support greater opportunities.

If a complementary niche were to open, someone in the community would learn the skills to fill it. Our lifecycle is designed to ensure this. This works the same way in organisations, as employees develop capability to align to strategy. If culture is left to develop freely, you can guarantee that niches will emerge to support life in its many shapes and forms. This may seem philosophical, however few organisations have defined their identity to determine how they positively influence people's lives and support community opportunities. This responsibility falls to the marketing department to define and the PR department to communicate. Leaders need to embody this understanding in the organisation.

Why do I think this? Our cultural mind – our ability to freely express and adapt our physiological form – has developed in response to our emerging custodian obligations and ability to support life. Not only are our bodies equipped to undertake this responsibility, so is our psyche. If we interact with the environment, if we connect to life socially, if we fulfil our contributory purpose, we experience a strong sense of satisfaction and develop positive, if not proactive, temperaments that support our ongoing guardianship responsibilities. Think of a mother throughout pregnancy: she develops a positive, compassionate temperament to care for a newborn. A positive temperament supports not only relationships, but also nurturing. Hormones help to put the expectant mother into a positive state of mind for nurturing.

Culture is an expression of how we do things and is closely aligned to our environment. While emotion permeates our bodies providing self-awareness and resilience, cultural awareness gives us the inclination to respond to opportunities in our environment. Misunderstanding of the essential balance between the individual and the environment has been evident since the beginnings of the industrial age, when mass production represented life as productive units underscored by personal materialistic desires. Throughout this period, left-hemisphere capitalist characteristics have become the new norm, with the undeveloped right-hemisphere social characteristics taking a back seat. On a personal level, competitive instincts can mask the need to collaborate for the greater good. Without understanding their merits, the social right-hemisphere attributes have been discounted, if not feared. Sharing is caring, but also promotes less consumption and more sustainability. In this age, people are fast coming to terms with this.

Identifying with the environment

In our age of mass production, have consumerism and standardisation reduced our sense of custodianship and our cultural identity? This low appreciation of culture is affecting the human need to identify with the environment. In a world where self-interest rules, the loss of environmental attachment is echoed in hierarchies of conformity across entire populations. Populist campaigns can easily substitute reality with fantasy, and some may even profit from adversity. Materialism, standardisation, self-importance and intellectual supremacy will continue to unleash world disorder unless the cultural mind can relate freely to the environment. By directing the mind to the abyss of the global market, we distract it from its guardianship role in the community where security and awareness can be more easily represented. Balance needs to prevail.

Instant gratification

Western culture is addicted to instant gratification, and governments ignore the damage it causes. External value prevails and risk/reward relationships are confused. Indifference and a lazy mind are consequences of the failure to identify the need to invest in self-value. In his book *Emotional Intelligence*, Daniel Goleman refers to the famous marshmallow study by Walter Mischel. The 10 per cent of children who delay self-gratification and do not eat the single marshmallow but wait for the second succeed in later life. While this study was challenged by new research in 2018[7] suggesting affluence or socioeconomic factors play a part in children delaying gratification, what is important to note is environmental influences contribute to our ability to delay gratification and these need to be understood. The risk/reward associations of sacrificing gratification for greater rewards and meaning are an essential life skill and a conduit to maturing emotionally. The new study tends to focus on affluence and class structures rather than the influence of parenting skills. Research comparing the attributes of parents who develop these important life skills in children would be more beneficial. Comparing how emotional intelligence influences parenting ability would provide valuable insights.

Understanding what behaviours promote self-sacrifice is an essential learning for governments and parents. Self-interest and instant gratification can be compounded by our divisive democratic systems,

---

7 'Revisiting the Marshmallow Test', Tyler W. Watts, Greg J. Duncan, Haonan Quan.

the controlling nature of some religions, and the supremacy of many Western academic systems. In excessively competitive environments, and without development, emotions can become a weakness too easily categorised into simplistic love and hate, and good and evil associations. In life, we often have to sacrifice short-term gratification to appreciate greater rewards, understanding and maturity.

What we really lack in this day is positive leadership role models who express hope, charisma and future pathways, and the organisations to support them. Those who move us beyond life's simple pleasures, wants and needs. As children, adolescents and employees in the community and in work we have all experienced them. Their stories have shaped our experiences, challenged our understanding and inspired us to grow. If our outdated systems don't support these leadership characteristics then we need to create ones that do.

OUR EMOTIONAL DEVELOPMENT

These simple life lessons which promote deeper emotional understanding are portrayed in the following diagram, which shows our biological journey to self-awareness or emotional maturity from stage 1 infant to stage 3 adolescent. This is further defined in the subsequent paragraphs.

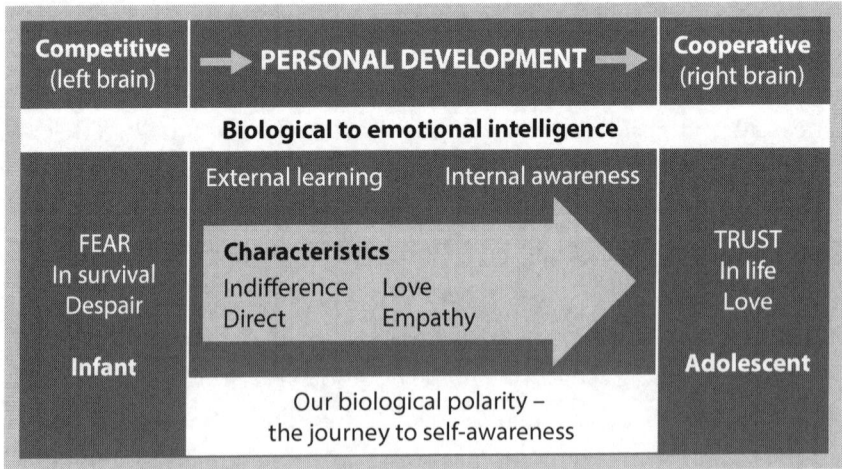

Extending the polarity of our emotions

From fear to trust

Like happiness, *fear* is relative. As infants, we start from a narrow base and broaden our emotional polarity throughout development.[8] To start, fear predominates as a natural survival mechanism. *Trust* begins with attachment and develops over a long period, and that is a measure of our maturity.

In our early development phase, when we are most susceptible to our environment, our fears are directed externally. We override fears and vulnerabilities in childhood development by learning a complexity of physiological skills while identifying with our personal belief system. Without our broadening emotional trust into adulthood, this knowledge can remain naive and prevent us from exploring our true potential.

In the absence of personal development and learning our life skills, we can keep holding onto the past when our beliefs were guileless. Building relationships in stage 3 helps us live in the moment, increase the currency of our connections, and also to understand more about ourselves. Hierarchy, power and authority promote a social pecking order and can harbour insecurity. In the absence of strong leadership, organisations may be too focused on problems and governance rather than promoting trusting relationships and a greater social good. Adult insecurity may too easily be precariously substituted for external security diversions; for example, guns over emotional strength, walls over compassion, fear over trust.

We have reason to feel insecure when leaders unnecessarily divert public attention to victimising minorities or display egotistical authority. Too often, leaders who publicly abhor bad behaviour only identify their own unresolved insecurities. Seeking to disregard feelings or empathy may neglect the deep emotional attachment underlying our humanitarian feelings and happiness. The insecurities that preoccupy our childhood can also help to define and influence our performance as adults at work.

People who suppress their insecurities or seek to ratify them externally invariably deny the need to resolve their weaknesses internally.

---

8   'Building Trust in Your Infant', Elizabeth Gutierrez, Michigan State University, January 2013.

Hate expresses unresolved insecurities. Personal development is a fundamental requirement for growth. Left unresolved, insecure childhood thoughts lead to insecure adult behaviour, and together with naive belief systems, anchor comfort zones and influence life decisions. Nowadays some leaders elected to powerful and responsible positions have difficulty illustrating positive future directions and expressing hope, and instead express their own limiting beliefs. Leaders who fail to come to terms with their own weaknesses may never have learnt the right-brain executive attributes to represent the future in strategy.

6. ATTITUDE, TRUST AND TRUTH ON THE JOURNEY TO SELF-DISCOVERY

FROM BELIEF TO TRUTH

Trust is cheaper than control and more empowering, so give employees access to information.

We are born knowing little more than a basic biological survival mechanism. Fight, flight or freeze are our predominant responses to challenging stimuli. The provision of sustenance and parental bonding begin the broadening of our biological polarity from fear to our emotional opposite, trust. Fear teaches us caution and directs our attention backwards in search of answers. Infants and children are unable to imagine the future before their feelings evolve. At the opposite extreme, trust and love are emotional responses that provide a strengthened foundation, allowing adolescents to begin to look to the future in search of answers. To exhibit trust in relationships and our environment allows us to adopt a positive attitude and become more aware of the present. This heightens our nurturing and coaching ability.

The following personal development model adds the physiological growth profile to the model in the previous chapter to complete the growth profile, representing a complete alignment of opposites: our biological to emotional growth – from stage 1 to stage 3 – and our physiological to cultural growth – from stage 2 to stage 4. This ties in the emotional stage objectives of fear to trust and the cultural stage objectives of belief to truth. The reflective left-hemisphere objectives of past-to-present characteristics (external to internal) aid in learning life skills while the right-hemisphere awareness characteristics (internal to external) enhance our application and doing.

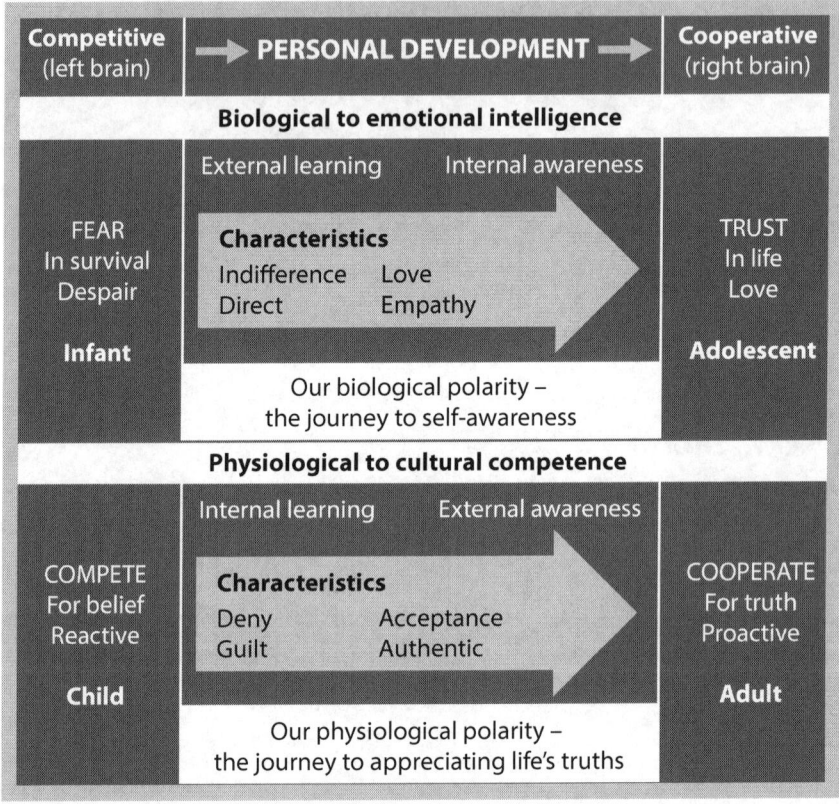

Distinguishing our biological and physiological development pathways

ESTABLISHING OUR PRIMARY DEVELOPMENT OBJECTIVES

Our biological to emotional development progresses from dependence to independence and occurs typically between infancy and the end of adolescence. Let's have a look.

Stage 1: Brain expansion – balancing fear

Mastering fear initiates stage 1 of our biological development, and it happens during the significant infant brain expansion. Our brains act like a sponge, accumulating environment data while the brain system is being structured, and with limited communication and in the absence of being able to process events it's very rare to remember anything before three years old. In the absence of a sense of self and strong identity, reflection and contemplation are undeveloped, and infants live in the moment.

Infants start from a narrow base and quickly broaden emotional polarity throughout development. Fear of detachment is the initial underlying instinct, and trust instincts are only learned over time, beginning with a bonding parent. Successful attachment helps to broaden our emotions and be more assertive and driven.

While our brain and cavity continue to grow throughout stage 2, they do so at a reduced rate.

Stage 2: Body expansion – balancing insecurity

The same may be said for our body growth, which slows in adolescence and completes as we enter adulthood. The structure of the brain and body only change slightly past these secondary growth stages.

Our primary body expansion accelerates from about the age of three, when we are more mobile and more responsive to our environment. Our primary physiological growth phase continues until the onset of adolescence, when our body development is most pronounced.

Mastering insecurity initiates our physiological childhood development. Vulnerabilities and insecurities anchor our development throughout this stage while our thoughts extend our emotional associations, and it's important to understand that we build associated skills to cope with them, known as our strengths. It's only natural for a young child to feel exposed as they come to terms with their growing body. While learning to build a strengthening sense of self as our bodies take shape, there is a strong connection between our developing identity, skills and body. Insecurity is relative, and specific to the individual, their associations and way of life.

As young children, we have a natural tendency to confront our world, as our fears are not fully defined. On learning new fears we sometimes mask them as we have a limited capacity to process them. As our bodies mature, we perfect new skills and our success is a measure of how we position ourselves and respond to our environment. At an early age, insecurities are our physiological responses to our world, and playing to our strengths is central to the development of a strong physical identity.

Self-belief or confidence is our essential childhood development objective and proof we have completed stage 2. Our identity is now fit for purpose, and we have the confidence to use it. We are now ready to step up to the next stage to start the journey to self-awareness and understand who we are.

Trust and love

The paradox of behaviour is that it must be learned and embodied before you can apply it. **To have self-respect is to understand how to respect other people. To show respect is to care how other people characterise you.** This paradox is evident in one of humanity's most widely used words: love. **How are we to love other people if we have not learnt to love ourselves unequivocally? And to selflessly allow others to love us?** This is an essential understanding for developing emotional maturity. The words trust and love are interchangeable, and central to our emotional development. To love yourself is to trust who you are, your instincts, your capability and your authenticity, without question. Love can too easily become a need or a dependence if we have not developed our emotions to a level of selfless maturity.

To achieve these objectives we must address the negativity and noise (negative self-talk and anxiety) in our left brain and put a positive spin on it. Learning to relax our mind, directing our attention inward, understanding our belief systems and coping mechanisms, and revisiting our childhood vulnerabilities establishes self-belief as we begin to understand who we are. This step towards self-confidence is a prerequisite to initiating the stage 3 emotional development objective of self-awareness.

Resolving your past to understand your life skills

As this objective is all about self-reflection and being comfortable in your own skin, set aside time for yourself, to begin to contemplate and appreciate who you are. If you need help in this area, try mindfulness or read personal development methods or books that resonate with you (chapter 18), to understand the vulnerabilities and limiting beliefs that defined you. Subjects may include low self-esteem, being amiable, low motivation, self-doubt, excessive worrying, insecurities, shyness, the need for validation, problem avoidance, unwanted habits, time management and procrastination. Identify with what is represented in the method or book if it applies to you. Write down your vulnerabilities and analyse your reactions to awaken your understanding. Awareness is a strong enabler, and meditation is also a great way to self-reflect. Seek advice if problems or past events seem insurmountable. Seek out self-help methods or books that provide structured activities to practise new behaviours and to progressively challenge your belief systems and comfort zones. If you feel you have a good understanding of yourself and are not held back by inhibitions then you have likely mastered this stage.

Stage 3: Emotional expansion and balancing trust

The ability to trust is a measure of emotional maturity and self-awareness. On entering adolescence, we start the journey to know ourselves and become self-disciplined and self-controlled – learning to regulate ourselves and come to terms with who we are.

Reflection and mindfulness improve our self-control, objectivity, tolerance, spontaneity, equanimity, concentration, mental clarity, emotional awareness and the ability to engage with kindness, acceptance and compassion. Our belief system and coping mechanisms may be fabricated fantasies and not necessarily life's truths. They should be revisited during our adolescent development stage 3 as we discover our independence, reveal our life skills, and come to know essentially who we are. To discover our authentic, self-aware selves, we must appreciate what is factual, and understand what our true role in life is. This role fuels our passion.

This is why the bond between parent and infant is so important. Trust is learnt through nurturing and caring whereas our primary fear is a given or prevailing survival factor. Trust starts from a very low base but broadens and strengthens throughout our development.

Learning to trust our capability and who we are
Entry into adolescence indicates our readiness to develop our creative right-brain capability and extend our awareness. The structure and wiring of the brain has reached a point where it can support the strengthening polarity of emotions. Our thoughts influence our emotional growth. Although the brain adjusts and will continue to be rewired, the expansion of the brain volume at this point is largely complete. This signifies the completion of our biological stage and entry into our emotional stage. The ambush of hormonal changes not only prepares the adolescent for reproduction, but also for nurturing.

This is a time of great transformation. The transition from learning left-brain to right-brain characteristics represents the passage from *knowing* to *doing*, from the *accumulation* of knowledge and skills to their *application*. We start to completely change perspective, from a reactive view looking for answers in the past to a positive view evolving a powerful awareness of the present to nurture, and the ability to reason for problem-solving. Emotional intelligence and reasoning skills allow us to distinguish and achieve this positive state.

Reasoning between our positive and negative states in stage 3 allows us to dig deep, address myths and bring understanding to what may be holding us back. Reasoning also develops our intuitive ability. The conclusions and associations we come to when revisiting the past are essentially associated intuitively or assimilated as part of our identity. As we learn to trust our intuition and discover our authentic selves, this understanding becomes part of our value-based automatic decision-making process. We are most creative when we are developing our emotional maturity and coming to terms with who we are. Our multidimensional, intuitive capability presents creative responses to problem-solving. Our growing sense of self and independence delivers personalised views and a wealth of experience. What may be of value to one self-aware individual may not hold value for another. Authentic, independent views can be powerful enablers to solving a problem that holds personal meaning.

Without self-awareness, without learning to trust our emotions in adulthood, our beliefs may remain naive so that we never discover our true potential. Lack of trust reflects our point of focus to the past. Without trusting relationships we may fail to achieve or even explore the currency of our passions. The need to internalise personal beliefs in childhood can be substituted too easily by external beliefs. Our conscious bias or cognitive dissonance can mask reality as beliefs from a bygone era hide a lack of self-belief in adulthood.

HOW OUR ADULT CULTURAL DEVELOPMENT REPRESENTS OUR AUTHENTIC TRUTH OR WORK PURPOSE

At the opposing extreme of internal childhood insecurity is external adulthood security, life's ultimate cultural objective and the fourth and final stage of development.

Stage 4: Work expansion – balancing our truth for future security

Culture represents life's truths, our why, an expression of our collective identity and purpose. Culture has emotion at its core. Stage 4 big-picture leadership characteristics help define future strategy and environmental security. When we reach this stage of development, we can exploit growth opportunities around us. Our environmental interactions and associations define our cultural identity, our capability, and give meaning to life.

Adult cultural competence and future-focused environmental awareness are achieved through a cycle of learning. Our youthful fears – and insecurities caused by what may be missing in our lives or our susceptibilities – direct our adult perception: the things we longed for, the car we wanted to have, what played on our minds in our youth. Our childhood identity supports the realisation of opportunities in adulthood. While our stage 2 reflective left brain is geared to

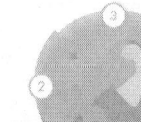

discovering problems, our stage 4 big-picture right-mind searches for solutions. A cultural competence allows us to use every aspect of our executive brain function.

Think about fear of spiders and why a child may have developed this fear. This fear was not evident at birth. Something or someone taught the child to be cautious around spiders. The interesting thing is, this fear plays on the growing mind. We have a fascination with fear, which we usually resolve once we have weighed and considered the likelihood the spider will not cause us harm. We program skills to help us balance our fears and insecurities. Once we know which spiders are not dangerous, we prod harmless spiders with a stick and realise they are more fearful of us than we are of them.

Fundamental life skills define us, for our brains are wired during stage 2 with skills, processes and procedures. This programming forms the foundation of our future-focused adult awareness. For our brains to be malleable and adaptable, we must ensure this programming does not limit us. As adults we are secure around spiders and respect their purpose. The insecurity we endured as children promoted personal skills so our adult awareness allows us to feel secure in our environment with spiders. Some people may not develop this awareness if they are not practised in dealing with spiders or do not challenge themselves to resolve their vulnerabilities.

THE PROGRESSION OF BEHAVIOURS REPRESENTED IN PHILOSOPHY

The ancient Chinese first observed the significance of matter, that objects have two opposing states, that duality recognises a polarity of determinations between two extremes with a simple balance being desirable. They called this balance Yin/Yang. The concept of dualism in the Middle East can be traced to Zoroastrianism, Islam, Gnosticism and Judaism. According to Babylonian legend, the goddess Ishtar was asked, 'Why was the division so?', and replied, 'We are divided for the chance of union'.

6. Attitude, trust and truth on the journey to self-discovery

In ancient philosophy and Buddhism, all life moves in cycles between natural polarities – seasons, pleasure and pain, love and despair, life and death – and this is apparent in our opposing biological states of fear and trust, and our physiological states of discovering and influencing life. As with our development cycle of infant, child, adolescent and adult, our journey through life moves from the lower aspects of left-brain prevalence to higher right-brain states: from negative Yin/Yang to positive Yin/Yang – and in some instances vice versa – as represented in the following table highlighting some behavioural extremes.

1. NEGATIVE YIN (SELF-WORTH)	2. NEGATIVE YANG (SELF-BELIEF)	3. POSITIVE YIN (SELF-AWARE)	4. POSITIVE YANG (SELF-EXPRESS)
Hurt	Rigid	Loving	Empowered
Depressed	Neurotic	Compassionate	Disciplined
Rejected	Angry	Forgiving	Assertive
Moody	Competitive	Joyous	Discerning
Defensive	Controlling	Cooperative	Focused
Fearful	Attacking	Authentic	Self-mastery
Negative	Critical	Self-trusting	Responsible
Worried	Superior	Accepting	Unattached
Lazy	Impatient	Humility	Patient
Low self-worth	Hateful	Modesty	Secure
Guilt	Vengeful	Gentleness	Decisive
Victim	Intolerant	Peacefulness	Big-picture
Needy	Patriotic	Flexible	Persevering
Self-pitying	Resentful	Intuitive	Giving
Lonely	Jealous	Receptive	Confident
Shy	Selfish	Open	Co-creator
Procrastinating	Workaholic	Feeling	Non-judgemental

Adapted from *How to Clear the Negative Ego*, Dr Joshua David Stone

* * *

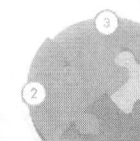

By appreciating that everything external is in a state of change, we learn to obey and understand our natural states when manoeuvring between polarities to discover a higher sense of purpose and happiness. Your purpose is to trust in who you are and to identify and assimilate your understanding of life – to express your identity and truth. We are the observers of balance and imbalance. At maturity, we live in the present with an eye to the future, and need to be consciously aware of a state of change in our internal and external environment. We supplement present understanding with meaningful goals and realistic career pathways to focus on the future.

Our attitude to learning is what underlies the growth and broadening of our behavioural capability. As we grow up, we learn what education means to our development, and over time we appreciate the necessity of education as we develop an identity and distinguish ourselves from our peers. Some find it easy to learn; others find it difficult – but we all recognise that success will come from our motivation. That is the spark that energises us. HR practitioners and managers must value this potential to grow and acknowledge these motivators and their growth objectives.

7. HOW OUR TEMPERAMENT INDICATES OUR LEVEL OF DEVELOPMENT

Our prevailing mood or temperament determines our locus of control and point of reference – the extent we connect to life. Our temperament indicates and influences our four stages of development and environmental positioning. On the whole, temperaments tend to mature through four development phases: negative, reactive, positive and proactive. Our temperaments are matched by development objectives through these four phases.

Our stage objectives throughout our development are shown in the table on the following page.

DEVELOPMENT	OBJECTIVE	PROFILE (DiSC)	REFERENCE	TEMPERAMENT
1. Dependent	Self-worth	Dominant	External	Negative
2. Control	Self-belief	Compliant	External to internal	Reactive
3. Independent	Self-aware	Steadiness	Internal	Positive
4. Intra-dependent	Self-express	Influencing	Internal to external	Proactive

How temperaments indicate our level of development

We start life completely dependent. When we sense we are worthy (self-worth), we begin to control our thoughts to build a strong identity and self-belief. The journey to independence begins the transformation to free the mind where self-awareness is the objective. Intra-dependent leaders realise the value of the collective beyond the independent mind. **Charismatic and secure leaders are masters at influencing, expressing their purpose (self-express) and contribution.**

A prevailing negative mood initiates our development as a newborn and is evident when the dependent infant is uncomfortable, hungry or tired. Research to back up this claim provides no clear direction and only adds complexity by searching for a genetic basis, prenatal influences, arousal, fluctuation and intensity of moods. Suggesting temperaments are also a class of personality traits only further confuses the basis for prevailing moods. What is agreed is environment and biological influences play an important role in determining our prevailing mood.

HOW WE DIRECT ENERGY

In the absence of clear research objectives and findings, I will go out on a limb to offer my understanding. Our temperament or mood represents how we direct energy. For the benefit of offering a generalised view of development for HR professionals, I represent the characteristics of our base moods for ease of identifying them. There are four ways we direct energy:

- negatively (biological)
- reactively (physiological)
- positively (emotional)
- proactively (cultural).

In physics, the natural energy flow is from negative to positive. Humans are no different; our temperaments start from negative. Our physiological state refracts the negative to positive continuum to represent a reactive to proactive continuum.

Humble beginnings

As a newborn, our prevailing mood is negative so as to master our primary fears and initiate our growth cycle. These humble beginnings promote essential sensory learnings and found values around bonding and safety. Other infant moods present with bouts of energy and respond to environmental stimuli. An infant quickly returns to a prevailing negative mood as energy resources are drained or biological factors ensue. I see the same behaviour in adolescents, and even in adults who do not exert a high level of self-control. They typically return to their prevailing mood when tired, hungry or threatened. Without a sense of self, associations are many-to-many.

Creating an identity

The inability of infants to moderate their energy means periods of inactivity are replaced by periods of high activity. In general, infants experience an array of emotions to broaden their temperament to reactive as they enter childhood. A reactive temperament helps the child analyse, judge and identify alongside other children. Learning to self-reflect and direct energy internally helps to moderate behaviour as the child develops self-control, an identity and self-belief. This is when children may become self-absorbed, always switching the conversation back to themselves, a normal characteristic of children who are

creating an identity and wanting to be unique. Associations start from many-to-one at this stage as the child starts to develop a sense of self through observing others. Many-to-one associations are also about perfecting repetitive tasks and improving productivity.

Forging deeper relationships

Adapting a positive attitude as we enter adolescence enhances intellectual, physical, and social awareness, allowing us to forge deeper relationships, and to reason between positive and negative perspectives. Now we are more creative as we learn to respond to problems automatically with a strengthening intuitive capability. Opposing our sensory ability, intuition represents a lifetime of emotionally associating actions, events, decisions and experiences. Perfect for nurturing, a parent's positive mood deploys a calmer, more tolerant, generous temperament to bond with an infant or guide a child's reactive mindset. The cooperative one-to-one associations help carers, coaches and HR professionals exhibit trust.

A strong proactive spirit

As we enter adulthood, we switch back to our primary physiological cultural growth objective and work purpose becomes our priority. Assuming we have achieved a prevailing positive outlook and are aware of our motivators, drivers and what defines us, once we align goals to our purpose, our temperaments deliver a strong proactive spirit. **Leaders who have achieved this stage of development are radiant, driven, charismatic and adaptive.** Jacinda Ardern, Oprah Winfrey and Bill Gates are great examples of culturally competent leaders, selfless and uncompromising in their endeavours. They have a strong sense of social values and intellectual awareness, and express themselves and their purpose with ease. Associations at this stage are one-to-many. Whether this temperament prevails over extended periods, I'm not certain. It would make sense for this level of energy to present in bursts, returning to a prevailing positive equilibrium for social engagement as goals and contributions are asserted. This positive state would focus our creative and social characteristics to broaden strategic initiatives.

When aligned in the BBDM, the sets of opposing temperaments, objectives and characteristics are in complete balance. The aligning and grouping of attributes encourages the development of associated stage objectives. For HR or management professionals as an example – who are honing their stage 3 emotional ability – a positive outlook supports one-to-one relationships and promotes self-awareness.

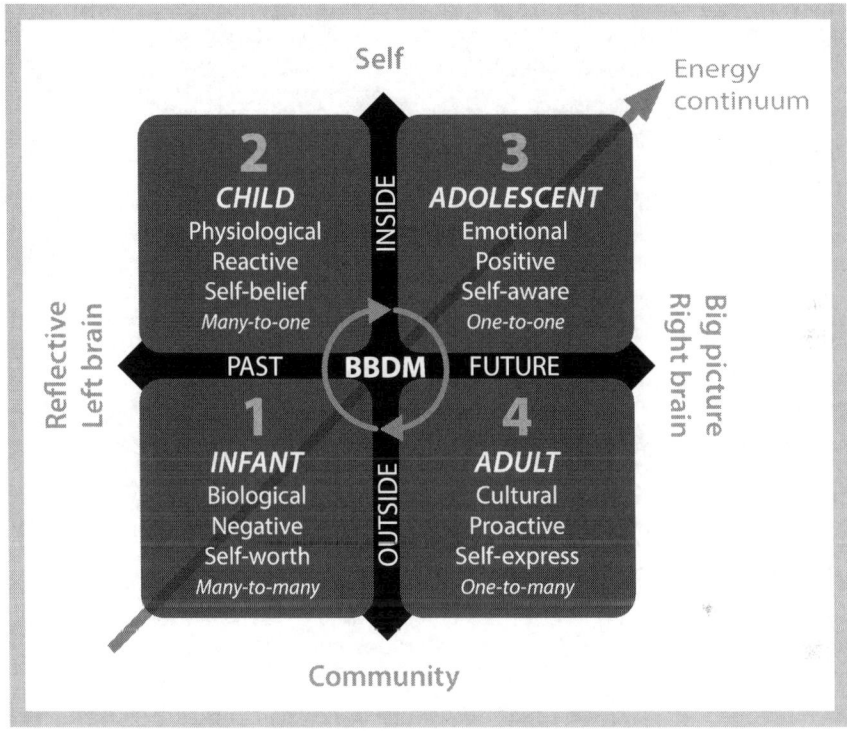

**Our temperament tracks our associations
and development stage**

THE BENEFITS OF HAVING A PREVAILING POSITIVE TEMPERAMENT

People who are positive are often healthier, live longer and enjoy their jobs more. People in a good mood set higher goals, do better at them, and continue to direct their future path for longer. In a positive mood, they can endure more discomfort and pain. As opposed to negative people, positive people tend to enjoy a rich and fulfill-ing social life. Employing life goals by actively pursuing a purposeful, fulfilling lifestyle fosters a positive outlook. A strong sense of self and a well-directed future provide the necessary foundation to indepen-dently direct a prolonged period of wellbeing. Attitude and gratitude are defining factors, and adapting a positive outlook has little to do with fate, chance or which side of the bed a person sleeps on. Far from being an expectation – with life, *you* make it happen.

A reactive mood in an adult can stem from unresolved physiolog-ical or intellectual sensitivities, or a lack of confidence or self-belief. A proactive mood is stimulated through setting goals and having achieved all the previous primary objectives: self-worth, self-belief, and initiating self-reflection to become self-aware. Our maturity or state evolves from dependence and control – independence through to intra-dependence.

Our mood defines us in many ways. The way we interact and emotionally associate, how we position ourselves relative to others, and our level of maturity. Reaching a positive, balanced state should be our goal: to appreciate all the health and wellness benefits that come from a prevailing positive outlook, having mastered stress and anxiety, and freed the mind.

8. CHANGE: THE NEW PARADIGM

OUR WILLINGNESS TO CONFRONT CHANGE INFLUENCES OUR GROWTH

I have always aspired to change, and viewed individual change milestones as some of my greatest accomplishments. Change has been about avoiding the mundane, confronting life's hurdles, and craving new experiences – what I hadn't tried, I wanted to explore. I just wanted to be different and to be my own person, so it's no coincidence that, 30 years later, I should be in the field of change management. The role of Change Facilitator encompasses a lifetime of learning and emotional maturity. Relationships are key to implementing change, and social connection is an absolute requirement for exhibiting trust, having other people's interests at heart, and gauging the readiness of an organisation for change.

'Change management' is the term used in business to describe the transition to a new model that enhances an organisation's relationships with its customers, employees and shareholders, using the power of strategy to drive performance. Its rise in prominence came after the widespread adoption and repeated failure of business process re-engineering (BPR) in the late 1980s and early 1990s. Change management principles were designed to position the employee at the centre of any process and system, to effectively manage change from the inside out so as to encourage continuous improvement ideals.

Growth comes from within

Today, change has become a constant in the business environment and is a requirement for leaders to master going forward. Change is a fact of life, representing evolution and adaptation throughout our lifecycle. However, while change may come from the outside, growth always comes from within. Change is inevitable, but growth is optional. Outside support may help and encourage people to grow, but ultimately it's up to the individual to want to progress. Rather than being a quick fix, change takes energy and effort over an extended period and requires determination. At times we may need to face up to radical changes, painful to endure or even to contemplate, but on the other side of change lie big-picture understanding, self-awareness, a multi-dimensional spatial capability, and the application of knowledge and skills contributing to a better, more fulfilling life.

If we humans challenge ourselves to do things differently, whether right or wrong, we learn from the experience, assimilate this understanding and flourish. Employees may resist if they do not see the risk/reward relationships, but – when change is managed properly – they are usually willing to test themselves and adapt. Change and growth provide certainty and job security when employees believe in the reasons for them. According to a survey of 6,600 employees across the world by CEB Global, 74 per cent say they are willing to adapt to support organisational change.

Many reasons can underlie change in organisations:

- Leadership changes often result in restructuring.

- Industry or technological disruption or declining profitability may result in rationalisation or outsourcing.

- Mergers and acquisition activity may also drive change.

Whatever the cause, organisations and the people in them must not only be prepared to adapt, but actively *seek* to adapt. Providing innovative, change-adaptive environments, agile teams open to challenges, and curious, self-aware, change-ready employees is the way to lead and meet change head on. Developing these characteristics prepares an organisation for change, and opens new markets. CEOs are more able to accept risk and develop new strategies when they can count on an adaptive, supportive workforce. Human resource professionals and managers can build the right skills and mindsets to implement new initiatives and systems, and even products and services.

THE SIGNIFICANCE OF SELF-AWARENESS

Employees typically first understand brain function and how change affects the individual through an introduction to personal development techniques. Personal development, mindfulness and accelerated learning techniques may help them realise the power of their mind, and their potential to maximise brain function and manage emotions. By understanding this core capability and directing brain function, it's possible to see how to leverage future career planning. Personal development can be applied to all situations, including growing self-awareness and success in relationships. By adopting strategic principles, including milestones and vision, the brain can be a powerful enabler of a desired purpose. Central to successful change management is the ability to cultivate a vision that is enlivening, compelling and meaningful for a qualitative lifestyle.

Traditional top-down approaches to managing change in organisations have been proven not to work, especially in an age where hierarchical organisations are being replaced by flatter matrix organisations and agile teams. In 'The Irrational Side of Change Management' by Carolyn Aiken and Scott Keller, a McKinsey survey of 3,199 executives around the world found, as John Kotter[9] did, that only one transformation in three succeeds. Other studies over the past 10 years reveal similar results. It seems that, despite many change projects and

---

9 'Leading Change: Why Transformation Efforts Fail', John P. Kotter, *Harvard Business Review*, May–June 1995.

challenges, the field of change management has not led to more successful change outcomes.

Change occurs at the individual level

What Carolyn Aiken and Scott Keller found makes complete sense. Firstly, there must be a compelling story or reason for change that is built from the ground up. What motivates management may not motivate employees, so why not let them create their own story? The story needs to be real and accepted by a majority, and it doesn't matter if there are both positive and negative influences. People will accept the factors that support the story.

Open-source change

Secondly, avoid top-down implementation. Involving employees in change and role-modelling required behaviours through open-source or inside-out change is the way to go. In top-down implementations, leaders may mistakenly believe they already are the change, but this is not necessarily the solution. To succeed, you must drive change at the individual level, using reinforcement mechanisms. To be effective, these mechanisms must take into account that people will not always behave rationally. Money is the most expensive way to motivate people. Motivations take many forms but, overall, processes and outcomes must be fair.

The transition away from top-down approaches to focus on your people greatly increases the chances of success. The open-source change approach is a response to these findings and provides a clear strategy for HR professionals and managers to implement change.[10] Staff are called upon to execute change, and also to influence and improve it. Open-source change originated in the 1990s, and the outstanding benefit of using this inclusive approach for change implementation is that participation from all levels of an organisation provides a diversity of expertise and perspectives. This method may be accompanied by collaborative tools such as Yelp messaging to facilitate the exchange of

---

10 'Making Change Management Work', Gartner-CEB 2017 white paper.

ideas and allow the exploration and grouping of outcomes aligned to organisational values and objectives.

Employees are actively involved in implementation and planning, and leaders proactively include them in change strategy decisions. Communication is about supporting rather than commanding. Convincing team members to agree to change, implement it and be rewarded for it develops strong working relationships.

Thirdly, employees are what they think, feel and believe in. When managers attempt to drive performance by changing the way employees behave, they all too often neglect the thoughts, feelings and beliefs that drive their behaviour. Good intentions aren't enough. Training should not be a one-off event. Robert Kegan and Lisa Laskow Lahey describe in *An Everyone Culture: Becoming a deliberately developmental organization* how training and development can be woven into the fabric of working life and a company's regular operations, daily routines and conversations. They describe fashioning a culture of development and growth through the everyday activities of employees.

Carolyn Aiken and Scott Keller go on to define a 'field and forum' approach, in which classroom training is spread over a series of learning forums, and fieldwork is assigned in between. Focus groups with participants at similar development stages can be extremely powerful when challenged to resolve problems, as well as improving skills, knowledge and competence, and creating fieldwork assignments requiring them to put into practice new mindsets and skills in ways that become hardwired into their responsibilities. Encouraging employees to work on business improvement projects according to their strengths will also motivate them to learn new skills outside their typical functional activities.

Open-source change management principles and open workplaces should encourage:

- self-empowerment
- self-awareness
- an understanding of motivators
- freedom of choice

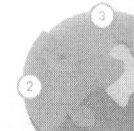

- positive outlook

- understanding

- problem-solving

- learning from experience

- communicating an intention to change for reinforcement

- learning, forgiving and moving on

- imagination

- knowledge – attainment and assimilation

- trust.

Fourthly, creating an environment of change and growth is central to supporting high-performance cultures. Every workplace is different, so creating the right culture depends on overall objectives and how they can be aligned to support the greater good. Every organisation has its own way of establishing values, concepts, meaningful stories, norms and practices. Being specific about the business's niche and how it positively influences the community it serves can be workshopped from various functional objectives. For example, HR can be made accountable for developing and training staff, thereby improving employees' wellbeing and encouraging them to engage more positively. Customer service can be responsible for measuring how the organisation's products or services affect customers' lives. Employees can be asked, or even incentivised, to provide examples or ideas of how to better target customers' positive experiences to improve sales processes, products and services. Giving this responsibility to customer service team members allows them to develop the skills and capability to engage with the community.

Change is the new paradigm: to change is to grow.

9. HOW TO MOTIVATE CHANGE AND GROWTH

Rather than being an expectation, happiness is a product of our engagement with life. Loving life is an indicator of our propensity to grow. Whereas growth is an incremental, adaptive process, change can happen overnight and may not be in our control.

In *Mindset: The new psychology of success*, Carol S. Dweck introduces the comparison of growth mindsets as opposed to fixed mindsets. Growth mindsets find challenges exciting rather than threatening. Rather than fearing to reveal weakness, you recognise an opportunity to grow. These attitudinal differences are evident in our hemisphere selection. Dweck also debunks the idea that intelligence is fixed or predetermined by your gene pool. She suggests people with a growth mindset develop intelligence and abilities, that they challenge themselves and are not afraid of making mistakes. On the other hand, people with fixed mindsets are afraid of making mistakes and of moving out of their comfort zone. Dweck describes fixed-mindset people as preoccupied with outcomes – for instance, with a final grade or successful work project – over the process and experience.

DEVELOPING A GROWTH MINDSET

One of the biggest inhibitors to achieving a growth mindset is self-confidence, and a lot of what underlies a lack of self-confidence – as Dweck describes in her book – is management or teacher styles. She says that telling students they are smart and intelligent and giving constant praise can lead to a fear of making mistakes, fear of failure and a fixed mindset. Praising or command styles may limit the exploration of broader outcomes. Learners can be taught a growth mindset. Dweck developed a program to teach growth-mindset principles – intelligence is not fixed, and students are encouraged to organise their own instruction and to test themselves in order to get smarter. Students taught a growth mindset performed better academically.

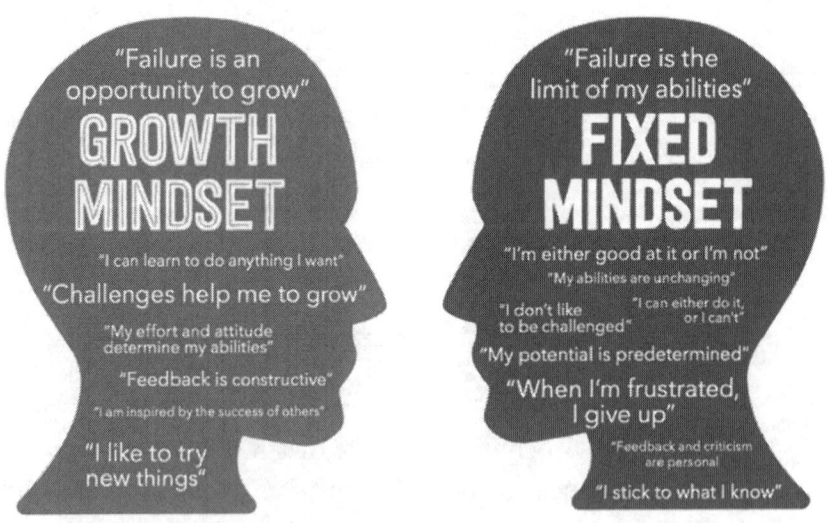

Mindset: The New Psychology of Success, Carol S. Dweck

The BBDM employs a growth mindset approach, suggesting our minds are adaptable. Even when left to our own devices we can accomplish our purpose and adapt traits to promote our cause. Neuroplasticity, or brain malleability, signifies the brain's ability to reorganise itself by forming new neural connections.[11] These are largely influenced by recent situations or changes in the environment.

In a fixed mindset, people believe their basic qualities such as intelligence or talent are simply firm traits, and they spend time documenting instead of developing them. They also believe that talent alone without effort creates success, but they're wrong. Having a growth mindset – the belief that you are in control and can learn and improve – is the key to success. Hard work, effort and persistence are all crucial, but it's more important to believe you are in control of your own destiny. Adopting a growth mindset is about challenging yourself to grow.

How self-awareness influences a growth mindset

Until we reach a certain level of self-confidence and understand our capability, we may not always believe what other people say about our ability. People will make their own judgement and need to come to their own conclusions about their ability. One of the key elements this book focuses on is the progressive development of capability through a succession of behavioural opposites. We all start life at a similar point, essentially a blank canvas, and over time we build up the confidence to know and trust our own and other people's understanding. As evident in the BBDM, a strong identity or sense of self developed in stage 2 supports a greater depth of emotions, allowing a higher awareness of what empowers and motivates the individual.

Employees' different motivations should be considered when asking them to participate in change activities. Dr John Demartini is a respected human behavioural specialist who describes the underlying motivators of people as 'voids'. Motivators or values are an attempt to fill what is missing or to solve what is unknown. Our motivations originate from whatever we perceive to be missing in our lives. Your

---

11 *Soft-Wired: How the new science of brain plasticity can change your life*, 2nd edition, Dr Michael Merzenich, PhD.

perceived emptiness drives your search for fulfilment. Dr Demartini was a special needs student and therefore particularly values knowledge.

I tend to describe voids differently. The insecurities we harbour as children are a product of having to learn to feel secure in our environment. Over time, we build life skills to balance our vulnerabilities, so we can move on to bigger and better things. Insecurities increase when we believe something in our lives is missing, or that something will provide more security. Insecurities exist so we can balance them to grow secure in our environment.

Values express our motivations to overcome our insecurities

Voids, motivations, insecurities, vulnerabilities – all express underlying emotions that keep us moving forward and form the foundations of our values. Understanding your motivations will also provide insights to your career purpose or self-actualisation as Maslow defined (chapter 19).

We all experience voids. In 1928, Eduard Spranger wrote a book entitled *Types of Men* (just a little sexist), identifying six major motivators or world views giving rise to the Why behind our behaviours and actions. These motivators show how we view the world and seek fulfilment. If we participate in a discussion, activity or career in alignment with our values, we respect the experience. Conversely, if we are in a conversation, activity or career that conflicts with our dominant attitudes, we are indifferent or even negative, and possibly stressed.

Every experience, decision and action is determined by our hierarchy of values and based upon what we feel will provide us with the most advantage and reward over risk to our highest values. The more managers understand their own and their employees' motivations, the more they can communicate, educate and empower themselves and their employees. Therefore it is important to ensure employees' values are not only aligned to their role, but also to the organisation.

9. How to motivate change and growth

The six basic personal interests, attitudes and value motivators are:[12]

1   *Theoretical:* A passion to discover truth. The chief objective in life is to order and assimilate knowledge and the meaning behind that knowledge.

2   *Utilitarian/Economic:* A practical interest in money and a passion for what is useful. Time and resources are considered with an eye to efficiency and future economic gain.

3   *Aesthetic:* Interest in form and harmony. Life is a series of episodic events, each enjoyed for its own sake. A heightened sense of beauty and inner vision, though not necessarily creative talent.

4   *Social:* Inherent love of people. Seeks to eliminate hate and conflict. Considers other people as ends and not means. Altruistic, kind, empathetic and generous, even to their own detriment.

5   *Individualistic/Political:* Primary interest is self-improvement or power, not necessarily politics in the traditional sense. Research indicates that leaders in most fields have a high-power value. Other people may be seen and used as the means to an end.

6   *Traditional/Regulator:* Unity and order. The need to be regulated or for structure from an outside source. Seeks to comprehend the universe as a whole and to relate to a global totality. Dislikes change and chaos and may be inflexible.

Each of these motivations can be designated in a job role. Most employees tend to align themselves accordingly, although disenfranchised employees may simply be in the wrong role. There are many assessment tools on the market to assist people to understand their motivations. Here in Australia, I am accredited to use TTI Success Insights to conduct Motivators Assessments; however, other organisations offer similar testing.

Aside from understanding motivators, behavioural assessments and development can also be targeted to assist employees to

12 Adapted from TTI Motivators Profile.

understand their limiting beliefs and progress, as I shall cover later. Managers need Ei to show empathy in coaching development objectives. Providing an open, supportive environment for employees to express their vulnerabilities and be encouraged to grow creates an inclusive, high-performance culture. Allowing them the freedom to be imperfect, make informed mistakes, talk through resolutions and challenge themselves is all part of creating a 'deliberately developmental organisation' (Robert Kegan and Lisa Laskow Lahey).

HOW DIFFERENT MOTIVATORS INFLUENCE EVERY ASPECT OF OUR LIVES

Motivations are the personal drivers or 'the Why' of what we do to pursue goals with energy and persistence. The more we know our likes and dislikes, the more we begin to understand our feelings towards other people and situations. We can then apply this awareness to manage relationships and to help achieve our goals. Motivators or our values are the things we are passionate about; they motivate our strengths that we perceive as important, or the associations that provide us with purpose and direction in life. Our values or motivations can change over time as we grow and become familiar and comfortable with them. They also influence our happiness.

Many studies have found that enough money to cover our basic needs influences happiness.[13] People who pursue material things above other goals tend to be less satisfied with life. The positive effects of generosity and building relationships influence our happiness over the long term. Emotional objectives such as being socially connected are positively and strongly correlated with happiness. Cultural objectives such as leading purposeful, goal-orientated lives also make people happier.

Gratifications express our motivations, and as opposed to pleasures, are learnt senses and emotions, deeper than sensory pleasures. Gratification stems from positive, purpose-driven actions and requires awareness of what motivates someone's personal interests. Unconscious

---

13 'Can Money Buy Happiness?', Rin Hamburgh, *The Guardian*, 7 January 2016.

biases in right-brain-dominant people are much less disruptive than in left-brain-dominant people. A person who acts on a sense of purpose is usually more confident and more likely to gain longer-term gratification from their role. Setting and displaying positive affirmations certainly distracts attention from negative behaviours.

* * *

Encouraging employees to be reflective and allowing them to discuss their motivators, vulnerabilities and strengths will build their identity, self-confidence and awareness, and is essential to their personal development. Challenging ourselves to change, grow and adapt is the natural course of evolution, where the rewards are greater certainty, security and therefore wellbeing. HR and managers can promote supportive environments where colleagues can talk freely about their challenges and strengths. This will help to address their concerns and allow them to move on to greater things. Employees will be at various levels of emotional maturity and self-awareness, so it is important that HR oversees the employees and ensures they are led by Ei-qualified people who abide by ethical standards.

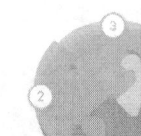

10. PERSONALITY AND BEHAVIOURAL OPPOSITES

LIFE EXISTS AROUND CAUSE-AND-EFFECT RELATIONSHIPS

Duality of characteristics or the instance of opposing or contrasting states is a pathway for human development. Dominant/recessive, primary/secondary, left-brained/right-brained and biological/physiological are all examples of the duality that exists in humans. Life is not entirely random: even in nature, life is ordered. From our very basic building blocks there is structure and there are patterns. There are relationships and associations in every aspect of life, and this is why symmetry and mathematics applies to our development. Life evolves to fill niches, and so does human development.

While our genetic makeup lays a strong foundation to assist us in our environment, it is the behavioural characteristics that evolve over our lifetime that help us adapt to our changing environmental circumstances.

We are built to adapt and change – it takes leadership to show the way

The world is composed of many dualities. We learn pleasure in the absence of pain, happiness due to the absence of sorrow. It's this dichotomy that cultures and religions have understood and built their belief systems around. The mind has two opposing hemispheres: posi-tive/proactive mental states and negative/reactive mental states. If you adopt a positive outlook then you strengthen the mind by engaging your creative hemisphere. People who work in the humanities like HR and medicine tend to develop positive temperaments. They have learnt to respect their social right brain through caring, nurturing and mutual respect. I am drawn to positive people and often they are in the humanities. There is plenty of research to support how giving back, listening effectively, learning to trust, and surrounding yourself with positive people enhances social connection and wellbeing, but little research on how a positive temperament or attitude enables functional roles like HR.

Personality characteristics correspond in primary ways to how people's minds process information. This book presents some ground breaking assumptions which are only now being researched. **There is a definite link between brain function and behaviour.** According to Michael Merzenich, practising a new habit under the right conditions can change hundreds of millions – and possibly billions – of the connections between the nerve cells in our neural pathways.[14] The table on the following page represents how divergent characteristics contribute to programing the neurological pathways for the four types of intellectual capability, which are:

1   conditioning

2   logic

3   emotional

4   cultural.

---

14   'The Brain that Changes Itself', Michael Merzenich, June 2010.

INTELLIGENCE	FUNCTION	ASSOCIATIONS	REFERENCE	APPLICATION
1. Conditioning	System and organisation	Many-to-many	External	Copy and conforming
2. Logic	Procedures and skills	Many-to-one	External to internal	Analysis and sequential processing
3. Emotional	Relationships	One-to-one	Internal	Reasoning and creative
4. Cultural	Executive and strategy	One-to-many	Internal to external	Awareness and adaptability

How divergent characteristics influence our intellectual preferences

I define the development of our logical capability by referring to stage 2 characteristics in the table. During childhood, when our primary physiological or body growth stage is most pronounced, skills development is our objective. Our growing ability to sequentially organise, analyse and process data supports the development of our long-term memory and identity. As we begin the journey to internalise our thoughts (external to internal) and broaden our sense of self, many-to-one associations support this.

How can I claim these characteristics support the development of our logical intelligence? Because when all the supporting attributes are aligned in this way, it becomes obvious. And for HR professionals who recognise these very distinct attributes in people, they can create the environment in organisations and coach the individual to optimise learning and capability in the same way. For example, promoting supportive teams to improve decision-making helps stage 2 individuals learn to make better decisions in their own right.

Strategic human resource management and high performance

To HR leaders and managers employing candidates in high-profile jobs, the value of a 'bit better' or a 'bit worse' performance can be significant in monetary terms. There is a strong connection between strategic human resource management and high performance. The relationship between innovation capabilities, innovation efforts and firm performance is also significant and substantial.[15] Look at productivity and gross domestic product (GDP) from a country's perspective: increases in productivity allow firms greater output for the same input, higher revenues, and – ultimately – higher GDP. The level of productivity is the single most important determinant of a country's standard of living, with faster growth leading to a better standard of living.

When we consider the duality of nature, we see that too much or too little light or dark, matter or energy, male or female would make our world a more difficult place to live in. Plants wouldn't grow; children would not be conceived, born or raised in a balanced environment. The predominance of conservative attributes in leaders and organisations are proof of this imbalance. Read on to understand how balancing these characteristics will supercharge our growth in the future.

THE DUALITIES OF BEHAVIOURAL CHARACTERISTICS

In HR, management and even in day-to-day life, the term 'type' refers to a person's general disposition. Most theories describe only a few types. The term 'trait' also describes a characteristic or tendency, but a person may have many traits, needs, motives, talents or handicaps. Indeed, Raymond Cattell's 1965 factor analysis found that over 50 human traits could be summarised by 16 major personality factors. Other academics and researchers say only five factors describe our personalities:

1   nervousness vs feeling secure

2   sociable vs reserved

3   independent (flexible) vs conforming

4   helpful (trusting) vs hard-hearted

5   conscientious vs disorganised.

---

15 'Relationship Between Innovation Capability, Innovation Type, and Firm Performance',
   R.P. Jayani Rajapathirana, Yan Hui, 2017.

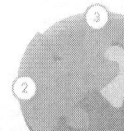

Whether it is 50 or 5 is arbitrary, but 16 has a mathematical basis when linked to the four development stages.

All traits can be learned, with the more mature, learned right-brained traits delivering the most rewards and happiness. Right-brain traits developed much later in our evolution exhibit our social, progressive, adaptable, growth mindsets, while our left-brain traits tend to align to conservative, competitive, fixed (controlled) mindsets. While we all have predispositions when adopting traits, we should be open to learning new ones. I personally know examples of right-brained people who, after successful creative careers in graphic design or art, found they lacked confidence in their left-brained skills, but later went on to pursue left-brain careers in law or psychology to balance out their creative preference.

There are many misunderstandings when it comes to traits. Right-handed people are said to be more left-brained. This would make sense as 90 per cent of the population are right-handed and evolution would indicate we develop our left-brain characteristics first. Left-handed people are said to be more creative, and maybe the 10 per cent of left-handed people are an adaptation to broaden creative dispositions. Or is the fact left-handed people grow up feeling different the cause of their creativity? Imagine growing up in the left-handed minority and seeing yourself as different from your peers. Some children may develop what's known as an 'outsider's mindset', or a tendency to have a more individualised self-image rather than a group-oriented one. This may predispose them to develop qualities such as independence and non-conformity, which psychologists have linked to creative reasoning and innovation. The same may be said for the creativity of homosexual people who grow up knowing they are different. Discovering independence during adolescence is part of our emotional maturity. Being independent includes independent thought. Your own authentic thoughts are likely to be distinct and creative.

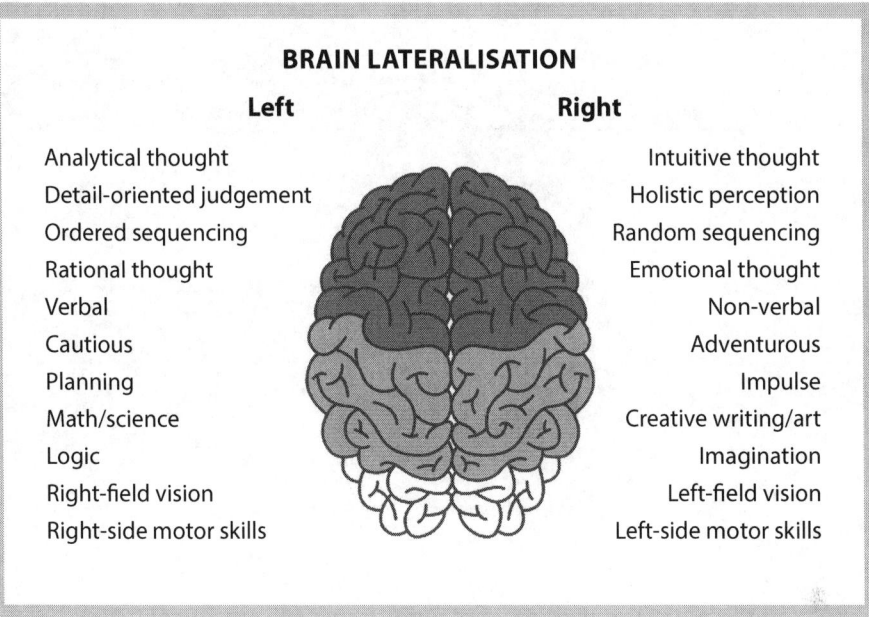

BRAIN LATERALISATION

Left	Right
Analytical thought	Intuitive thought
Detail-oriented judgement	Holistic perception
Ordered sequencing	Random sequencing
Rational thought	Emotional thought
Verbal	Non-verbal
Cautious	Adventurous
Planning	Impulse
Math/science	Creative writing/art
Logic	Imagination
Right-field vision	Left-field vision
Right-side motor skills	Left-side motor skills

Brain hemisphere distinction

THE ORIGINS OF PERSONALITY PROFILING

Carl Jung, the founder of analytical psychology, was the first to discover that central to appreciating your position in the development process is understanding your personality type. He researched a combination of eight personality types. This was later expanded to the 16 personality types of the Myers–Briggs Personality Type Indicator (MBTi) by Katharine Briggs and Isabel Myers, a mother and daughter who studied thousands of characteristics over 22 years. MBTi measures four sets of preferences, as shown in the table on the following page.

These four sets of personality characteristics are available to us to develop a strong character. What is not represented is how these characteristics can be aligned to maximise our development.

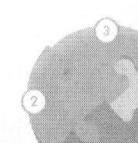

MYERS–BRIGGS TYPE INDICATOR (MBTI)	OUTSIDE COLLECTIVE FOCUSED		INSIDE PERSONAL FOCUSED
1. Orientation of energy/focus of attention	Extrovert (E)	⬅️➡️	Introvert (I)

MYERS–BRIGGS TYPE INDICATOR (MBTI)	LEFT BRAIN REFLECTIVE	PAST – FUTURE	RIGHT BRAIN BIG PICTURE
2. How you deal with your outside world	Judger (J)	⬅️➡️	Perceiver (P)
3. Preference for information uptake	Sensory (S)	⬅️➡️	Intuitive (N)
4. How you direct your decisions	Thinker (T)	⬅️➡️	Feeler (F)

Myers–Briggs Type Indicator – development pathways

The most popular personality tests tend to be based on generalised notions of different personality types. The most widely used, MBTi, tests subjects' responses to questions about their tendencies and behaviours on four opposing scales:

- introversion and extroversion
- judging and perceiving
- sensing and intuition
- thinking and feeling.

The first two characteristics determine your position relative to the environment (judger, self-reflective; perceiver, outside awareness); the remaining two influence how experiences are associated and how knowledge is stored and retrieved for decision-making.

A person is then assessed as being within one of 16 possible four-letter personality categories. For example, it has been said that ESTJ – extroverted, sensing, thinking, judging personality types – are natural leaders in the way they direct action and organise projects logically. This statement is probably true for a rational leader whose logical problem analysis and quick decisions are at the core of their role – for example, an economic or scientific researcher (left-brain) – but not for a visionary, resourceful leader where promoting employee development, diversity, flexibility to changing situations, solutions and big-picture strategic awareness (right-brain) are key to their leadership success; for example, ENFP (extraverted, intuitive, feeling, perceptive).

THE MISCONCEPTIONS OF PERSONALITY TYPING

The BBDM challenges the view that ESTJs are natural leaders, and suggests that a well-developed leader is more likely to be right-brained with mature visionary characteristics including social skills (Ei), perception and strength of character (feelings). A right-brained leader is more likely to be authentic, charismatic and big picture, whereas the left-brained leader may appear factual, logical and predictable.

Furthermore, the right-brained leader may be more able to select between INFP and ENFP preferences to foster communication on both personal and collective levels. This is a known peculiarity to the INFP and ENFP preference – many sit on the cusp of Introvert and Extrovert selection. I myself am an INFP, but sometimes present the characteristics of an ENFP because I appear outgoing and passionate. When I first completed the MBTi test as a fledgling accountant I was an INTJ.

Some experts believe that while the test captures valid aspects of personality, it is too simple to be of practical use, but I disagree. The purpose of learning your type is to develop self-awareness and enhance understanding. MBTi allows an organisation to define a balanced framework of best behaviours to promote development within ethical guidelines.

Some experts think that the MBTi has generalised personality, making people appear walking 'types' when most people are blends. **Few, if any, have suggested personalities change over a lifecycle by adapting characteristics to a changing environment**. While there are no right or wrong types, what distinguishes the *Best Behaviour*

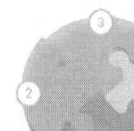

interpretation is the assumption that all the types can be learned, through broadening and moving between their primary and secondary preferences. Moving from left-brain to right-brain preferences provides pathways to maturity. This is where the BBDM is substantially different, and why it will empower a new model of HR practice and thought.

THE DEVELOPMENT OF SELF-AWARENESS

Sensory to Intuition is the most obvious pathway for emotional maturity. We are all born with a primary sensory capability. During our infant years our brains are populated with sensory information. Intuition develops over a lifetime of emotionally associating experiences and actions, but intuition is not available to us until we start to respect, analyse and understand it. This is part of developing self-awareness, which typically occurs in adolescence and involves a complete transformation in the way we process the world – from thinking to feeling, from judger to perceiver. More than being supported, we need to challenge ourselves to transform.

Few people elect to initiate the journey to self-discovery. Many people move on to the right-brain attributes in the absence of mastering personal development. For adult learning or leadership development, if we miss mastering a development stage, we should revisit the earlier stage characteristics to realise wellbeing, self-confidence, self-awareness and, ultimately, self-expression. Revisiting stage objectives may also occur when an employee is inducted into a new role in a completely different industry, and may mean starting as a trainee if they are not self-confident or knowledgeable in the ways the organisation works.

The following model suggests a balanced development selection from an ESTP sensor to an ENFP perceiver. Perceivers and sensitive people tend to externalise, while judgers and intuitive people tend to internalise.

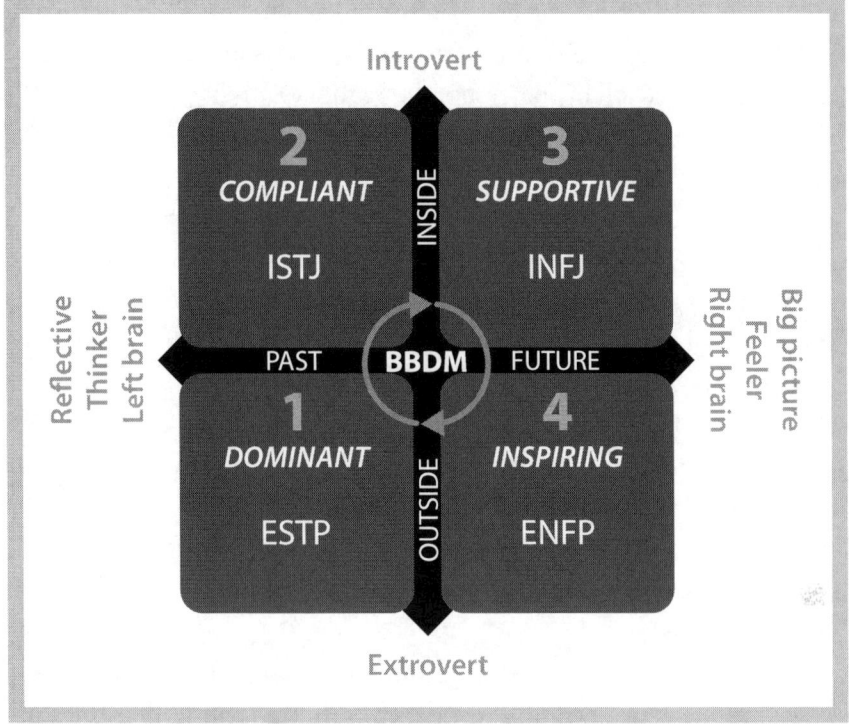

Distinguishing various engagement styles (DiSC and MBTi)

We have a natural inbuilt development mechanism, which has evolved over millions of years to identify a balance between opposites. Our behaviours are represented as opposites:

- inside and outside (introvert or extravert)

- face value or deep appreciation (sensory and intuition)

- the learning and the doing (thinking and feeling)

- the calculated or visionary (judger and perceiver).

These behaviours have been well documented by Jung and Myers–Briggs. The opposing four sets of behavioural types are preferred as primary and secondary selections. Each of the four preferences is interwoven and does not develop in isolation. The coordination of these behavioural growth pathways is powerful. For example, interactions in our environment deepen our senses over time. Judgement and thinking add meaning to our sensory and emotional development. As we mature and begin to understand the basis of our life skills and purpose, we accept deeper emotional understanding as part of our identity, and assimilate this until it becomes intuitive or second nature – it becomes who we are, our role in life.

Biological and physiological, feminine and masculine, IQ and EQ are evident in our development, and the balance of each is essential to our success. What is right or wrong, what is truth or fantasy, what is positive or negative? Our experiences, actions and decisions influence our identity. We weigh up our responses and actions in accordance with an internal compass, navigating our pathway though life. The broadening and maturing of the behavioural opposites develops our identity, and also our environmental positioning. At first we don't have an identity and are completely external, without a sense of self. But after comparing, developing and differentiating ourselves, we begin to define ourselves.

Our identity is dependent on our interactions and the environment we are brought up in. As we move along the spectrum of behaviours, our identity is programmed. No behaviour develops in isolation, and each one influences the development of other behaviours as we move along the continuum. Our intelligence and measure of capability are functions of our willingness to transform and adapt our capability throughout our development cycle.

In the same way that we are victims of our own circumstances, we also have the superior ability to guide our own destiny. By respecting our intellectual capability we develop an independent view: our own truth around our own sense of purpose to achieve self-actualisation. Our purpose is closely associated with the life skills we learnt in our childhood to overcome our insecurities.

Our level of self-assurance is a measure of knowing our capability, together with a willingness to extend ourselves and to influence posi-tive change in the future. In directing our perceptive mind and spatial awareness to the future, we can release ourselves from limiting factors and judgements, and strengthen our identity and executive functions.

10. Personality and behavioural opposites

To understand why the prevalence of today's left-brained, transactional, command–control 'boss' styles are more likely to be fixated on past problems, cost control and tactical objectives is to understand that these defensive styles may be ill equipped to represent their right-hemisphere big-picture spatial awareness which supports strategy, vision and the search for solutions. The diagram below displays why 'boss' styles are not focused on the apparent causes (being the solution) but more so the effects (problems). Is this imbalance of leadership styles the cause of many of the world's problems? The transformational right-hemisphere cultural leadership styles are the enablers of sustainable strategies, growth environments and secure futures.

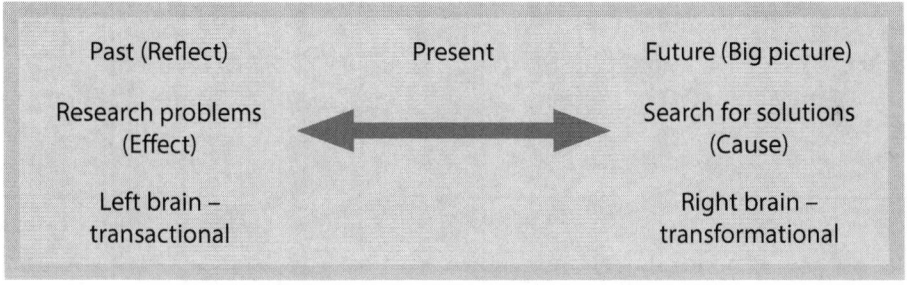

Balancing cause and effect analysis

11. SYMMETRY AND BALANCE IN THE BRAIN HEMISPHERES

HOW OUR HEMISPHERE SELECTION INFLUENCES OUR PERSPECTIVE

The brain's left and right hemispheres have numerous interconnections, especially through the corpus callosum, a bundle of about 200 million nerve fibres that transfer information back and forth between the two hemispheres. Most of the nerve fibres connecting the brain to various parts of the body cross from one side to the other. This means that the right side receives sensory messages and controls movement in the left side of the body, and vice versa.

The two hemispheres make different contributions to the same functions. Both hemispheres contribute to language and memory functions, to perceptual and awareness functions, and to emotional functions. Although the two hemispheres have similar functions and compositions, typically the left brain processes data analytically, while the right brain associates experiences emotionally.

11. Symmetry and balance in the brain hemispheres

Over the last decade numerous studies have found differences in male and female brain development.[16] Considered key to intellectual development, the corpus callosum develops at different rates in boys and girls. Until recently, the corpus callosum was said to have a greater surface area in men than women; however, this theory has now been discredited. Scientists also now accept that the emotional, right side of women's brains are more in touch with the analytical left side.

It appears size does not matter when it comes to intellectual ability. While men's brains are on average 10 per cent larger, size does not modify intellectual performance as was once thought. Men and woman perform similarly in IQ tests. In fact, in some regions women's brains are more tightly packed and appear to have more connections between the two hemispheres.

Even though each hemisphere contributes to different functions, our locus of control and a selection mechanism in the processing of associations allows one hemisphere to dominate. Research by Professor Ornstein revealed that the ongoing strength and weakness of cortical or perceptive skills **were more a function of habit than of basic brain design**. When training people weak in either area, they also simultaneously strengthened their performance in other areas. For example, if a person with poor drawing skills was taught to draw and paint, their academic performance increased overall, especially in subjects such as geometry where perception and imagination are important. Ongoing research suggests that when people have been trained to use either side of their brain to the exclusion of the other, they tend to form dominant habits favouring activities controlled by their chosen brain side, and to describe themselves in those terms.

It's unlikely the brain works exclusively in either hemisphere. We just tend to be more aware or developed in one hemisphere. We tend to have hemisphere preferences because we haven't been taught to optimise both.

The following table shows some attributes of the left and right brain hemispheres (according to Professor Roger Sperry and Professor Robert Ornstein, after an extensive study of the human brain).

---

16 'Sex differences in intelligence', Wikipedia.

LEFT BRAIN (ANALYTICAL)	RIGHT BRAIN (EMOTION)
Words	Rhythm
Logic	Spatial awareness
Numbers	Dimension
Sequence	Imagination
Linearity	Daydreaming
Analysis	Colour
Lists	Holistic awareness (gestalt)

Attributes of the left and right brain hemispheres

In the 20th century, educational systems all over the world favoured left-brain skills – mathematics, languages and the sciences – over the arts, music and teaching intuitive skills, especially creative skills. In focusing on only half of the brain's capability, it may appear we only use 50 per cent of our capacity. It has been said that the average human utilises only a fraction of their intelligence, but research to support this is questionable. Numerous studies have proven all areas of the brain are used, but how can research investigate or prove our overall capability, the way we engage the brain?

The key to our capability

There is little doubt every part of the brain has a function and all areas of the brain are used, however it's how we use it that counts. Some areas may remain underutilised if brain function is not used purposefully. Comparing how intellectuals such as Einstein used their brains can be telling. We know a person who is driven and has direction and purpose will achieve multiple times more than a person who is not. The key to our capability is how well we are developed in all quadrants and how we apply our learning to maximise our purpose and explore meaningful solutions.

Studies of geniuses (for example, 'The Corpus Callosum of Albert Einstein's Brain: Another clue to his high intelligence' was published in the journal *Brain* – the research was led by Dean Falk) have shown that, invariably, they use both sides of their brain. Being of strong character,

emotionally mature and self-aware encourages the use of 'both sides', 'aft and fore' and 'upstairs/downstairs' to explore and develop your own genius. The left and right sides of the cerebral cortex shuttle messages back and forth between the hemispheres, creating a synergetic formula for thinking and growth.

'We should take care not to make the intellect our god;
it has, of course, powerful muscles, but no personality.'

Albert Einstein

The cerebral or prefrontal cortex is also referred to as the area of second thought, the CEO of the brain, or 'executive' function. Women may use the prefrontal cortex more often in conjunction with the amygdala when processing emotions. The amygdala is essential to your ability to feel certain emotions and to perceive them in other people. As men age, they tend to lose more tissue from this region behind the forehead, which concerns itself with consequences and self-control. Generally, the female brain is more interlinked and better suited to cautious diplomacy and emotional awareness.

Today, science expands our concept of balance. It is a scientific fact that humans think differently with the right side of their brains than with the left. The right side of the brain is creative and empathetic, supporting solutions and artistic tastes with original ideas. The left side supports problem discovery, linear thinking, mathematics and logical analysis. Because all brains have two sides, all humans have a creative side and an analytical side, although most people are not fully cognisant of the power of their creative minds. The creative mind can best be appreciated in a positive, goal-oriented person where right-brain vision and inspiration are used to leverage knowledge from the left brain for understanding.

While at least one neurological scientific study[17] discredits the prevalence of left- and right-brain dominance, and although the brain may or may not be symmetrically opposed, primary characteristics

---

17 'An Evaluation of the Left-Brain vs Right-Brain Hypothesis', Jared A. Nielsen, Brandon A. Zielinski, Michael A. Ferguson, Janet E. Lainhart and Jeffrey S. Anderson, *PLOS One* journal, August 2013.

are diametrically expressed in different people. The brain is much more complex and works to provide a multidimensional holistic view of the world. How we see the world depends on our conscious and unconscious bias, and our stage of development. Certainly, primary behaviours align to a past-to-future and inside-or-outside preference. Our primary sensory ability alerts us to external stimuli in the past to present (left brain).

Does our sensory function back up our present-to-future internal right-brain intuitive capability? Absolutely. Our sensory memory associates past actions and experiences, enabling our deeper intuitive ability. Just because we have a behavioural preference at any stage of our development doesn't mean the rest of the brain is deactivated. As adults we all have intuitive instincts, often intentionally ignored. We engage perception, depending on our level of self-assurance, in a more limited capacity for safety and protection (past) or to alert us to opportunity (future). The brain draws on all regions to represent our world in the way we want to see it.

All behaviours can be learnt

This concept of a person with a tendency to lean towards either of these modes rings true for many people, including myself. Just as there are left and right sides to politics[18], we know this distinction to be true in personalities. Most of us make an assessment of left–right, past–future, reflective–big picture, competitive–collaborative, thinker–feeler and judger–perceiver in personalities. We see these elements as either/or, but in fact they're not. All behaviours can be learnt and work as a combination of primary and secondary preferences.

Behavioural characteristics define us. While our genetic makeup may influence our lives, as well as where we are born and the parents we have (or don't have), by and large we are all born with the same biological and physiological attributes, which we can adapt to succeed.

---

18 The modern usage of the political terms left and right comes from the 1789 French Revolution, when supporters of the King stood to the President's right, and supporters of the Revolution to his left. This political divide is at odds with the brain hemispheres.

12. MASTERING A 360° INSIDE-OUT OUTLOOK

DOES OUR ENVIRONMENTAL REFERENCE INFLUENCE OUR BEHAVIOURAL PREFERENCE?

The left-brain/right-brain distinction in human behaviour is perhaps more easily understood than the inside-out distinction. Where do you direct your attention and get your energy? Do you like to spend time in the outer world of collective thoughts and tasks (extraversion), or in your inner world of personal ideas and images (introversion)?

Extraversion and introversion were terms used by Carl Jung to explain the different attitudes people use to direct their energy. Jung applied the words extravert and introvert differently to their meanings today. Extraverted has been understood to mean sociable or outgoing, and the term introverted has been referred to as shy or withdrawn. Jung used the terms to describe the preferred focus of one's energy on either the outer or the inner world. Extraverts oriented their energy to the outer world, while introverts oriented theirs to the inner world. Do not confuse introversion with shyness or reclusiveness. They are not related. I would define introversion as being more considered, intro-spective, independent, personable and selfless.

Introversion and extraversion

One of Jung and Isabel Myers's great contributions to the field of psychology is their observation that introversion and extraversion are both healthy variations in personality style. Everyone spends some time extroverting and introverting:

- *Extraversion (E – From MyersBriggs.org):* I like getting my energy from involvement in events and having a lot of different activities. I'm excited around people and like to energise them, **to move into action and make things happen**. I generally feel at home in the world and often **understand a problem better when I can talk about it and hear what others have to say**.

- *Introversion (I – From MyersBriggs.org):* I like getting my energy from dealing with the ideas, pictures, memories and reactions in my inner world inside my head. I often prefer doing things alone or with one or two people I feel comfortable with. I **take time to reflect**, so as to have a clear idea of what I'll be doing when I decide to act. Ideas are almost solid things for me. **Sometimes I like the idea of something better than the real thing.**

What makes the BBDM distinct is the suggestion that we should challenge ourselves to encompass both styles throughout our development. Evolution dictates we are all born with our energy directed to the outside world. This is not random; it is a survival mechanism to support a quick response to our 'fight, flight or freeze' reaction. **Many academics would have us believe that some people are born focusing energy inwardly (introverted), but there is no evidence to back this up.**

Sensing

It makes perfect sense that we should be born extraverted, without an identity, as one with the environment. Our brain system and structure are unformed and malleable. When information from the outside world enters an infant's extraverted brain, it travels a shorter distance, passing through the areas of the brain where visions, smells, sounds, tastes and interactions are processed. This external focus optimises the use of our youthful sensory traits to fill our brains with untainted sensory information:

- *Sensing (S – From MyersBriggs.org):* Paying attention to physical reality: what I see, hear, touch, taste and smell. I'm concerned with what is **actual, present, current and real**. I notice facts and remember details that are important to me. I like to see the practical use of things and learn best when I can use what I'm learning. **Experience speaks to me louder than words.**

Over time, the environment will dictate whether we maintain our extraversion or begin to direct our energy inward. Encouraging the younger generation to develop strong individual identities would inevitably lead to their focusing their energy inward. Introverts are known to deal with the world differently. They tend to overthink, processing information more thoroughly and deeply. This is about identifying personally, developing a personal point of view and learning to respond in a more calculated way. Introverts take longer to speak, react and make decisions. The brain's pathway to processing information takes much longer. Stimulation travels through many areas of the brain, including:

- the right-front insular, which is an area associated with empathy, self-reflection and emotional meaning – this is also the area of the brain that notices errors

- Broca's area, which plans speech and activates self-talk (our internal speech)

- the right and left front lobes, which select, plan and choose ideas or actions – these areas also develop expectations and evaluate outcomes

- the left hippocampus, which stamps things as 'personal' and stores long-term memories.

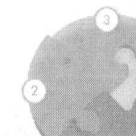

Children who are encouraged to develop a strong identity, reflect inwardly and find comfort in solitude are more likely to develop the traits associated with introversion, including being:

- good listeners
- more self-sufficient
- easily pleased
- more observant and attentive
- more trustworthy
- more thought-provoking when they get talking
- more in touch with their feelings.

Meditation and mindfulness are now being taught in schools and will help to build self-confidence. Ultimately, children who develop intrinsic traits will be better prepared to appreciate the benefits of emotional intelligence as adolescents.

HOW EXTRAVERSION AND INTROVERSION ARE EVIDENT IN OUR NERVOUS SYSTEM

The nervous system, particularly the brain in human beings and other animals, controls our behaviour and the way we respond. It receives information about changes in the environment from sensory organs, including the eyes, ears, skin and nose, and transmits directions, telling our muscles and other internal organs how to respond. The brain, as a repository for our memory, also stores information and provides the capacity for thinking, reasoning and creating. The nervous system issues commands through an intricate network of millions of nerve cells, called neurons. A neuron is a specialist cell dedicated to receiving, processing and/or transmitting information to other cells. The whole nervous system is interrelated, with the main influences on brain function represented in the divisions and subdivisions shown in the following image.

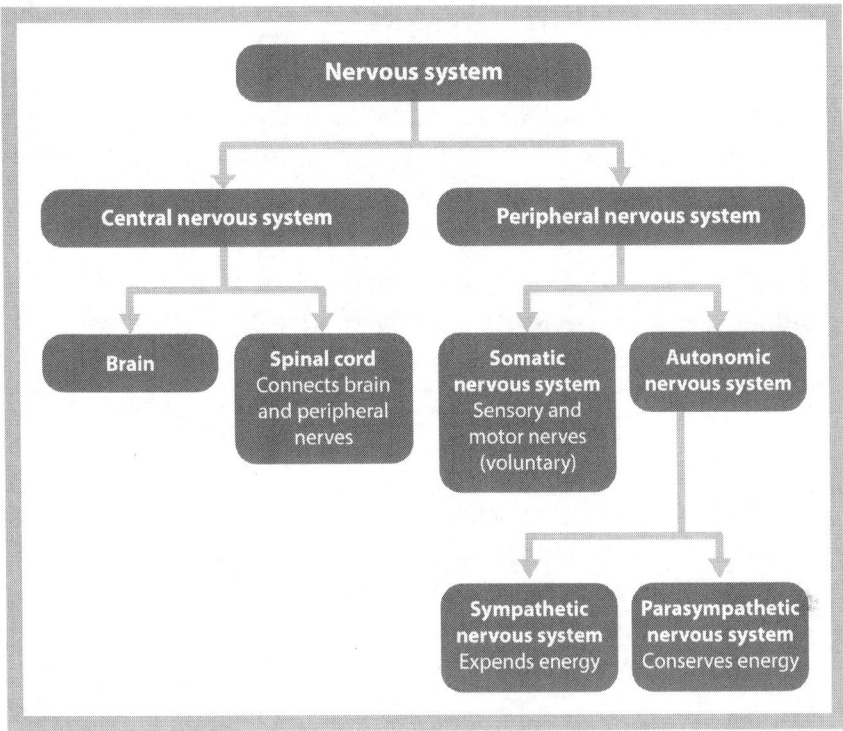

Our nervous system directs our internal-external reality

Like our brain hemispheres, our nervous system has two sides:

- the sympathetic side, which triggers the 'fight, flight or freeze' response
- the parasympathetic side, which is responsible for 'rest and digest' mode.

Think of the sympathetic side as applying the accelerator pedal and the parasympathetic side as pressing on the brakes. When your sympathetic system is activated, your body gears up for action. Adrenaline is released, glucose energises muscles, and oxygen increases. Areas of your brain that control thinking are turned off, although dopamine increases alertness in the back of your brain. But when you use the parasympathetic side, your muscles relax, energy is stored and conserved, and food is metabolised. This balancing act is likely linked to how well people employ emotions and exert self-control.

ACCESSING OUR INTUITION

While extraverts and introverts use both sides at different times, introverts are more likely to favour the parasympathetic side, which slows us down and calms us. One way of learning to engage our parasympathetic nervous system is to engage our intuition. Intuition is usually felt in the centre of the body, commonly referred to as the solar plexus. We often call it 'gut instinct', and it includes our most vital organs, including the heart, lungs and stomach. The body is connected to intuition and, by learning to respect our intuition, we increase our body awareness, using it to bring us into the present and be positive.

Intuition

Intuition is a natural and inherent part of our nature. When you strip back all the learned stress behaviours, pressures, mental projections, limiting beliefs and layers of coping mechanisms, you find the radiance of true self. Accessing intuition delivers a deeper understanding when processing. Intuition represents our centred, multidimensional capability. Intuition is about *the Who* and *the How* rather than the act:

- *Intuition (N – From MyersBriggs.org):* Paying most attention to impressions, or the meaning and patterns of information. I'm interested in new things and what may be possible, so that I think **more about the future than the past**. I like to work with symbols and abstract theories, even if I don't know how I will use them. I remember events **more as an impression of what they were like than as actual facts or details of what happened**.

The spinal cord regulates our implicit environmental awareness and connection to life. Sometimes referred to as our intuitive sixth sense, it controls basic reflexes such as reacting to sudden pain. Its most important function is to take messages to and from different parts of the brain to coordinate our bodily functions in response to environmental influences. As the vital link between mind and body, the spinal cord is a sympathetic receptor in supplying physiological data to the brain.

The medulla (brain stem) is a thickening of the top of the spinal cord and the beginning of the brain itself. The medulla controls basic bodily functions such as breathing, swallowing, digestion and heartbeat. It also centres our general level of awareness and temperature control while signalling incoming sensory information. Recent research suggests this area of the brain is far more intelligent than previously thought. Today's preference for external egoism or extraversion is probably related to the underdevelopment of this function. René Descartes's simplistic statement 'I think, therefore I am' may explain why our mind seems to have lost a vital bodily connection and why our right hemisphere capabilities tend to be unexplored.

Personal development supports greater awareness on a journey into self-discovery and higher consciousness. Tune into your core, understand your purpose and develop techniques for long-lasting wellbeing. By taking the journey to self-discovery, focusing intrinsically, relegating your overthinking and anxieties, and respecting your intuition, you can be more present, heighten your awareness and centre your reasoning skills.

These two systems permanently modulate vital functions, usually antagonistically, to achieve homeostasis. Some typical actions and characteristics of the sympathetic and parasympathetic systems are listed in the table on the following page.

External, extraverted characteristics are an essential requirement. Inasmuch as we encourage the development of internal, introverted characteristics, we must continue to broaden and diversify them, especially in our youth, to develop their identity of skills, processes and knowledge in conjunction with growing bodies. Competitive team sports, hand/eye coordination, speed and agility all build motor skills and a productive mindset. However, at some point these competitive characteristics need to take a back seat to personal growth and self-belief to ensure a deeper, more fulfilling life. Extraversion can then be relearnt in adulthood, and called upon and applied in a more meaningful, charismatic way as and when required.

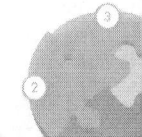

SYMPATHETIC SENSORY – COMPETITIVE	TRAITS	PARASYMPATHETIC INTUITIVE – COLLABORATIVE
Yes	Speed, agility, fast reaction time	No
Yes	Good hand/eye coordination	No
Yes	Physical and mental quickness	No
Yes	Aggressiveness, competitiveness	No
Yes	Good concentration, controlled motivation	No
Yes	Strong will to win, high emotion (external)	No
No	Large muscle bulk, strength, power	Yes
No	Good immunity, good health, instinctive	Yes
No	Stamina/endurance, rejuvenating	Yes
No	Fast repairing, rebuilding, healing	Yes
No	Strong intuition, creative	Yes
No	Team player, caring, strong feelings	Yes

The nervous system – characteristics of sensory and intuitive behaviours

Left-brain thinking (reflective), right-brain feeling (empathy) preferences

While thinking backs up our sensory and judgement capability, feelings and empathy for life extend our social intuitive and custodian perceptive capability:

- *Thinking (T – From MyersBriggs.org):* When I make a decision, I like to find the basic truth or principle to be applied, regardless of the specific situation involved. I like to analyse pros and cons, and then be **consistent and logical in deciding. I try to be impersonal**, so I won't let my personal wishes – or other people's – influence me.

Over time, thinking supports the development of emotions and a strong identity. Our interpretation of a progression of events defines us. As we mature, impersonal becomes personal as we learn empathy and to engage our feelings:

■ *Feeling (F – From MyersBriggs.org):* I believe I can make the best decisions by weighing what people care about and the points of view of people involved in a situation. **I am concerned with values and what is the best for those involved.** I like to do whatever will establish or maintain harmony. In my relationships, **I appear caring, warm, and tactful**.

It's interesting to note the Myers–Briggs classification for feelings is purely people-focused and does not include a general environmental classification for all things. Maybe this had something to do with the line of questioning, or environmental sustainability may not have been an important factor during their research. Feelings or empathy enable greater connection and more meaningful outcomes because holistic perspectives are applied. People and the environment are important to outcomes. Feelings fuel our awareness.

How our language references our environmental positioning
Our language inferences or linguistics distinguish between past, present and future tenses to determine a person's relativity or point of reference. Reflection, observation and inclination are all part of our natural ability to choose a point of reference. Do you make past references when you speak or do you listen and observe in the present? Or are you focused on the future, referring to hope or the direction you are headed? We grow through different references as our mind matures, allowing us to develop distinct characteristics as we view the world from different perspectives. Only after achieving each stage's objective can we use what we have learned to tackle the next stage of development. This allows the individual to establish a 360-degree view of the world through a complete cycle of development.

THE PROGRESSION OF OUR CAPABILITY INFLUENCES OUR POINT OF REFERENCE

The following BBDM tracks our point of reference as we develop through the four stages. We initiate life from an external reference without an identity and start our journey concerned with what is actual, present and real. We tend to externalise our conversation to seek confirmation of our thoughts. As we enter childhood we develop an internal judger mindset by association. Our associations become familiar as we program our logical mind and develop a strong sense of self; we become more self-assured and can process decisions more efficiently. The transformation to self-awareness throughout adolescence allows us to understand who we are and what defines our decision-making processes. As products of our authentic selves, decisions become automatic or second nature. Reasoning allows us to search for meaning, associate patterns and to understand how we are affected. We recognise the positive associations of a decision and automatically sense its negative implications. On entering adulthood, a strong sense of purpose opens our mind to opportunity.

How we deal with our outside world – Judger/Perceiver

Take a moment to fully appreciate how completely balanced the BBDM is when the primary and secondary personality characteristics are aligned to the quadrants and reference points. You will soon conclude that our personality also indicates our environmental point of reference: past, present, future, inside, outside. You will also appreciate how behaviours and personalities likely evolved because the growth pathways cannot be associated and combined any other way, and remain holistic, symmetrical and true to the definitions:

- *Judging (J – From MyersBriggs.org):* I use my decision-making (Judging) preference in my outer life. To others, I seem to **prefer a planned or orderly way** of life, like to have things settled and organised, **feel more comfortable** when decisions are made, and like **to bring life under control** as much as possible.

- *Perception (P – From MyersBriggs.org):* I use my perceiving function in my outer life. To others, I seem to prefer a flexible and spontaneous way of life, and **I like to understand and adapt to the world** rather than organise it. Others see me as staying open to new experiences and information.

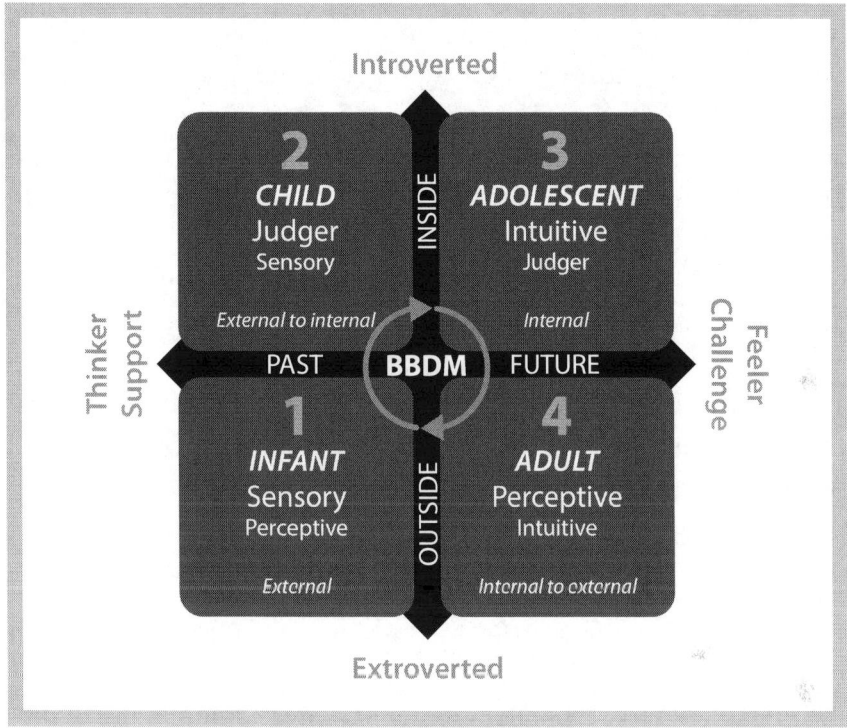

How our personality indicates our point of reference

This classification tends to point to perceptive types being readily adaptive and change-tolerant. In the MBTi classification, 'perceiving' means 'preferring to take in information'. It does *not* mean being perceptive in the sense of having quick and accurate perceptions about people and events. In my view, perceptive people are aware, understanding and accepting of the diversity around them, and more attuned to taking advantage of opportunities. With a strong sense of self and strength of character there is little need to pass judgement or to feel vulnerable.

Fully adapted, forward-focused, perceptive leaders have bigger fish to fry. Their objective is to change the world and make a purposeful contribution. These leaders are culturally aware.

The judgements and logical processes we form early in life influence the environmental data we amass in adulthood. Our thought processes, our judgements, our knowledge, our identity and capability we develop as a child will influence what we perceive as an adult, our external awareness, and the information we scan from the environment. As an example, if we grow up with a love of birds, we will always spot them in our environment while filtering out other data. Essentially, our perception feeds pertinent data into our brain to be processed: the subconscious processing of large amounts of data in a multifaceted capacity. When unusual situations occur or there is a match to preconceived passions, goals or visions, we are immediately alerted to inconsistency or consistency.

Our learnt behaviours influence our environmental positioning, as represented at any point on the BBDM cycle on the previous page. A personality test provides an indication of our point of reference falling into one of the four quadrants.

13. RETRACING THE EVOLUTION OF BEHAVIOUR (FROM FEAR TO TRUTH)

OUR EVOLUTIONARY PATHWAY IS EVIDENT IN A HUMAN LIFECYCLE

The Balanced Behavioural Development approach supported in this book asserts that the evolution of behavioural attributes guide the development of human capability and the programming of our intelligence. If we can map the key behavioural development objectives of each stage to organisational functions, we can equip graduates and employees better for change and growth.

Change programs fail when thinking, beliefs and behaviour are not changed at the individual level. Business methods and development tools can support an individual's career choice and allow them to broaden life skills to adapt to the unpredictability and uncertainty of changing environments.

The BBDM approach brings together philosophy, mathematical symmetry and organisational and leadership development by defining an optimal pathway mirroring our biological and physiological evolution. It establishes a simple and compelling framework around a balanced, holistic objective.

An adult can leverage all the executive functions and a cultural competence by emulating the human evolutionary pathway. This is accomplished by embracing the primary and secondary objectives of each developmental stage, as represented in the following BBDM.

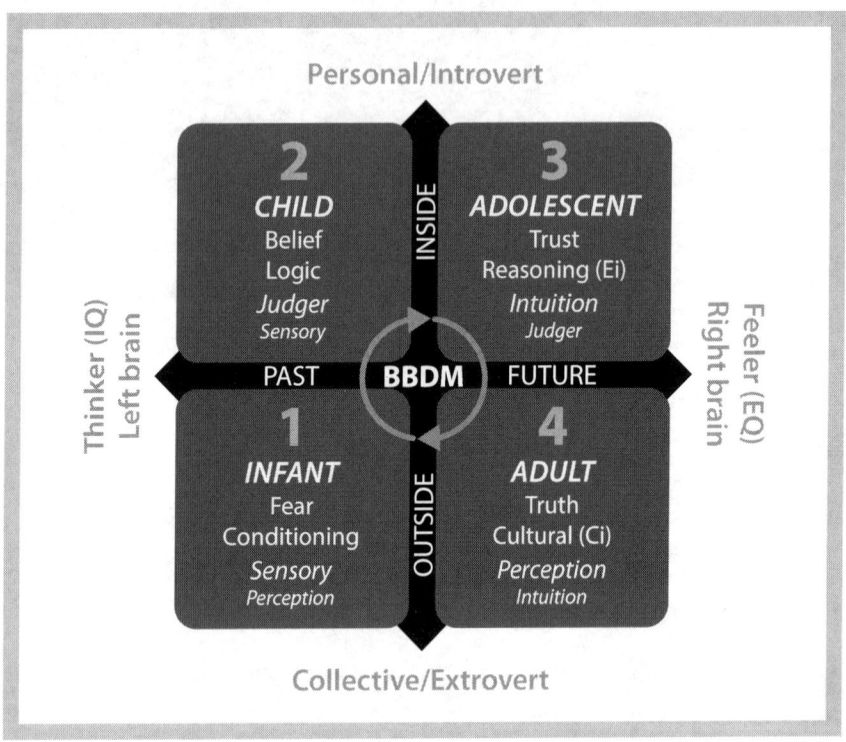

How personality influences our intellect

Establishing an optimal development pathway

This model was developed as a symmetrical construct from the development pathways – biological to emotional and physiological to cultural – and knowing that we all start from a baseline of biological fear: our survival instinct. I have represented a progressive model of opposing development objectives: fear to trust or love as biological objectives, insecurity to security or truth for physiological objectives. Objectives were based on balancing primary instincts:

- fear–bonding

- insecurity–self-belief

- trust–self-awareness

- security–expressing our purpose or truth.

The theory uses the Myers–Briggs Personality Type classifications of behaviour by slightly varying the definitions of characteristics. The BBDM maps the four polarities of behaviour to the four development stages (brain, body, emotional, cultural), and establishes how our identity and environmental relationship underpin the progress of learning. When this is presented as a cyclical development framework, we understand how behaviours have influenced our intellectual evolution. The outcome is a progressive intellectual development supported by prevailing temperaments; that is, a positive temperament supports emotional intelligence in the third stage of the model.

Each stage encompasses optimal development and relational objectives associated with how we identify in our environment. The BBDM theories challenge the view that personalities are resolute throughout a lifecycle. Jung believed all functions are largely unconscious and undeveloped in infants. As we grow and mature, different functions develop.

What directed the evolution of human capability was the relationship between the four opposing sets of personality characteristics, as presented in the complete holistic lifecycle in the BBDM. The lifecycle symbolises how all behaviours align in a compelling sequence of development embodied in the distinct intellectual stages. Inasmuch as the brain has evolved along this path, you would expect – if we were to replicate the development in an individual's lifecycle – to realise the full potential of the mind.

How the primary and secondary behaviours in each quadrant interrelate and how environments influence the drivers of individual and organisational capability and performance should be recognised. Do learning behaviours guide your locus of control or environmental positioning? Absolutely.

HOW DEPENDENCIES SUPPORT THE COMPLETION OF EACH STAGE

Our evolving intellectual ability programs and associates our capability. During infant brain structuring, primary sensory characteristics fill the mind with experiences and associations. Most people are familiar with five senses: sight, hearing, smell, taste and touch. However, we also receive input through two additional senses: the vestibular, or movement and balance, sense gives us information about where our head and body are in space; our proprioception, or body awareness sense, tells us where our body parts are relative to each other. Our sensory ability helps develop our copy/conformist conditioning intellect. If you have ever been beaten at the card game Concentration (Match Up, Memory or Shinkei-suijaku in other parts of the world) by a three year old, you will appreciate this ability is well developed after the infant stage. Basic language, bonding, coordination and organisation are key learning objectives and assist in developing the conditioning capability.

As we advance into childhood, our primary conditioning intellect takes a back seat to an emerging logical ability associating linear risk/reward relationships. This stage is about moderating instant gratification and self-interest, and understanding the consequences of our actions. In childhood, a prevailing reactive temperament allows us to construct linear associations and judgements to program a logical capability, aiding the development of an identity. The protectionist judger personality assists the child to develop and identify skills well beyond copying and conforming. With an undeveloped identity, children initially see themselves through other people's eyes, and the constant reinforcing of their self-image and individuality ensures the development of a strong sense of self, a personal identity. Self-control and regulation is also an objective.

The cycle of human objectives

In the following diagram I represent an optimal succession of a typical person's life objectives as Maslow represented in his Hierarchy of Needs, starting from infant inception. The cycle is more attuned to the transfer of knowledge, learning and skills to ensure the success of evolution and the growth of humanity. However, attitude and the willingness to learn to know and apply yourself ensure success, and the sequence of learnings supports this understanding. Leading a purposeful, fulfilling life delivers our unique view of causation and our view on life, our contribution being the knowledge and understanding to broaden the growth cycle.

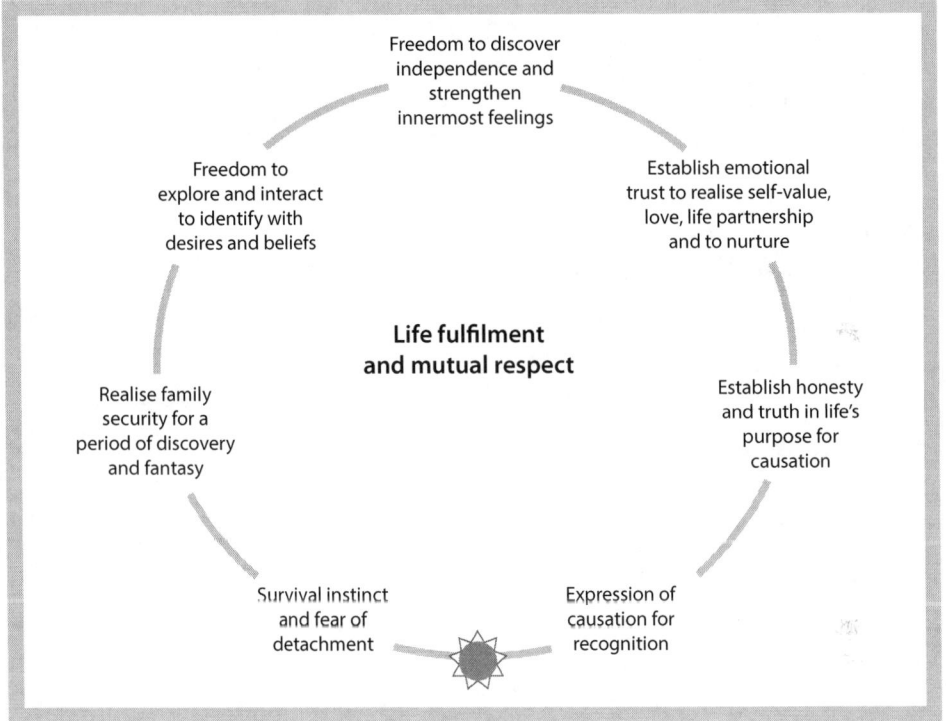

Freedom to discover
independence and
strengthen
innermost feelings

Freedom to
explore and interact
to identify with
desires and beliefs

Establish emotional
trust to realise self-value,
love, life partnership
and to nurture

**Life fulfilment
and mutual respect**

Realise family
security for a
period of discovery
and fantasy

Establish honesty
and truth in life's
purpose for
causation

Survival instinct
and fear of
detachment

Expression of
causation for
recognition

The cycle of human objectives for self-expression and recognition

It's at the childhood stage that we adopt a productivity mindset of continuous adaptation and improvement, and develop specialist skills to differentiate ourselves from the community. A child supplements personal values with cultural and family insights, including photos, stories and legends from the past, evolving a distinct identity from the community and environment.

A child's growing need to identify independently, and determination to make a place in the community, soon relegates infant sensitivities. An emerging judgemental personality constructs a diagnostic timeline of associations to identify any inconsistency in the social or physical environment that fuels insecurities. Meanwhile, emerging emotional desires develop environmental associations to guide the development of essential skills. Over time, through teamwork and play, strengthening self-assurance overrides personal insecurities and relegates infant fears to the back of the mind. Children of strong character will seek out and play to their strengths while the less motivated may avoid challenges. A culture and environment that supports the growth of strong, personable, balanced identities will help guide children through this difficult stage.

MASTERING OUR TRANSCENDENT RIGHT BRAIN

Daydreaming provides an induction to the creative mind and symbolises entry into adolescence. Rising hormonal activity encourages emotional experimentation. Adolescent desire initiates the broadening of trusting relationships, and with this the experimentation with love. The love we generate outside our families is supported by common interests, mutual respect, capability and acceptance. A broadening polarity of emotions gradually emerges throughout adolescence. As we wrestle with emotional intelligence, we learn to confront our deepest childhood regrets and disappointments and realise the power to resolve them.

Eventually, by confronting fears, insecurities and disappointments, the adolescent develops a strong sense of self to prepare for adulthood responsibilities. A toolkit of emotional associations (body awareness) provides an intuitive foundation. Social rehearsal and challenging our limiting beliefs throughout adolescence transforms weak emotional associations into a strong, independent, intuitive core, which guides a growing sense of self-value and purposeful relationships.

Understanding a typical journey to emotional and cultural maturity and representing how behaviours interrelate to encourage the completion of each stage and broaden capability is the power of the BBDM. Aligning behavioural development in this way programs the software (intellectual capability) during hardware development (your physical attributes). As an example, the judger personality approaches life in a more structured, controlled way, enabling a child to identify and connect skills while the body develops. Procedural memory is integral to learning the cognitive, perceptual, motor and linguistic skills that contribute to school achievements.[19] Also, as our skills develop, our bodies adjust; for example, when playing football or riding a bike.

Demonstrating and developing a succession of behaviours is supported by Maslow's Hierarchy of Needs[20] and is similar to the way Buddhists are educated to self-realisation. Not discounting age-old philosophies, the four development phases are represented in a cycle as the polarity of opposing behaviours interacting and aligning, enabling a complete toolkit of environmental and complex perspectives. The four stages are supported by mathematical symmetry, biological understanding, personality typing and Kolb's four learning styles in chapter 26.

All human beings start off with the same personality characteristics: infants are born extraverts, at one with their environment and without an identity. Historically, psychologists suggested a preference for extraversion into adulthood, however the BBDM view is that introspection in a child and adolescent should be encouraged to promote individuality, identity and self-awareness.

Introspection is followed by relearning extraversion in adulthood to view the world from the inside out. Extending the polarity of learning between the four sets of opposing behaviours – Extraversion and Introversion, Judging and Perceiving, Thinking and Feeling, Sensing and Intuition – is fundamental to realising our true potential. There may be prevailing functions; however, we can learn opposing traits to reach self-realisation and a leadership cultural competence. Career choices tend to align to the stage where people find most comfort and success with their associated traits (their strengths). These career choices may change as each stage is mastered and the capability is learnt and becomes habitual. Leadership is about addressing weaknesses and mastering all stages for a cultural competence.

Every human trait has a purpose – none is redundant. The current most progressive education systems have individualist programs at their core; for example, in Finland every student need is assessed

19 'Contributions of Memory Circuits to Language', M.T. Ullman, 2004.

20 'A Theory of Human Motivation', Abraham Maslow, 1943.

independently and provided for locally. Finland has developed a strong sense of independence and self-reliance through education. Accepting individuals' vulnerability and promoting self-reflection encourages accepting behaviours to embrace feelings.

Thousands of human traits are known to exist, and if they were aligned to the four quadrants during the optimal stage of development to support learning we could enhance capability. Cognitive behavioural therapy is proof that behaviours can be learnt. Growing emotional awareness is the key to confronting change. HR professionals who appreciate this understanding will be pivotal to supporting the learning organisations of the future.

OUR DEVELOPMENT THROUGH THE AGES

Our environment has a big influence on our development stage. Today, stage 2 characteristics rule as the digital age extends the bounds of the information age. Throughout history, stage preferences have influenced human development, with a recent preference for competitive left-brain characteristics to the detriment of collaborative right-brain characteristics. In the late Middle Ages, plague, autocracy, conspiracy and witches preceded a period prior to the 14th-century creative renaissance. Today it is climate denial, standardisation, conformity, overpopulation and the rise of populism that indicate we are overdue for a stage 3 creative awakening. When this happens, life will flourish in its many diverse forms. There is nothing wrong with this cycle of development, but we need to know how to balance the left brain with right-brain characteristics so the natural development cycle can occur naturally in the individual.

Stage 3 Ei will define the next Age, whether it's called the Collaborative or Creative Age. It will happen because the most progressive and knowledgeable organisations will encourage employees to develop these soft skills and bring meaning back to the communities where those employees live and develop their identities. The most progressive organisations realise the true value definer lies above the process layer and that the right-brain characteristics of Ei will drive this through innovation and connectivity.

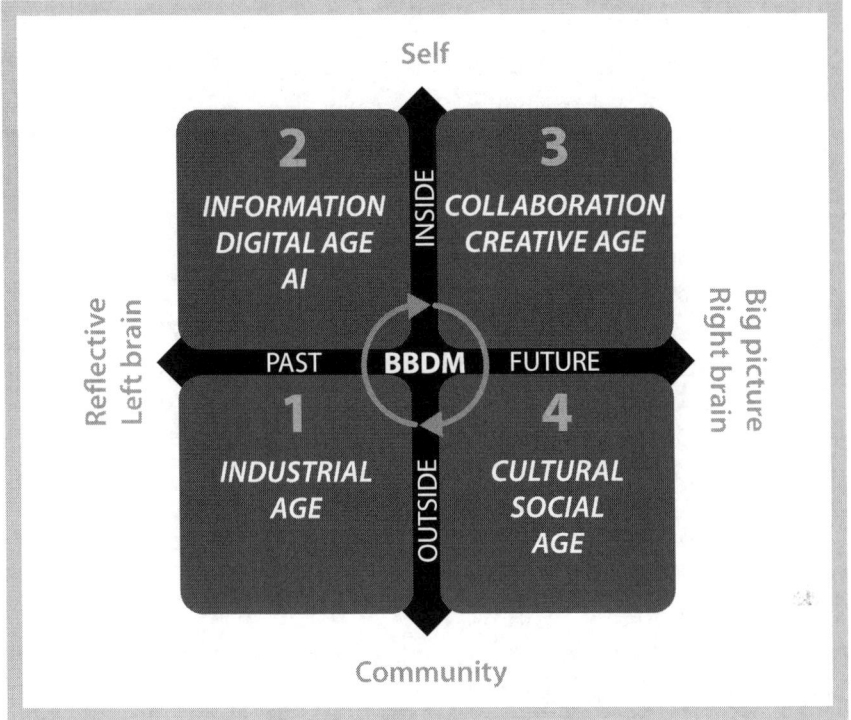

The natural progression of Ages

The reason this full right-brain evolutionary adaptation will be welcomed is that the characteristics of Ei and social connection are positive and uplifting. Numerous studies indicate social connection is at the heart of human happiness.[21] People like myself have spent significant time thinking about how Ei can be developed collectively through development programs. The work of George Elton Mayo and, more recently, Abraham Maslow (humanist theory) introduced the psychological needs basis to directing employee performance in both social and work contexts. Organisational development and behavioural change management emerged in the 1980s, but took a back seat to globalisation and productive value from the 1990s. However, today humanist theory as represented by Ei is again redefining the importance of developing social values to empower business success.

---

21 Matthew Lieberman, neuroscientist. Gillian Sandstrom and Elizabeth Dunn, *Personality and Social Psychology Bulletin*, July 2014. Art Markman, PhD, *Psychology Today*, July 2014.

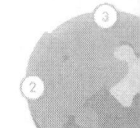

DISC PERSONALITY PROFILES

If you have ever completed a DiSC Personality Profile, you will have noted there are four pure behavioural styles:

- dominance
- compliance
- supportive (steady)
- inspiring (influence).

The behaviour of most of the population is a combination of two or more styles, however the core behaviour is the factor that trends highest above the energy line, meaning a person does not have to exert energy to display the trait.

What is emphasised under the DiSC approach – and the many other personality profiling tools – is that each behavioural style brings strengths and weaknesses to every situation. Each can be a winner, but a team or business needs all four styles to win. All four styles are important to our personal growth. DiSC distances itself from behavioural ethics, concluding right and wrong behaviours are not within the scope of the tool.

Along with management, HR should be accountable for defining and promoting the behaviours necessary for the success of an organisation, and needs to be open and honest about the objectives of behavioural learning. The trainee will understand this and will likely align to the quadrant according to their motivators. However, while these four groupings may be represented as core behaviours, all behaviours can be taught and indeed leveraged for the benefit of the individual and the organisation. Behaviours may be broadened and developed systematically as we progress to the right of the following table: they are specific to the organisation and community.

While there are many differences in the language between the columns, we should look for the connections in each of the four groups as we move to the right of the table and the language becomes more mature and positive. Behaviour is not an exact science. There are differences between communities, cultures and populations.

The BBDM introduces a conceptual framework to provide a generalist view on how behaviour and the environment influence human development. The approach starts with basic balanced assumptions to construct a symmetrical picture of how an individual can develop a holistic, multidimensional, cultural capacity. The starting point is augmented over time by accounting for the four development stages. One assumption is that each development phase is defined by an underlying mood or temperament influencing the primary behaviour or unique point of reference. The opposing biological and physiological states (biological–emotional/physiological–cultural) are combined in a progression ranging from negative to proactive to provide a complete cycle of perspectives.

The BBDM is completely balanced. As we develop through four intellectual capabilities from conditioning (copying, conforming), logic and Ei to a multidimensional collective awareness (cultural competence), the BBDM approach also supposes that there are optimal behaviours, temperaments, objectives and dependencies to support each of these intellectual milestones, as outlined in the following table.

STAGE	DOMINANT	COMPLIANT	SUPPORT	INFLUENCE
Development	Biological/ Mind	Physiological/ Body	Emotional/ Relationships	Cultural/ Work
Associations	Many-to-many	Many-to-one	One-to-one	One-to-many
Temperament	Negative	Reactive	Positive	Proactive
Identity	External focus	External– internal	Internal focus	Internal– external
Intellect	Conditioning	Logic	Reasoning–Ei	Cultural–Ci
Core type	Sensory	Judger	Intuitive	Perceptive
Instinct	Fear	Insecurity	Trust	Security
State	Dependent	Control	Independence	Intra- dependence
Objective	Self-worth	Self-belief	Self-awareness	Self- expression

A balanced progression of development objectives and capabilities

* * *

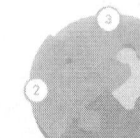

The behaviours we learn when we fail any stage tend to allow us to excel in the opposing stage. My case in point is the amiable, timid behaviours I learnt failing stage 1 Dominance helped me to excel in stage 3 Support. I still had to relearn how to be assertive and communicate effectively (stage 1) in adulthood. This is essential to know for HR professionals and managers for their personal growth and their team. And for the cotton-wool millennial generation who feel leadership is a rite of passage, revisiting stage 2 Compliance to build a strong, confident identity may be required. This may also indicate their under-preparedness for STEM (Science, Technology, Engineering and Maths) subjects at school.[22] According to the US Department of Commerce – Economics & Statistics Administration, STEM creates a nation of innovation and global competitiveness because it drives the generation of ideas and propels the creation of new industries. Smart organisations will create the sales, service and technology roles in-house in employees' communities to ensure skills and knowledge support the vital connection to the customer. These smart businesses will likely shun artificial intelligence (AI) if the technology prevents experiencing and learning new skills.

Although regression may occur following life or relationship trauma, at any point in our lives we can revisit a stage to reinforce our knowledge or lay the foundation to challenge the next stage. A positive mind may be difficult to maintain, and a proactive temperament requires the constant assertion of goals and purpose. Awareness of what supports both temperaments will help to maintain our right-brain preference. Cultivating emotional intelligence in stage 3 is all about developing a strong sense of self, trusting in your instincts and centring yourself in the present to realise the power of intuition. To build this strength of character and self-awareness requires a solid appreciation of which skills were developed in stage 2.

---

22 'Millennials Are Failing Because We Are Failing Them: The STEM Gap', Neale Godfrey, *Forbes*, April 2015.

14. INTUITION IS AT THE HEART OF CREATIVITY AND EI

THE DEVELOPMENT OF INTUITION

Our customary instincts and common sense are the culmination of a lifetime of sensory experiences and associations. They represent the development of our intuition. We instinctively learn to identify patterns and assimilate learning habitually.

To develop emotional awareness, humans need a sense of social capital. What emotional awareness is to the person and social awareness is to the organisation or the community is something I explore and develop throughout this book. A strong respect for social values in the community supports the development of Ei. You just need to define your passion. Since sensory characteristics instil values from our earliest memories, intuition (the opposing sensory characteristic) embodies our deeper social values. The more we trust our intuition, the more likely we are to develop heightened social awareness and association skills. Learning to trust and to extend intuition is learning to be self-aware. It's believing in who we are right to the very core, so that intuitive decisions and thoughts are made automatically and instinctively.

A positive mind uses intuitive instincts to assist with childcare. Familiar environments and emotions spark past associations as an expectant mother practises her intuitive ability. She may find recalling childhood events that once prompted fear apt or humorous due to their naivety. Centring emotions through the parasympathetic nervous system heightens awareness of the present, calmness and intuitive skills. The mother uses her imagination to plan how her child will develop. If she is self-assured and only wishes the best for her child, confidence and intuitive instincts come naturally so that the unborn already has a strong bond and sense of survival.

The autonomic nervous system determines our level of interaction with the environment, allowing an individual to focus inwardly (para-sympathetic) to associate and assimilate knowledge, and externally (sympathetic) by increasing their metabolism for greater awareness and environmental interaction. Coming to terms with the autonomic nervous system may indicate a level of maturity or self-awareness whereby people subconsciously learn to trust their instincts. It also indicates that some decision processes are intrinsic and adapted to respond automatically to external factors in the absence of conscious analysis, as the nervous system is connected to and regulates all our other body systems, mainly subconsciously.

The autonomic system also helps our environmental positioning and centres our point of reference in the head (left-brain) or solar plexus (right-brain). Once the brain has reached its full size, the onset of puberty identifies the beginnings of the adolescent transformation. Over time, social centring and independence help direct our relativity from the head to the centre of the body or solar plexus.

The mind has built-in mechanisms to hinder growth as expressed as stress, which may also hinder the immune system. When discon-nected from the body, our ability to retrieve and analyse data through the skin or to exhibit self-regulation is limited. Is this why many of us tend to engage only a fraction of our brain capability in a complex age? Why does a substantial part of the brain connected to the spinal cord lie underutilised? Does this indicate underdevelopment of this part of the brain, concealing a possible mind/body connection or spiritual sixth sense? These observations should form the basis of scientific research to discover what overpopulation or a lack of personal space is doing to our health.

BEING YOUR AUTHENTIC SELF

Our intuitive processes define our authentic self, because they are independent, instinctive, spontaneous decisions and a measure of internal and external trust. They also help us to better understand people and situations. It takes time to develop intuition and learn to analyse it, to comprehend our decision processes and indeed ourselves. It may take weeks to come to terms with a gut decision, but these choices are often correct and are in tune with our value system. We need time to go through intuitive decisions to give them currency and perspective, and time to discuss our instincts with other people.

The complexity of the mind will never be automated or replicated. Emotion is what distinguishes us from machines and regulates how our brain is uniquely engineered for purpose. Throughout childhood we build up a complexity of knowledge and skills for a belief in an individual identity to balance and innovate in support of an adult niche and purpose.

As a measure of emotional strength and social values, intuition is also used in problem-solving, a flow-on effect of experience and expertise. We may not remember solving a similar problem or reading about it, but our mind makes the connection. Since we do not have a specific memory of the solution or method, we link it to intuition. Terms such as muscle memory, instinct, gut feel, second nature, common sense, mind/body connection, body awareness and body consciousness describe intuition at work, and signify a lifetime of learning, actions, experiences and associations.

Intuition adds feelings and personal experience to rational thought to help solve complex problems in a multidimensional way. It is also powerful when conversing because, while focusing on a subject and expressions (perception), we subconsciously use all our senses for recall while intuitively appreciating how the subject feels relative to our own experiences. This is called *reasoning*, and allows us to respond appropriately. Its power comes from trusting our intuition.

Academics and scientific researchers seem to have discounted or completely overlooked the importance of intuition to self-awareness and extending our Ei. This may be because the nature of their role is to *know* rather than *do*. Left-brained people who have not undertaken a right-brained transformation may label feelings as a weakness, not understanding how a strong intuitive core allows an individual to extend big-picture feelings to support a strong, multidimensional capability. Two hundred million years of evolution and a 10-year adolescent development stage would indicate the importance of our intuitive development. We just have to learn to trust intuition; otherwise it holds limited meaning and application.

INTUITION IS CENTRAL TO CREATIVITY

Trusting your intuition will unlock your creative core and broaden your feelings and strength of character. This is the embodiment and power of self-awareness.

As one of the last bastions of socialist government, Sweden proves the all-important link between Ei and creative value by regularly topping the Global Innovation Index (2011–13). A creative group of Northern European countries is challenging the economic power of the US and 'old Europe', according to a report 'Europe in the Creative Age'. Nordic countries such as Finland do well as open and tolerant societies, although they are not ethnically diverse. What the report fails to identify is the developed emotional value that comes with living in inclusive, accepting, collaborative societies. Ethnic diversity adds a variety of skills and emotional associations to better align strategy, just as inter-racial diversity contributed to the US's creative prevalence.

Tolerant societies attract talented people who contribute to technological innovation. In *The Rise of the Creative Class*, Richard Florida explains how jobs now follow people, rather than the other way around.[23] His emphasis on tolerance comes from realising that creative people prefer to live in places that are ethnically and socially diverse.

---

23 *The Rise of the Creative Class*, Richard Florida, June 2012.

Since the mind is the control centre that determines our success or failure, it seems apparent that our subconscious mind provides our conscious mind with a very individual, personal view of the world. The more respectfully we free the mind, the more we appreciate its emotionally elevated, intuitive decision-making powers that deliver multifaceted outcomes on impulse. These also give a sense of free-riding a superior capability as we learn to trust its innate ability to take and add meaning to life-defining decisions. Relationships provide social currency and a means to reason around vague solutions so as to progressively construct logical understanding supporting creative problem-solving.

Our cycle of maturity in an inside-out (internal to external) perspective supports a particular view of the world, from a learning/knowing left-brain perspective to an application/doing right-brain perspective. People who develop an internal locus of control believe they are responsible for their own success. Those who maintain an external locus of control believe external forces like luck and fate determine outcomes. You often hear that everyone has a book in them, and I agree, but I also suggest everyone has creative powers to balance their lives. When we change direction and transform into our right brain, when we release our stress and worries, and identify how insecurities have defined our life skills, we are at our most creative.

Once revealed, the life skills or strengths that help address our uncertainties and vulnerabilities are put to work to balance our perceived shortcomings and bring back equilibrium and environmental security. We are unlikely to think it – the creative solution will more likely come instinctively, perhaps as a thump in the chest. Or we may suddenly realise a huge injustice to stop us in our tracks. The solution delivered to our front of mind may be incomplete, but we have every tool to bring understanding: conceptualisation, reason, independent thought, planning and positive energy. This is the power of self-awareness and a product of understanding our social mind and intuitive, liberated free spirit. Heightened creativity will provide solutions to balance out the insecurities of childhood. Transitioning to stage 3 sets us up perfectly for stage 4 delivery and to market and strategise a collective solution.

WHAT DOES THIS MEAN FOR BUSINESSES?

Progressive organisations realise that offering creative opportunities and lifestyle choices is important in developing employee commitment and securing future growth. Appealing to an employee's lifestyle preferences and strengths enhances wellbeing, and will be supported by the community and result in better outcomes for the business. Employees are a business's principle asset for tapping into the all-important value link between business and community. Developing strategies that incorporate a measure of social capital and promoting cultural meaning also motivates and appeals to our innate sense of wanting to contribute and give back.

A well-defined HR strategy will not only inspire employees to deliver, but also create customer loyalty. The most powerful stimulus to employees and customers is combining organisational and community cultures. Few organisations do this well. One exception is Air New Zealand, which promotes the Maori culture and community in safety videos that often go viral. The company uses humour, and showcases the New Zealand trait of not taking itself too seriously. This targeted digital marketing creates a strong sense of identity for its customers, and even for Australians, who voted the airline the most trusted company in the Australian Corporate Reputation Index in 2017.

As organisations harness human potential better and develop high-performing, inclusive cultures, they will see that superior performance is tied to the local community.

* * *

In respecting its free plasticity, the mind can completely transform a person's life – including personality, capabilities, relationships and status. Once someone begins to realise what supports superior ability, they appreciate the pivotal role we play as guardians of life's environmental diversity and balanced growth. Inasmuch as there is an external expansion of diversity, the mind assimilates and associates the growing diversity, increasing our ability to process a growing complexity of multi-relational arguments.

By understanding the creative mind's purpose in ensuring balance for sustained growth, we unlock its adaptive power.

15. PERCEPTION DRIVES OUR STRATEGIC LEADERSHIP FUNCTIONS

Perception is the lens we view the world through. Our perception is our fit-for-purpose radar tuned into a lifetime of learning and experience to associate pertinent data-capture in our environment. Human perception is a masterpiece of intellectual support. Perception supports a part of the brain called the amygdala or executive functions. Perception forms part of the intellectual capacity of humans, therefore a highly intelligent person can perceive their environment better compared to an 'average' person, because a highly intelligent person can identify, organise and interpret their sensory information more easily.

So how did we develop this capability, and how can HR assist aspiring leaders to hone their perceptive powers?

OUR ENVIRONMENT INFLUENCES THE DEVELOPMENT OF OUR AWARENESS

Our ancestors were subjected to abrupt climatic changes every few thousand years after the more gradual Ice Ages began two million

129

years ago. A rapid decline in the environment would have met with a corresponding increase in competitive behaviour as survival instincts switched the mind into productive mode to conserve diminishing provisions. Prolonged periods of cooling may have resulted in a complete breakdown of any established social order, ending cooperation outside family allegiances. Only the hardiest, most resourceful tribes or families could have survived.

This sudden cooling reduced the mammal population and dislocated our ancestors' family groupings. The survivors were probably those most willing to adopt a nomadic lifestyle to seek improved conditions. By crossing many different territories, our ancestors' awareness developed, allowing them to understand life's complexity and inter-relationships. Eventually this increased intelligence has also helped us to survive as evolving capability anticipated and planned for changing climactic conditions.

What supported our final leap in intelligence was the ability to adapt and cooperate for strategy. Rapid physiological change developed our respect for life preservation and our future success as a species. William H. Calvin argued in *A Brain for All Seasons* that cycles of cool, crash and burn powered the enormous increase in brain size and complexity in human beings. Driven by the imperative to adapt within a generation to 'whiplash' climate changes where only grass did well, our ancestors learned to cooperate and innovate to support the hunting and fostering of large grazing animals. The planning and cultivation of the environment promoted a vastly different set of human characteristics and transformed human intelligence.

Sudden climatic change cultivated our custodian awareness

By adapting a guardianship role and valuing all forms of life, humans realised a huge expansion in capability and developed the ability to plan for the future, influence the environment and understand inter-relationships for sustained survival. The development of our future-directed spatial awareness represents the final stage of our intellectual evolution, achieving full capacity of our biological and physiological states. This search for truth has brought humans intelligence of the highest order. Our visionary freedom to look into the future so as to come to terms with the past and present enables us to adapt rapidly. Our transcendent creative hemisphere also allows us to imagine ourselves in a future environment and to innovate and change in favour of greater security. Our reward for creating greater certainty and sustainability is less stress, prolonged wellbeing and health to appreciate life.

Through learning to trust our humanist instincts, our search for understanding will naturally incline towards reasons to sustain life. The search for truth has elevated humanity to the position of guardianship, evolution's highest accolade. For our custodian role, we are equipped to use special reasoning skills to innovate and contribute to life's diversity. However, many of us have not yet developed a right-brained capability, and resource depletion, overpopulation, pollution, climate change and built-up environments are proof of this. Nevertheless, we have the capacity to put this right. The natural energy that fuels our evolution ensures we have the capability to do so. Evolution does not regress. We just need to direct our capability towards creating purposeful, sustainable life outcomes. By understanding how intelligence has evolved, custodian awareness and ability are available to everyone and not dependent on external influences. We need to respect who we are, the bounty around us, and to trust our ability for it to work.

Indeed, as with all evolutionary advances, respect for life's diversity and the ability to prize the environment supports the greatest innovations. Our innate ability to quickly adapt and innovate will ensure any experimental risks are rewarded with increased understanding and capability.

OUR STAGE 4 PERCEPTION SUPPORTS OUR EXECUTIVE FUNCTIONS

As we master one stage, we move onto the next. After balancing the previous three stages, mastering the final stage 4 focuses our perception and executive function on strategic objectives and the future. After mastering self-awareness, diverting your awareness externally makes cultural awareness the remaining objective.

To be personally strategic, we must align meaningful goals to our *why* or *purpose* to ensure our passion is ignited to associate a lifetime of development. From a collective perspective, we must harness the objectives of every contributor in the organisation or the community. They may not know these objectives yet, but the power of leadership is the ability to canvass the general feelings of the majority to drive everyone forward. For the HR executive, this means ensuring employees are appropriately aligned in support of a leader and their executive functions.

Engaging your executive function is about mastering your cognitive control of behaviour for the attainment of goals. These behaviours include:

- attention control

- inhibitory control

- working memory

- cognitive flexibility

- critical reasoning

- problem-solving

- planning.

Executive functions consist of a variety of 'higher-order' mental processes and behaviours that help the brain organise and act on information. Executive functions include:

- thinking 'outside the box' (cognitive flexibility)

- mentally associating ideas and facts (working memory)

- giving considered, deep responses rather than impulsive ones

- resisting temptations and staying focused (inhibitory control, including selective attention).

These skills enable a person to plan, organise, remember things, prioritise, pay attention, and get started on tasks. These attributes are evolving, and gradually develop and change across the lifespan of an individual, especially into adulthood, and can be improved at any time over the course of a person's life. These characteristics are essential for aspiring cultural leaders to master.

The BBDM stage 4 behaviours that
support our executive functions

PERCEPTION COMPLETES OUR INTELLECTUAL DEVELOPMENT

The following research gives support to the distinct stages of intellectual development, but also will help HR and behavioural professionals to better understand the attributes of each stage and how they present in employees. Dr Joshua Hartshorne and Dr Laura Germine at MIT's Department of Brain and Cognitive Sciences found raw speed in processing information appears to peak at the age of 18 to 19, which is when our secondary stage physiological development ends (primary emotional stage 3), also signalling the completion of our body's structural development.

STAGE	1. INFANT	2. CHILD	3. ADOLESCENT	4. ADULT
Age	0–3 years	3–12 years	12–20 years	>20 years
State	Dependent	Control	Independent	Intra-dependent
Hemisphere	Left brain (competitive)		Right brain (collaborative)	
CHARACTERISTIC				
Primary	Sensory	Judger	Intuitive	Perceptive
Secondary	Perceptive	Sensory	Judger	Intuitive
CAPABILITY				
Primary	Conditioning	Logic	Reasoning	Adapting
Secondary	Adapting	Conditioning	Logic	Reasoning
DEVELOPMENT				
Primary	Brain (biological)	Body (physiological)	Emotional	Cultural
Secondary	Cultural	Brain (biological)	Body (physiological)	Emotional
LOCUS OF CONTROL				
Positioning	External	External–internal	Internal	Internal–external

The BBDM cycle of primary and secondary development objectives

Closely associated with Ei, short-term memory allows us to be present in and focused on the moment. This begins to level off at 25, and starts to decline at about 35 (primary cultural stage 4/secondary emotional stage). This suggests the secondary emotional development stage is largely complete and the optimal age for nurturing is prior to this.

Our adult stage 4 cultural development directs our forward-facing perception in search of opportunity and gathers data in support of our goals. Intuition provides a secondary supporting objective to perception in our adult stage 4 development.

15. Perception drives our strategic leadership functions

Our adult future-directed perception starts at about 20. According to Hartshorne, 'social perception continues to get better well into middle age, and it doesn't decline much with age after that. This suggests that older adults may be better positioned to engage and understand others.' This is particularly important for gathering information on meaningful opportunities (perception) and connecting the opportunities through other people (social awareness).

Social awareness delivers on strategy and is available to us throughout adulthood. 'Vocabulary is peaking later and later with each generation.'[24] Surprisingly, Hartshorne and Germine's data identified a peak in vocabulary during the late 60s or early 70s.

In the previous table, the alignment and progression of learning objectives support the subsequent stage objective.

As we progress around the cycle, balancing each stage objective enables the next stage. Secondary perception supports an infant's primary sensory development and coming to terms with the environment. As distinct from forward-looking adult perception, infant awareness is both present and directed behind to enhance safety and security. This also ensures that the infant's mind assimilates the information it needs to balance its primary fears.

The information and representations an infant absorbs are pure and unfiltered, an unbiased representation of the environment, and these schemas form a foundation of our early existence. They influence our core values and motivations and the way we experience life, as they are fundamental to who we are. Our emerging sensory memory supports our copy–conformist, stage 1 conditioning capability and initiates our environmental positioning. Data on touch, sight, taste, smell, sounds, vestibular system (relative body movement and balance) and proprioception (flexibility and strength) are assimilated systematically to build a safe point of reference to begin our development. Our programming then starts in stage 2 (skills and processes), which is all about initiating procedural understanding.

An infant's perception or awareness supports and protects it. First and foremost, perception accumulates and organises all the sensory

---

24 'When Does Cognitive Functioning Peak? The asynchronous rise and fall of different cognitive abilities across the life span', Joshua K. Hartshorne and Laura T. Germine, March 2015.

data required to balance fears and construct a safety net, allowing progression to the next phase, which is developing an identity.

It's important to note that when our left-brained stage 1 secondary perception protects us, aside from safety it offers very little if we get trapped. The real value of perception is when it is focused on the future in adulthood stage 4. People encouraged to develop self-worth and allowed the freedom to discover a strong identity in their community in stage 2 should be able to push past the first stage.

How can I make these observations? Because we grow through a beautifully balanced, symmetrical and aligned cycle of development, completely dependent on our relative positioning and how we identify in our environments (locus of control, strength of character, resilience, and so on).

When you begin to understand the relationships between the characteristics and how their development is fully dependent on the systematic completion of stages, the purpose of each stage takes shape. The meaning jumps out like the solution to a mathematical problem. Picture an infant learning to walk: the sensory information and safety perception are front of mind and all the infant needs to take the first step. Reflective thinking will develop over a long period to associate past experiences and learn the most successful, productive approaches. Judgement, introspection (introversion) and intuition come later as we perfect our style and walking becomes innate.

As we master each intellectual capability, we relegate it and move on to the next, working our way around the cycle and adjusting our locus of control. These evolving capabilities become part of our identity, to be used habitually or by second nature when assimilated.

DOES PERCEPTION LURE OUR DEVELOPMENT THROUGH EACH STAGE?

What motivates us to advance through each stage of the cycle? Does the search for opportunity inspire us? I suggest our external environment, an inherent appreciation of life, opportunity and diversity are closely associated with life's meaning. Our naturally inquisitive nature encourages us to expand our learning, to grow in accordance with our values and challenge ourselves in the search for meaning (Where, How, Who, When, What and Why). Our propensity for the positive aspects of life motivates us, and perhaps the natural progression of objectives lures us forward through the cycle.

Our perception is tuned to life, where it subconsciously gathers information to ensure our success.

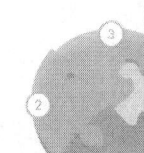

PART II

CREATING A HIGH-PERFORMANCE BUSINESS CULTURE WITH THE BALANCED BEHAVIOURAL DEVELOPMENT MODEL

16. WHY HR NEEDS TO OWN EI FOR STRATEGIC SUCCESS

EI DELIVERS ON FORESIGHT AND CONNECTS PURPOSEFUL OBJECTIVES

HR departments will lead the transformation of businesses as they refine their Ei capability and roll out developmental systems and programs to ensure managers and leaders are equipped to tackle the fast-changing, innovative workplaces of the future. Ei promotes greater clarity of work objectives and trust, which benefit from more productive, supportive relationships. Increased competitive agility arising from cohesive teams that can evaluate and respond better to competitive threats will drive successful organisations in the age of artificial intelligence (AI) and digital disruption.

Coaches and HR practitioners should strive to broaden their emotional intelligence to represent and role model Ei skills to employees; they should be aware of the methods and benefits. There is no time like the present to develop this capability. Educational facilitators or researchers may not exhibit high Ei if they are not actively engaged in the application of real-world problems. I have attended Ei training where the facilitator did not score highly on the Ei assessment.

It's more than learning or knowledge: it's all about challenging, applying and engaging with people to influence unforeseen outcomes. A lifetime of learning, knowledge and skills becomes instinctive and habitual in our intuitive ability. A multidimensional capability develops and our intuition stores these experiences, associations and understanding. It is not a logical, reflective ability. It's a relational, creative, instinctual ability, which is all about spontaneity, applying a complexity of capabilities, being in the moment and being as one with our surroundings.

Active involvement in Ei programs and organisational strategy raises the level of Ei in the HR department to a leadership ability. HR is best placed to take on the responsibility for developing Ei because someone must be accountable. Evolution indicates we develop our relationship and nurturing skills during adolescence, which is also when our maternal parenting skills are formed. Hormonal, emotional and body development heighten our senses, connect our mind and body, and polish our intuition. These are all core competencies that not only assist in nurturing, but should also be respected and promoted by HR coaches. HR needs to become a leader in these cooperative, emotional characteristics to develop the qualities in the organisation.

HR AS THE TRUSTED ADVISOR AND COACH

To fulfil its role as a purveyor of Ei, HR needs to be a trusted advisor acting not only for the benefit of the company, but also seeing the potential of each employee and how employees ensure the success of an organisation.

To develop Ei ethically and responsibly, HR professionals must be made independent coaches. To be seen to act independently for the benefit of the employee ensures the success of their HR Ei responsibility. Ei is best facilitated in one-on-one coaching sessions, guiding subjects through difficult life decisions. Ethical approaches also require training in Ei coaching techniques.

The most progressive organisations are awakening to HR's influence on directing superior business performance and long-term strategic success. Google and Facebook are examples of companies leading this transformational change. The traditional compliance role of HR is being raised to a strategic development role, encompassing personal development, change management, business transformation, and balancing and aligning capabilities for strategic success. Leading organisations are adopting Ei, and many businesses are realising that they have been narrowly focused on creating marginal value through process efficiency and competitive advantage. The power of Ei will change each and every transaction, bringing greater meaning to employees and customers. And, oddly enough, the internet, selective AI and data analytics provide the tools to facilitate this.

By defining value as productivity and continuous improvement alone, globalisation has largely ignored cultural meaning as a competitive value and disregarded traditional cultural boundaries. Communities are starting to see that culture is inextricably linked to their local environment. When culture is bound to a work ethic or purpose, people collaborate to innovate and realise significant value for both employees and company. Humans are designed to create and grow, and they want to contribute to their local communities. They are at their happiest when encouraged to connect their objectives to a purposeful contribution. This explains the growth of values-orientated companies. Where they conduct their business is an integral part of their business model, as is the impact they have on their communities.

THE IMPORTANCE OF INTUITION

Intuition connects humans to value, and is our natural inbuilt software programmed to innovate over a lifetime. Whenever an action or thought presents itself as a variation to our programing (or second nature), we are instantly made aware of the inconsistency. When we discover an injustice or different way of doing things or an improvement, the realisation presents as a thump in our chest and stops us in our tracks. Intuition allows us to take on tasks instinctively, so that we complete them subconsciously, which frees us to explore new ways of undertaking activities while thinking personally or engaging with other people.

To develop the use of intuition purposefully for innovation and strategic implementation is to teach self-reflection, to trust our instincts, to feel empathy and to respect self-awareness. The journey to self-discovery begins with an analysis of intuition. Some of my intuitive decisions have taken months to understand, but then taught me a lot about who I am. When coming to grips with intuition and facing a key decision, take the time to sleep on it. If the next morning the decision still feels good, then go ahead. On the other hand, if you have a sleepless night then perhaps you should reconsider. Take the time to analyse why the decision does not sit well with your values.

In the future, value in business will be created above the process layer, with innovation being the vital word. Despite the rapid introduction of digital technologies, millennials are learning to integrate these tools and leverage them for purpose. Their power will be clear when people use them to personally connect and collaborate rather than remaining disempowered and disconnected.

THE NEW STRATEGIC ROLE FOR HR

HR's newfound strategic role promotes inclusive work environments, aligning employee strengths to their function, and developing formal and informal learning programs targeted to the individual's growth needs. HR's role is also to identify opportunities to network skills across the organisation and ensure they are bound into its culture.

When surveyed to research this book, a cross-section of business executives believed employee wellbeing is linked to fulfilling goals and encouraging growth. Survey participants overwhelmingly responded that a workplace should provide the environment for employees to flourish and that recognition of contributory value strengthens self-awareness. They also felt that more motivated, self-assured employees would significantly influence business growth. Social awareness, self-confidence, trust in ability and a sharing, independent nature are the positive attributes of an emotionally astute employee. In motivating employee performance, Ei places itself firmly in the present and supports enhanced listening skills, reasoning and awareness of other people's values. To speak is to know, to listen is to learn. An inclusive work environment develops emotional awareness and trust in personal ability. Since employees should celebrate winning, a workplace culture should encourage development risks and open discussion of making informed mistakes, strengths, weaknesses and vulnerabilities.[25] Survey respondents supported this objective overwhelmingly.

HR and managers need to embody trust by being a cohesive, neutral, independent voice, acting on behalf of the employee and the organisation without question. This is an absolute requirement for any person or group representing Ei. Emotional maturity can be challenging, and employees need support from strong ethical values. Coaches who have high Ei should be available for guidance and to discuss issues preventing self-acceptance and respect. The coach should know how to direct the best interests of the trainee, and a consultative approach is recommended. An open, inclusive, accepting culture with strong social values supports emotional development. (Practical Ei techniques are discussed in chapter 18.)

These are the requirements of an HR core competence that identifies and develops desired behavioural characteristics, while encouraging cultural connection and social interaction to explore and associate individual contributions and creative value. In the table over the page, I introduce the concept of balanced development objectives. I'm big on frameworks to simplify what can be complex behavioural interactions.

A balanced cycle of learning

As represented in the BBDM, our 200 million years of human evolution have delivered a completely balanced cycle of learning, allowing us to develop a holistic 360-degree, inside-out view of the world, positioning our awareness from past to present to future as we mature. In this time we have learned right from wrong, that for every positive there is a negative, from fear we can develop trust, and what is revealed as a truth can revoke a belief. There is a natural balance and

---

25 'Embracing Vulnerability at Work is the Key to Employee Engagement', Monica Parker, *The Guardian*, September 2013.

we need to consider the full spectrum of behavioural objectives in our organisational development programs. In the recent past, too much attention has been given to left-brain characteristics, to the detriment of the right brain.

HR development objectives: aligning characteristics for balanced growth

BALANCED DEVELOPMENT	LEFT BRAIN (FIXED)	RIGHT BRAIN (GROWTH)
Growth value	Productive value	Cultural value
Capability value	Intellectual value (IQ)	Emotional value (EQ)
Leadership value	Competitive value	Collaborative value
Sustainable value	Standard value	Diversity value
Employee value	Self-value	Collective value
Economic value	Past value	Future value
Business value	Expense control	Revenue growth

Balanced objectives to optimise growth

The power of representing a balanced behavioural framework is broadening behaviours along the spectrum of opposing behaviours and objectives. An HR advisor can work with functional leaders to define an optimal set of balanced behaviours for the department and across the organisation. For example, competitive characteristics are important for sales teams to develop skills and teamwork and build strong identities. A collaborative style is also required in certain circumstances to moderate behaviours; for instance, when team-based KPIs promote teamwork. Customer service may define their optimal behaviours when surveying customers. These behaviours can be encouraged in the organisation through programs led by the customer service team to reinforce and ensure they become part of the culture. A behavioural framework allows the HR advisor to work with the business to define a balanced approach to promoting optimal behaviours across a functional group.

16. Why HR needs to own Ei for strategic success

By encouraging a supportive work environment, HR can stimulate creative interaction to solve problems and explore growth strategies. By encouraging diversity and independent thought to overcome groupthink, opportunities are created to broaden capability in the workplace. Encouraging employees' appreciation of how the business can serve the community and develop future opportunities enhances the work culture, and incorporating employee development in the same objective is doubly rewarding. For example, customer service and sales representatives networking in the community also develop their own decision-making skills and build a strong identity.

Once a business or division assembles a diverse array of capabilities around a vision, employees can collaborate towards a common goal. If the goal includes community or developmental benefits then the objective will be shared, meaningful and more powerful. Strategy is sustained by the creative mind (right brain) responsible for inspiration, imagination, understanding and humour (positive/negative distinctions). People may develop skills in support of a common belief that comes from a strong emotional bond within both the family and community. The time required to achieve this depends on the level of backing and coordination within the organisation or community.

Our creative mind supports all aspects of strategy:

- *inspiration* to construct a vision endorsing our knowledge of the environment

- *humour* to enhance diversity of thought and provide left-of-centre alternatives for understanding

- *understanding* to construct a strategic map and milestones in support of knowledge to achieve the vision

- *brainstorming* to present multiple causes that may be influencing an effect.

The strategic attributes of our right brain, accessed by our Ei capability, will define and empower the successful organisations and communities of the future. Those who accept that this is inevitable will flourish in the new world of social values and connection.

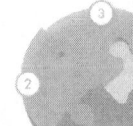

17. HOW HR LEADERS CAN NURTURE EI AND SOCIAL DEVELOPMENT

EI AND SELF-AWARENESS ARE OUR REWARD FOR NURTURING LIFE'S DIVERSITY

We are the product of our environment: highly evolved social mammals, each developed to serve a custodian purpose. Our unrealised intelligence is our higher ability to adapt and change. Humanity's highest life recognition is cultural intelligence founded on the courage, compassion and empowerment of the collective to build a strong belief in the future.

The evolution of human intellect to early adolescence has been going on for about 2.2 million years, while our adult intellect, as indicated by the rise of civilisation, is around six thousand years old, or 1/360 of our species' entire lifespan. Our success as a species depends on our willingness to accept our higher guardianship responsibilities in an adult executive capability. The rewards of a greater sense of purpose and sustained happiness may be understood at the individual level, although as a species the battle to move beyond our left-brain, competitive animal instincts can only succeed with complete coopera-tion using our right brain humanitarian capability.

Emotional intelligence – a term coined by Dr Daniel Goleman, who co-founded the Collaborative for Academic, Social, and Emo-tional Learning centre (originally at Yale University, but which later moved to the University of Illinois at Chicago) – does not refer to cog-nitive ability, but to how well we manage ourselves, our empathy and our motivation, and how we engage with others. It includes:

- self-awareness

- self-confidence

- knowing our strengths and limitations

- integrity

- ability to handle emotions

- being able to work through conflicts.

When asked which is more important, cognitive ability or emotional intelligence, Dr Goleman says both are vital, and that IQ predicts how well you do in an academic setting, but in life it's not as strong a predic-tor. In his book *Working with Emotional Intelligence*, he says he looked at 500 organisations and studied what made a star performer or leader. Cognitive ability and technical skills were only half as important as emotional intelligence in these settings – the higher up in the organisa-tion, the more important Ei became.

Goleman says IQ can predict the job you can get and hold (the knowing). To be a doctor, for example, you need a relatively high IQ to clear cognitive hurdles such as medical school. However, IQ does not predict how well you'll do in the field (the doing). Dr Goleman says doctors who leverage their right mind for emotional connection and reasoning skills are more likely to be successful in diagnosing patients.

He also points out that there has been a decline in the qualities that make up Ei in children. In studies done in the mid-1970s and late-1990s, researchers found that this set of abilities in American children had declined across the board. Some schools call this 'social devel-opment', and teach kids to manage their anger, work out agreements

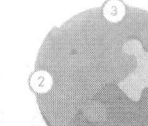

and empathise. Research by Dr John Gottman from the University of Washington showed that, at one of these model programs, rates of violence had dropped, teen pregnancy declined and drop-out rates were reduced.

HOW COMPLEXITY HAS DISTRACTED OUR HUMANITARIAN RIGHT-BRAIN DEVELOPMENT

In uncertain times, many demands are placed on organisations in their struggle to compete, but intense competition during 15 years of globalisation has confused the essential role the community plays in:

- defining a distinct social identity
- developing behavioural attributes such as social esteem, relationship trust and social awareness
- defining a collective purpose.

Comparative advantage has focused investment on value creation alone, and aggressive competition has dehumanised value as purely material. Much of the problem lies with the companies themselves, trapped in an outdated, narrow approach to value creation. Focused on optimising short-term financial performance, they overlook the greatest unmet needs in the market as well as broader influences on their long-term success.

In every culture, the importance of independence has been represented in ceremonies and rituals to formally recognise an individual's emotional maturity, and in turn allow them to appreciate adulthood and make a contribution. Recognition of a child's success in identifying with a niche as supported by our competitive instincts is rewarded in adulthood with a collaborative role in developing the niche. An individual's ability to actively contribute to the community is relative to the willingness of the community to accept and develop the contribution.

Our brain has evolved to develop emotions that support our parental and social responsibilities. Selfless caring, nurturing and respect for life are in complete contrast to the fear the parent manages in a newborn. Without the security of a lifelong commitment to sharing and family, our intellectual growth and subsequent success within the environment would not happen. Established cultural rituals and ceremonies in support of collaboration, sharing and commitment have played a vital role in advancing our intelligence. A growing appreciation of how life created a strong sense of purpose laid the foundation for the next major leap in intellectual capability: the need to understand life's truths. This development was probably in response to increased understanding of environmental custodianship and our survival through extreme climatic changes.

Relationships and community

Relationships and community are extremely important to our social development. They teach us to balance our temperaments, to collaborate for a purpose and to be trusting, self-aware and respectful. Fortunately there are now many initiatives to develop more functional, purposeful businesses and communities. 'B Corps' are for-profit companies certified to meet rigorous standards of social and environmental performance, accountability and transparency, and the United Nations 17 sustainable development goals to transform our world. In their article 'Creating Shared Value', Michael Porter and Mark Kramer claim that companies could bring business and society back together if they redefined their purpose as creating 'shared value': 'Firms can do this in three distinct ways: by reconceiving products and markets, redefining productivity in the value chain, and building supportive industry clusters at the company's locations. Shared value could reshape capitalism and its relationship to society.'[26]

The following BBDM shows how development responsibilities may be shared among a community to maximise individual growth. From family to community, to government, to leadership, every social unit plays a distinct role in nurturing a succession of opposing, often incompatible objectives.

---

26 'Creating Shared Value', Michael E. Porter and Mark R. Kramer, *Harvard Business Review*, Jan.–Feb. 2011.

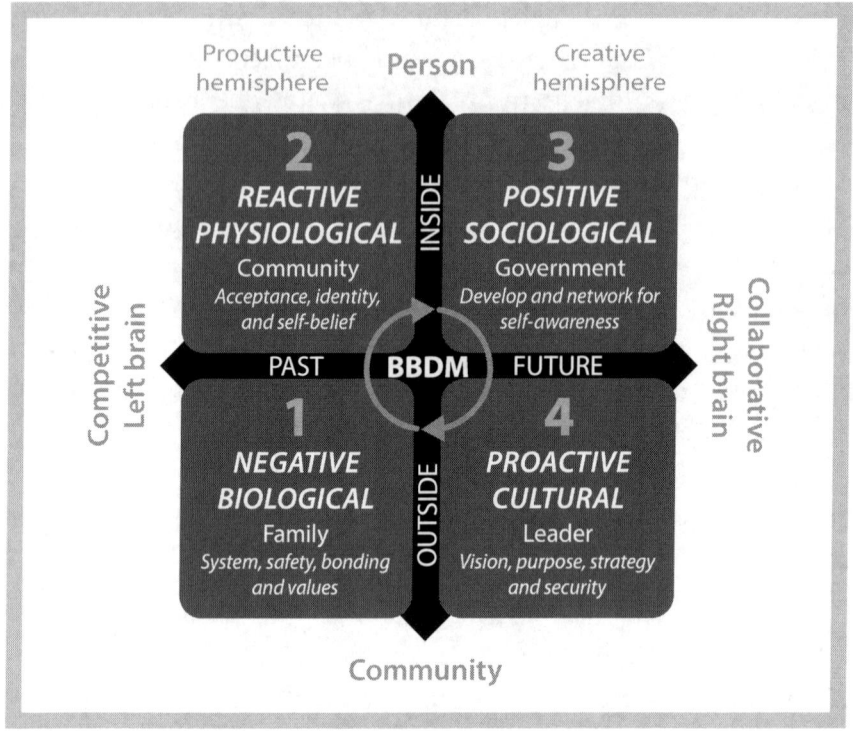

The shared responsibility BBDM to
align development objectives

EMPLOYEE GROWTH

So why is this important to HR and organisational leaders? Because it's important to know what environmental factors can influence employee growth, and then strategy can be adjusted to incorporate every aspect of employee growth. This may go some way to understanding an employee's motivation. Employees may either be family orientated (stage 1) or community focused (stage 2) when they prefer mingling with prospective customers.

Everyone has a capacity for the passion and empowerment that would allow them to leap out of bed in the morning and lead a full life. It's important to understand what your life motivators are and how they can align your role to purpose. By applying one's strengths and leveraging the creative mind for meaning and purpose, this book defines the human need for happiness as the security of fulfilling a work purpose and success in belonging.

STAGE	1. BIOLOGICAL	2. PHYSIOLOGICAL	3. SOCIOLOGICAL	4. CULTURAL
Responsibility	Supporting family	Supporting community	Supporting government	Supporting leadership
Development	Master fear	Master insecurity	Master trust	Master security
By promoting	Bonding for safety and values	Teamwork for skills and practice	Socially develop for relationships	Purpose and direction

Sharing supervisory responsibility to coordinate development objectives

The role of the HR leader is to appreciate this need and assist the individual to discover and develop their strengths, and confront weaknesses once confident. Strategic principles, supported by the creative right brain, encourage independence of understanding in mapping a future path to success. These principles respect freedom of choice by allowing an individual to make independent, informed decisions to support a balanced, positive lifestyle and a strong organisation and community culture.

Identifying disengaged employees

Most individuals join an organisation with similar values, wishing to make a contribution. Employees usually do want to play a part in the success of their company. According to Gallup, in world-class organisations the ratio of engaged to actively disengaged employees is 9.57:1, while in average organisations it is 1.83:1. Identifying disengaged employees is an important role of the HR practitioner. Coaching is the best way to understand whether an employee is actively working to benefit the organisation or to its detriment and why.

The progression that is evolution dictates we must grow and push the boundaries. The BBDM provides a framework to develop emotional intelligence and the forward-focused creative attributes of our

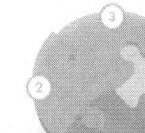

right brain, which make people happier. Failure to develop emotional maturity can prevent an employee from adopting a positive, healthy lifestyle and contributing fully. Emotion fuels the creative mind, however little is known about emotional intelligence adding multidimensional capacity to the brain and contributing innovative solutions to organisational problems.

Ongoing left-brain prevalence maintains a competitive, reactive temperament and can inhibit emotional growth. Without developing right-brain prevalence, individuals may associate emotions with weakness and remain emotionally naive. Reaching maturity enhances relationship collaboration and contributes to relationship success. Dependent minds seek security in co-dependent relationships, but without learning Ei, the inability to present an independent point of view disregards our essential freedom of choice to discover our life purpose both in and out of work.

To know yourself is to know what drives you. Just remember, you learn from others to learn from yourself. Be grateful; be caring. This will open your mind to opportunities.

These principles, built on a foundation of values and motivation, include:

- Look inward to learn your strengths.

- Respect differences as you find your place in the community.

- Build trust in yourself to ascertain your value in the community.

- Look to the past to learn the truth that guides your destiny.

- Learning to know and trust yourself grows trust or love in another.

In *Emotional Intelligence* by Daniel Goleman, these characteristics are shown to be essential to supporting trust in the individual and a positive, successful lifestyle. Those of us in business know that these principles underlie the successful development and execution of policy. Organisations where HR successfully plays a strategic role know the power to execute judiciously is closely associated with an individual's ability to perform.

An employee will only develop their creative mind when respected

The evolution of best practice in HR and management is moving to the next phase, one that dynamically and intuitively adjusts to individual expectations or acceptance of majority support within a distinct community. **To derive value from people, businesses must realise value in people.** Trust, open communication, input at every level and acceding to the needs and expectations of an individual will dictate the business environments of the future. The era of controlled knowledge and intelligence will no longer feature, as customers, employees and shareholders adjust to the benefits of individual attention and demand that organisations lead by example.

Successful organisations leverage the diversity of independent thought to provide a wealth of alternatives that map the most respected path to a common vision. My underlying theme is that the future of business is being challenged to accept and encourage diverse thought. Using differences to expand rather than limit organisational capacity is the key to future success. The future of business strategy involves capturing views and norms at the individual level to influence and target both personal needs and the majority perspective at the community level. This takes into account diversity within communities and requires a dedicated strategy to target customer preferences. Developing a strong, safe community allows individuals to roam freely and identify growth opportunities.

By respecting creative ability, an individual is better able to use resources to represent the particular requirements of divergent communities. Whatever the future holds, it should value the individual's need to develop their right-brain capability. Without that, we are no better than the artificial intelligence that will replace our productive left brain. Governments must not allow automation to diminish us. Coordinated research should be conducted on how much using a calculator or tablets in class may limit the building of processing skills in the brain. If the mind is not fully wired or associated, do these tools encourage a lazy mind?

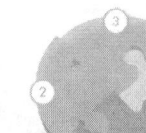

THE SIMPLE LIFE SKILLS THAT DELIVER EMPOWERMENT AND FULFILMENT

Learn to love who you are and to be grateful. You have the power within yourself to succeed in every aspect of life. You experience deeper trust when you learn to understand your capability and who you are. Express your gratitude often and compliment people, because the energy you create is infectious and captivating. Surround yourself with positive people and you will become optimistic with both feet firmly in the present. With an enthusiastic attitude and a genuine nature, people will be drawn to your smile and charisma.

By trusting your own intuition you will learn to respect your decisions, which are an extension of who you are. Analyse and understand your gut feelings and your decisions will become second nature, enlightened and habitual, freeing you to engage your superior reasoning skills and behavioural awareness.

The challenge of engaging your Ei

Ei is perhaps the biggest hurdle in most people's development. Initiating emotional maturity is typically associated with our adolescent development, when our hormones work overtime to fill out our bodies and create the attraction to connect to a future partner. A primary objective in adolescence is to practise relationships, and our physical and emotional development during this stage is geared to making this happen. Girls develop into women and become fertile, so the learnt behaviours during this stage assist a future mother to nurture a child. Boys follow a similar path. Their emotional development gives a mature outlook on life and how to nurture.

Emotional Intelligence 2.0 by Travis Bradberry and Jean Greaves provides a structured approach to learning Ei. It's important to note that developing Ei is a personal journey and the individual must want to challenge themselves to learn. A manager or HR practitioner can also provide the environment for people to feel comfortable with this challenge. Again, awareness is the key, and being empathetic to their vulnerabilities encourages employees to develop these skills. From the BBDM, understanding that feelings (empathy), self-reflection and trusting intuition initiate the development of Ei and assist in the journey to self-awareness. Ei is a function of all of these objectives, and cannot be achieved without all components. Our strength of Ei depends on how well we adapt all stage 3 objectives with an eye on the stage 4 objectives.

SELF-CONFIDENCE AND SELF-REFLECTION BEFORE SELF-AWARENESS

Since Ei signifies maturity and coming of age, it can be learnt. We are all at different stages of emotional development, but to develop Ei you need to change direction and adopt a more open, positive, empathetic outlook.

Self-reflection initiates the journey, and undertaking an Ei and behavioural assessment is a great way to kick-start the process and to understand what needs attention. Mindfulness is a fantastic tool to help with self-reflection. Mindful meditation improves the executive function of the brain, where we process information and regulate emotions. Mindfulness is also an important tool to coach managers in Ei and self-awareness, and for relating to staff better. Over-thinking situations and stress inhibit our listening ability so that we miss important nuances. A lack of self-confidence may also hold us back.

Self-reflection, caring and showing vulnerability are important first steps to engaging feelings and intuition. When we learn to trust our ability and instincts, we can centre ourselves in the moment and communicate more effectively. Self-awareness means trusting our instincts and understanding a lifetime of learning associations, but also allows us to focus on the bigger picture. Detail, analysis and judgement then become a secondary preference, although these relegated traits only need to be called on as required. Intuition, reasoning skills and Ei develop over time along with strength of character, positive feelings, individuality and creativity. For managers, leaders and directors, the need to relinquish detail holds strategic significance. Delegating and allowing staff to keep us abreast of the details develops their self-confidence, enhances our listening skills and builds trust. Trusting our ability and instincts helps to connect our skillset to strategic objectives and solutions through enhanced communication and rea-soning.

Letting go of the need to be perfect reveals our true selves and unlocks our creativity. **Although a catchword nowadays, being authentic is a product of self-awareness and demonstrates we know ourselves inside out.** Set development goals that include mindfulness and emotional intelligence, and, if necessary, employ a coach or mentor to help gain the clarity of purpose to interpret your motivators and passion. It will be money and time well spent.

Our mind and body instinctively connect when all the skills and understanding we learnt in our youth are understood and associated. As we learn to apply these skills and knowledge to career options, we develop a stronger sense of self, and the cycle of development con-tinues into this heightened phase of self-awareness. Youth is about self-reflection, and judging differences to develop a strong identity; adolescence is more about digging deep to understand who we are, and to appreciate how our motivators define our strengths and capa-bility. The relationships we forge and invest in will develop our under-standing of ourselves. Gaining proficiency in one-to-one relationships encourages a strong sense of self.

Hormonal changes can influence a positive temperament and teach adolescents to place both feet firmly in the present. Every adult can learn these positive attributes. Awareness of others is heightened, and so too are listening skills. People who challenge themselves through this transformative growth phase will be well placed in adulthood to experience the associated rewards. HR leaders and managers also need to appreciate this transformative life event when coaching employees.

As managers, we may have a resounding influence on an employ-ee's development, although it's important to understand what the stage objectives are and how to encourage them. To succeed in stage 3, employees must appreciate the complete change in focus as they begin to initiate a future orientation. It's important to be aware of what changes in behaviour are playing out.

I explain this phase from an evolutionary basis to show its pri-mary objectives, which will position the HR professional to target development programs. Self-reflection may occur through meditation.

Developing feelings and empathy, engaging in one-to-one relationships and learning to understand our intuition will teach us who we are.

Embarking on the road to emotional maturity can be challenging, but is ultimately rewarding. Ei is essential in today's constantly changing world. **Confronting Ei is about purposely changing direction to challenge ourselves to grow and to do rather than to know.** The transformational power of Ei is in its relational ability to influence people to define the optimal outcome and bring together resources and understanding to demonstrate and deliver results.

THE STAGES FROM SELF-CONFIDENCE TO EI

Before an employee's objective is self-awareness, they must develop self-confidence by mastering a set of skills and true understanding of their capabilities. On completing stage 2, employees who have grown confident in themselves and their work can embark on stage 3 since their skills and knowledge will become second nature and automatic. This confidence and understanding allows them to navigate to the next stage more easily. Intuition is at the core of Ei, and self-awareness and understanding the process make the journey significantly easier. Intuition represents a lifetime of learning and associations, a programming of our capability and a powerful resource, which must be respected before it works on our behalf.

To engage intuition for decision-making and completing tasks, an employee or manager requires a level of capability where they can undertake activities as if second nature or habitually. Intuition or 'gut feel' may be common sense, but common sense is specific to the individual. What makes sense to one person may mean nothing to another. The power of intuition is such that we can go about our activities and complete tasks subconsciously, free to consciously focus on other things, including listening and communicating with a deeper meaning.

The significance of intuition being at the very centre of your body is that it allows you to pivot your senses and really focus in the present. Think of your body as your subconscious, and how intuition centres your mind and bodily functions. Intuition records how you respond to various situations, and learns what you become accustomed to. The act of doing eventually becomes a fluid, automatic, multidimensional capability.

More than a technical ability, Ei distinguishes leaders who can monitor feelings and guide responses and behaviour. Ei sets high-performing leaders apart from average leaders, as high-performing leaders tend to be more selfless and genuinely have employee welfare at heart, which of course translates into better financial results as inclusive behaviour encourages trust and higher performances across the team.

The following framework represents the five components influential to mastering Ei and transforming capability with simplified What, Why and How messages to promote understanding.

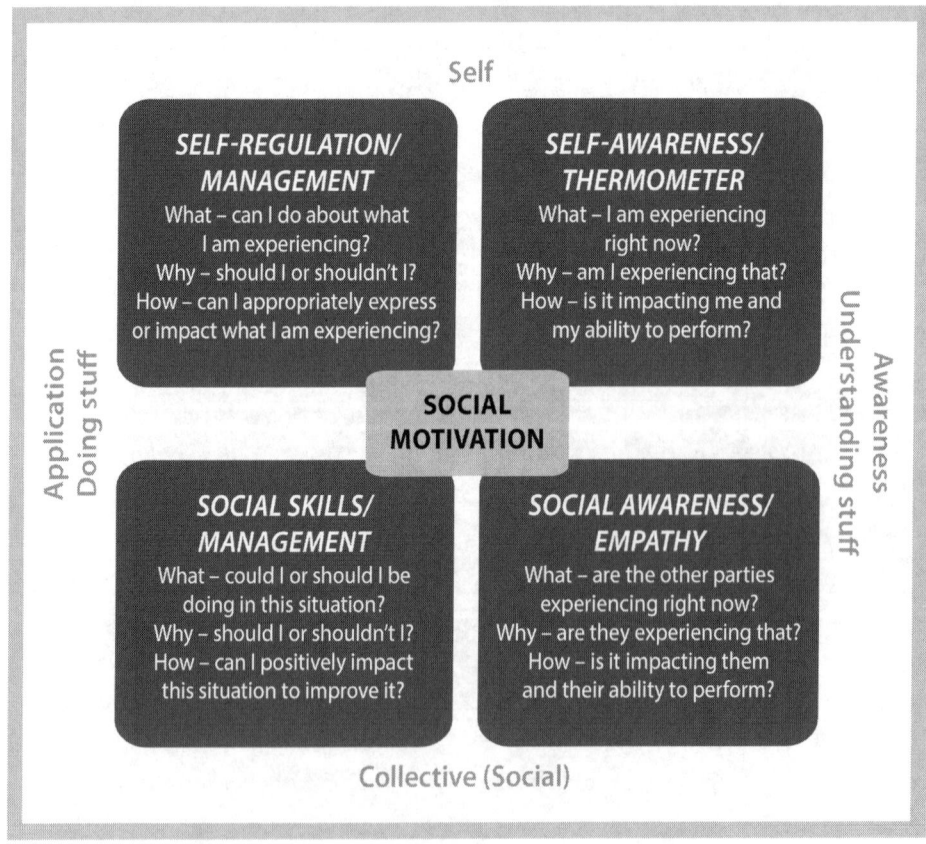

The five components influential to mastering Ei

It was Dr Daniel Goleman who originally identified five components of Ei. In extending his definitions, social is a subset of the collective or cultural definition. You can substitute cultural with social to include the wider environmental influences.

Self-regulation

The first, self-regulation, is the ability to control impulsive emotions and to think before acting. Rather than disciplining the team for a failed sales bid, a self-regulated manager considers what contributed to the failure and talks through a solution to ensure lessons are learned and the team is well placed for the next opportunity. This invariably increases the integrity of the leader and wins the support of the team. It also allows everyone to learn from mistakes, so they are more willing to contribute the next time around. Leaders who control their emotions are more likely to create a culture of fairness and trust, which is essential for encouraging employees to confront their biases, experiment with their vulnerabilities and develop the skills to balance them. They are also more likely to attract top talent.

Self-awareness

The second is self-awareness, which means thoroughly understanding yourself and your influence on others. If we don't really understand ourselves, we are unlikely to understand other people's emotions – and professionals who know themselves usually understand their company more clearly. This is an inside-out clarity, as the professional is more present and can more easily understand what is happening, admit to shortcomings and influence capability. Employees empathise with such leaders and managers and are more likely to support them.

Self-aware employees acknowledge their mistakes, welcome feedback and can generally laugh at themselves. Self-aware people are conscious of their abilities and play to their strengths, know their weaknesses and confront them as required. They know that if they have difficulty meeting deadlines they must plan accordingly. They tend not to overcommit, and to ask for help if necessary. Professionals ready to embark on the journey to self-awareness should have no problem challenging their fears and insecurities, and may even video

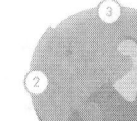

themselves to understand their weaknesses and encourage feedback on their public speaking. These are the challenges aspiring leaders use to promote strengths and address weaknesses.

Social motivation

The third is the element of Ei that almost all good leaders have: socially motivated leaders are driven to achieve beyond status or monetary rewards and want their contribution to the world to be permanent. This characteristic increases over many years. Intuition is an indicator of social value connecting us to likeminded people who can help us to fulfil our objectives. Intuition focuses energy and passion to connect purposeful relationships for the greater social good.

Dedicated, resolute leaders aim to achieve beyond expectations and are always looking to challenge themselves and raise the performance bar. They are optimistic, and their positive energy is both charismatic and contagious. Managers and leaders with this talent who believe in company values and goals are valuable to the organisation.

Empathy

Empathy or social awareness is the fourth constituent of Ei. People who are empathetic read between the lines and understand and support group dynamics. They are service-orientated, considerate and respect diversity of thought, taking time to understand other points of view.

Social awareness is increasingly important, and so is the need to attract top talent and create agile environments. With the rise of dynamic, diverse workplaces, empathy is an important behaviour to bind teams together and gain their valuable creative insights. Empathetic people have a good feel for cultural differences, including body language, when collaboration and political awareness can ensure the success of the team.

Since empathetic managers and leaders value enhanced employee wellbeing, studies show increased staff satisfaction and reduced staff turnover.[27] Empathy may play a big role in change projects.

---

27 'Proof That Positive Work Cultures Are More Productive', Emma Seppälä and Kim Cameron, *Harvard Business Review*, December 2015.

An organisation that is open and honest with staff and includes them where possible in decision-making is more likely to retain them. Demoralised staff may move on.

Social skills

The fifth component of Ei is social skills or social management. Social skills are about more than being friendly, and their ambitious collaboration draws on all the other parts of Ei. Socially skilled managers are great communicators, and use their empathetic, supportive and influencing skills to build lasting, committed, connected teams. Nurturing relationships is essential to the success of an agile, productive, creative group. A change catalyst accelerates business performance initiatives and growth, therefore conflict resolution and being able to negotiate disagreements are important traits of the socially skilled leader. Social managers know when to make an emotional plea and when to appeal to reason; Ei provides the basis for these distinctions.

A socially skilled manager also has positive drive and passion, which motivate and inspire the team to perform and to create solutions. Ei is about creating meaningful relationships, and the potential of a cohesive team is significantly more powerful than that of the individual. Committed relationships don't necessarily begin and end in your workplace or team, and Ei people always show an interest and try to make the most of any opportunity.

THE POWER OF EI

Emotion fuels the creative mind. From a simple mathematical basis, Ei associates the skills and knowledge accumulated during our early learning phase (conditioning and logical stages) to represent anything from eight (2^3) to twenty-seven (3^3) times the power of our baseline intellectual capability. The enormous commitment to developing Ei pays off when emotionally developed leaders have the most satisfied and engaged employees. If you like your leader, you're more likely to like your job. The opposite reality is an underperforming, disengaged workforce that may actively work to disrupt others.

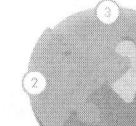

18. THE MIND'S POSITIVE TRANSFORMATION – INSIDE-OUT

'Once you understand your own unique values and align your life accordingly, you can achieve fulfilment in every aspect of your life: deepening your loving relationships, creating an inspiring career, establishing financial freedom, and tapping into a rich spiritual life.'

Dr John F. Demartini

Characterising the benefits of Ei in previous chapters provides some insights to how to learn Ei and what to expect from transforming your emotional capability. These observations form the basis of instructional learning to set expectations, however it is the methods we employ that will change our behaviours and perspectives. But what are the most practical approaches to learning Ei and how should HR professionals and managers apply them? Even if the HR professional or manager is already emotionally astute, knowing the practical methods to develop Ei are important to providing the right environment for change, but to also understanding how best to coach the employee.

Below I outline a list of practical activities to develop Ei and transform into a positive mindset. Not all methods may be required but it's important to understand how they work together to move an employee forward. An employee in this regard is any leader, manager or professional who decides to challenge themselves to further develop their Ei. This is a very personal choice, so the methods are focused on how the individual would approach each activity. Coaches can supplement the understanding if requested. Because there are implications outside of work, it's important to be aware of employees not willing to confront the change. This is especially important when considering coaching some activities in a team environment. The best outcome comes from when an employee approaches the coach with a willingness to change.

PREPARING FOR EMOTIONAL TRANSFORMATION

Transforming into a right-brain capability may not be for everybody. If you are an HR practitioner, a manager, or want to be a big-picture, spontaneous, charismatic, culturally astute and aware leader, then undertaking a right-brained transformation is right for you. If you are in a rut or sense the need for change, then maybe this is for you. If you are not happy in your career or relationship, you may want to change direction. Talk your intentions through with your partner, family or friends to see if this is the right course of action. It needs to be understood before embarking on such a transformational change. If you sense this change is too soon, then it probably is.

Developing our Ei ability allows us to be more authentic, instinctive, independent and happy in ourselves. Childhood is spent living up to and being defined by other people's expectations. We tend to live by cultural norms and conform to the behaviours represented in our community.

An awakening for most people is instinctively knowing they should confront this change, but no-one has shown them a pathway.

Once people are made aware of the need for change and are shown a course of action, the transformation usually begins in earnest. This is pure strategy at work. Most of the following suggestions make sense because the objective is to free the mind from complexity to enable a healthy, positive change. If you are a happy, compassionate, nurturing humanist with trust instincts then chances are you already appreciate life's meaning and are enjoying the rewards of a positive temperament, so the transition process should resonate with you.

THE STEPS TO POSITIVELY CHANGE YOUR LIFE AND DO WHAT YOU LOVE

Analyse each step in this chapter and the implications of each task and how they could influence your life positively. You may find you are already well on your way or have even achieved some of the objectives. Everybody is different, which is why the list is extensive, but only you know what should make your list of priorities and timeframes. Talk this through and agree them with someone you trust. A coach or accountability group can help you through the transition.[28]

The formula to transforming to a right-brain inside-out manager/ leadership capability is represented by the stage 3 objectives set out in the BBDM throughout this book, and shown in the following figure.

Mastering stage 3 self-awareness depends on how we internalise our thoughts and capabilities – we need to make them spontaneous and automatic by trusting our intuition, showing empathy (feelings) for life, and developing our one-to-one reasoning ability.

This process may take up to six months if you are ready to implement such actions, even longer if you implement them progressively.

Changing your lifestyle for the better:

1   Start from a base of self-confidence in your knowledge, skills and processes, so as to intuitively represent your understanding and experiences when you graduate to your right brain.

If you are at team leader or manager level and thoroughly know the ins and outs of your role and industry, you should have the experience to initiate the journey to self-discovery. Accept you are self-confident and have a strong self-belief. If you don't have the knowledge or procedural skills or judgement from a long period of working in your industry, see chapters 24 and 26 to develop these traits and self-confidence. Stick to the old adage, 'If you can't, then you must'. Always write down and prioritise your learning plan.

---

28   *Emotional Intelligence 2.0* by Travis Bradberry and Jean Greaves includes exercises and an EI test to track your progress.

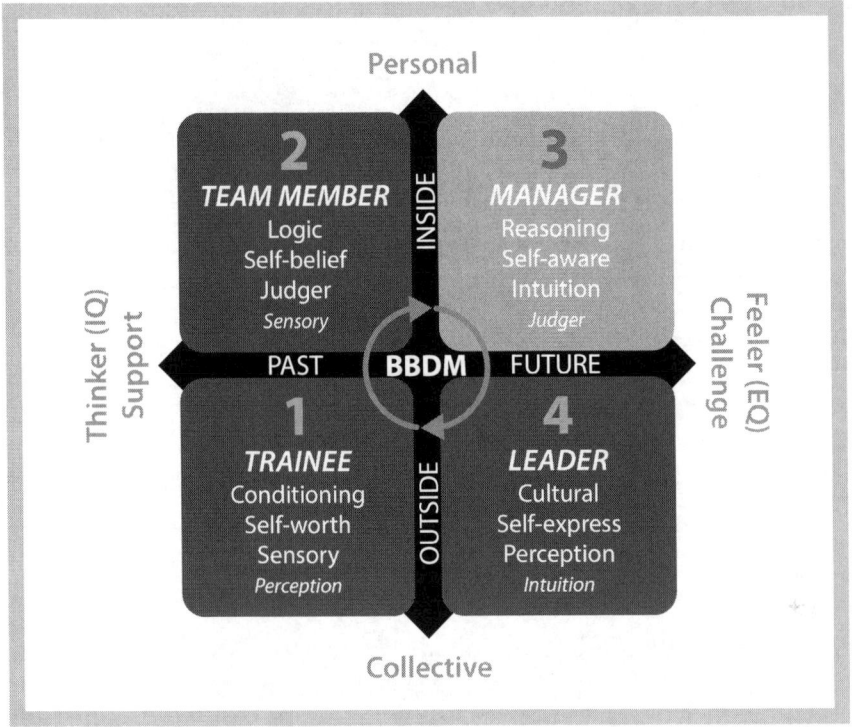

Mastering Ei using the BBDM

2 Be mindful of your body's needs. Eat healthy meals that include fruit and vegetables, and cut down on sugar, coffee and other stimulants. Many people try to survive on a diet of sugar and carbohydrates, which are another form of sugar. **Many behavioural disorders originate from a poor diet.** A detox is an excellent way to begin your transformation and raise your energy levels rapidly. See a nutritionist if necessary. A healthy body leads to a healthy mind, and if you initiate the change you will notice the benefits.

3 Start a personal cardiovascular exercise routine, acknowledging that even vigorous exercise can relax the mind and provide time to reflect. If your exercise regime does not provide the necessary downtime to relax your mind and invigorate your senses, find one that does. I find cycling a spiritually relaxing activity, because

while contemplating my goals and organising my life I can still engage my body awareness to keep me safe on the road. Apparently Albert Einstein conceived his Theory of Relativity on a bicycle. Choose an exercise routine that suits you and where your mind can wander safely.

Understanding the *who* – interpret your past to understand who you are:

1   The overarching objective of self-awareness is to be your authentic self. You must get to know yourself.

2   Take a behavioural and emotional intelligence (EQ) test to confirm your start point. I use the Behavioural Intelligence test (combines DiSC and EQ) offered by varying country providers. The Myers–Briggs Type Indicator® instrument and the TalentSmart EQ appraisal are other options. Be honest with yourself. The results will provide insights to what quadrants require work, and they provide activities to improve the behaviours to focus on. I recommend a certified practitioner who understands behavioural development to oversee the test and provide feedback on the results. The practitioner can also help you to prioritise the behaviours that require work.

3   Reflect and acknowledge your strengths and weaknesses, and the limiting beliefs holding you back. Once these are understood, you can begin to acknowledge what motivators define you. Understand what past events inspired your motivators to really appreciate your life skills.

4   Identify what you find most meaningful and the values most important to you. (Refer to the motivators in chapter 9 and the activity in chapter 21 to help you define and prioritise them.)

5   Listen in to your self-talk to understand the basis of and learn to cancel the negatives. Are these thoughts factual and realistic? You will become ever more present and in the moment as you address them. Your reflections will become constructive as you learn more about yourself and how to exercise self-control.

6   When confronting the past, accept that a lifetime of fears and insecurities may be unwarranted and naive. Otherwise, seek help from an accredited life coach or psychologist in your community.

7   Take mindfulness or meditation classes if you find it difficult to relax and reflect. Consider personal development methods and books for social anxiety, self-doubt, procrastination, lack of motivation, unwanted habits, and so on that may be holding you back from growth. The best approaches or books contain structured activities to help you change behaviours.

8   Write down your vulnerabilities and try to understand why they may limit or mask your feelings and intuitive instincts. This happens when your mind is preoccupied with unhelpful thoughts, noise and distractions:

   a)   Understanding the skills you developed to cope with your vulnerabilities or what you were missing as a child may identify your life skills and career choice. Dig deep to understand how they define you.

   b)   Understand how these relate back to your behavioural and EQ assessment.

   c)   Once you've identified your life skills, try to work out which activities you love and make you happy, and how to lead a meaningful life. Acknowledge your purpose.

   d)   Write a development plan addressing the areas of opportunity you need to focus on to hone strengths and address weaknesses. Include actions from your assessment.

   e)   Set goals around these activities to extend your understanding of what makes you happy. Mind map the milestones to get there.

   f)   Further reading: *The Values Factor: The secret to creating an inspired and fulfilling life* by Dr John F. Demartini.

9   Don't procrastinate or sweat the small stuff. Organise your goals into priorities and milestones to tick off as you accomplish them. Consider using an app for this purpose.

Take control, unclutter your life and release its complexity:

1   Free your life from complications and avoid unnecessary consumption:

   a) If driving your car causes unnecessary stress, travel on public transport or, better still, ride a bike.

   b) Only buy what adds value to your life.

   c) Organise your finances and live within your means, with the security of a savings plan for your retirement to provide peace of mind.

   d) Be a guardian: give back. Make a contribution to life and to looking after the world. It will make you happier.

   e) Unclutter your life and learn to get back to the basics with a healthy, meaningful lifestyle.

2   Use technology selectively, ensuring you are comfortable with your choice and it does not confound you. Use your smartphone to plan your day, take notes, make calculations and achieve goals. Use mind-mapping software to brainstorm and broaden your objectives, or a Trello board to organise your objectives visually.

3   Free your mind and learn to trust your instincts and gut to make decisions. Build this up slowly over an extended period. Sleep on the bigger decisions, but also try to understand why they feel right (or they don't). You will learn a lot about yourself and what values and motivations define you. This is key to developing your self-awareness and body awareness. As represented in the BBDM, your ability to centre a positive, strong, trusted, intuitive core influences the extension of your big, bold, future-directed feelings.

4   Delegate the detail. This increases the capability of your team or family and builds trust. Reason to understand outcomes. Hone your perception to determine what is true and what is not. Employ your judgement to support decisions if necessary. Leave deep thinking to your personal time.

18. The mind's positive transformation – inside-out

Directing your mind from the past to the present and future:

1   Start by being honest with yourself. Admit your flaws, but be your authentic self. Don't blame anyone else for obstructing your progress. Live with meaning and try to be a better person. Surround yourself with authentic people who promote your causes. Have meaningful conversations about personal and community development with your friends and colleagues. Be empathetic and try to tune into their needs too, thus opening your mind and learning about yourself.

2   Forgive yourself for past transgressions and ensure there are no ill feelings among your connections. Learn from your mistakes. Face and address any outstanding concerns with your social or work network. Initiate the conversations, and apologise if you feel the need. Avoid negative people if you cannot influence them.

3   Increase your awareness of the present and future by empathising with life's diversity. See how your goals can benefit your community, your work, your family and your relationships, and how each goal adds meaning and purpose to your own life. Be grateful for who you are and what you can achieve and contribute:

   a)   Before you go to bed at night, review your day and how your activities have advanced your goals.

   b)   Wake up in the morning with a positive attitude. Plan your day, and express gratitude at having the opportunity to make a difference.

   c)   The more you love what you can achieve, the more everything aligns to help you.

4   Enjoy the security of a defined pathway to improving yourself and the community you represent.

5   If these steps do not release your stress, worry and anxiety, then seek professional help.

6   Have fun and enjoy the fruits of this life-changing commitment; reward yourself in your community for your achievements.

Use any of the points above to start meaningful conversations with your partner, friends and colleagues. This will show your commitment and improve your reasoning skills and self-awareness. Reason why you want to change your life so as to clarify and reinforce your decisions. Hopefully the significant others in your life will join you in this positive process. There are substantial life rewards from being positive, and there is no going back.

THE POWER OF GOAL SETTING

The power of reasoning towards purposeful, meaningful goals and actions soon becomes apparent and helps in managing staff and setting strategy.

Studies indicate that successful people have clearly defined goals. Set achievable goals and analyse how your own mental processes help or hinder you. Set goals in both your business and personal lives and develop a plan of action to achieve your dreams.[29]

The power of the pen

To make your goal a reality, put pen to paper (or fingers to keyboard). Commit yourself even further – write it down to review every day, so that you stay focused and on track. Writing down goals may sound like surprisingly simple advice, however the outcomes are powerful. Billionaire entrepreneur Richard Branson says organising his goals is his top tool for success. 'Ever since I was a child I have made lists of all kinds, including short-term tasks, long-term goals and resolutions. It's how I make sense of the world, bring order to the ideas in my head, and start turning them into action,' wrote Branson in a 2017 New Year's Day post on his blog.

Physically putting pen to paper unleashes a psychological process that imprints on the unconscious mind – in psychology this is called a psycho-neuromuscular activity. This will activate a part of your brain called the 'reticular activating system', which will automatically guide you and keep you focused on your task.

---

29 Recommended reading: *Take Action* by Irene Vervliet, 2004.

Choosing the right goals

Most people find working towards and achieving a goal is motivating and satisfying, but that selecting the right goal and sticking with it isn't always easy. How can you develop meaningful, achievable goals? How do you become better at creating the results you want? Practise the three essential goal-setting skills: choosing, assessing and planning. Always structure your goals and organise, prioritise, discuss and record them for increased clarity.

Once you have established a goal, understand your motivation and set a plan of action, keep trying and never give up. No matter how many mistakes you make or how slowly you progress, you are still way ahead of everyone who isn't trying.

HOW WILL YOU KNOW YOU HAVE MADE THE POSITIVE TRANSFORMATION?

Regulating your thoughts, increasing your independence and positive outlook, and strengthening your character will transform you into a positive temperament. This can be a very spiritual experience. It happened to me over the space of two blocks while I was out walking. Six months before I had ended a relationship, which I had wrestled with and finally concluded wasn't right for me. We were on different paths, and my deepening anxiety prevented me from being myself. The moment I realised this, I rediscovered my independence and resilience. The tension in my body was released, my spine straightened, and I found myself walking tall and ready to face whatever came my way. I had discovered my trust instincts. The transition was uplifting; I felt centred and my mood was positive from then on.

This positive transformation may not happen to you in the same way. Before I was diagnosed with a social anxiety disorder, I suffered from stress and anxiety, which is probably why the experience was so defining. You may just wake up one morning with a positive attitude. However it happens, there will be no turning back. The feeling is invigorating, and the bounce in your step, your strengthening character, awareness of the present and clarity of purpose will define

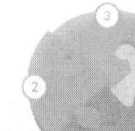

your sense of wellbeing and enable you to take on whatever comes your way.

THE FOIL OF PROCRASTINATION

Dr Piers Steel describes impulsiveness in his book *The Procrastination Equation* as 'the Achilles Heel of procrastination'. He goes on to say, 'Impulsive people find it difficult to plan work ahead of time, and even after they start they are easily distracted. Procrastination inevitably follows.'

According to the English Brain Bank blog published by scientist Dr Sarah Fox: 'These brief but powerful lapses in self-control govern the brain's preference for behaviours that provide instant gratification and avoid pursuing goal-directed achievement.'

To add another layer, according to an article in *Psychology Today*, procrastination, on a neurobiological level, appears to be a negative emotion and stems from an internal desire to protect ourselves from the negative feelings associated with fear of failure.

Often it's a significant event that we procrastinate most about, like changing jobs, relationships or moving to a new house. It's simply feels too hard. We may have been thinking about putting in for a promotion or applying for a transfer, but somehow the time has never felt right. The common theme is feelings – it's all about how things *feel*. This is where mindfulness comes in to help you start that looming project or make that change you've been avoiding. It will help you move forward and feel positive about what you've been shying away from.

FIVE STEPS TO OVERCOMING PROCRASTINATION[30]

If you can't organise your priorities by writing them down and ticking them off, then Sarah Salas sets out a mindfulness technique for procrastination:

1   Make a list of important tasks and see how your body feels.
    Write down what happens: 'I feel tightness in my chest/throat, buttocks/head or I feel an ache/pain in my…' Name an emotion if you feel one. 'I feel sad/anxious/angry…'

---

30 *Acuity* magazine. Sarah Salas is a Melbourne-based mindfulness expert.

2   Prioritise the list with the most unpleasant yet important task at the top, then go back to your body and see how it reacts and what emotions it reveals. Write them down. Concentrate on where in your body that feeling is.

3   Set a timer for three minutes and focus on slow, deep breathing. Try not to think, and concentrate on breathing. Reset the timer for 30 minutes, and during that time work only on the most unpleasant task at the top of your priority list. Turn off your phone and avoid any potential distraction.

4   When the alarm goes off, one of two things will happen:

   a)   You will give a sigh of relief and stop… or

   b)   You will decide you want to carry on because you're on a roll!

5   Whichever option you chose, once you have decided to stop the first task, give yourself a pat on the back (literally), take a deep breath and see how your body feels – alert, alive, relaxed, excited? Also write down any emotions like relief, contentment, happiness. Move down the list, chipping away at a few tasks or concentrating on one. The choice is yours, but there's no denying how good it feels to start. So what are you waiting for?

19. MASLOW'S HIERARCHY AND WHAT IT MEANS FOR MANAGERS

HOW LIFE CAN PRESENT IN HIERARCHIES

External influences such as instant gratification and consumerism can distract from our need to develop our social currency and to find deeper meaning. This can be exacerbated by the media and aggressive advertising. Our avoidance technique is called 'diversion', where our minds retreat to past events or happy childhood associations. Having spent our childhood developing fantasies and skills to cope with our insecurities, in adulthood we must move beyond these innocent beliefs to discover our purpose, for when we are passionate about delivering meaningful outcomes, posturing for status and personal agendas become futile.

Our creative mind continuously updates schemas or visions to create a mental representation of life and associations. Our perceptive visual system takes in data from the periphery of our visual field. The flipside of our superior perceptive ability to observe the laws of nature allows humans to disregard them by creating artificial environments. Once immersed in an artificial environment we become oblivious to the natural order of things.

When focused on social status, a pecking order emerges as the perceived privileged person in our community prevails and we feel emotionally inferior to them. Equality is lost in a world where volume, mass or size determines value. Structure and hierarchy only encourage inferiority and dependence, and consign our locus of control to reflecting on the past, impacting both our perceived social status and disempowering our growth. The more we distance ourselves from the laws of nature, the more we seek to standardise and structure our lives around artificial environments. Moreover, without a solid understanding of our connection to the environment, we may lose all sense of our development potential. This is an essential learning when designing open work environments in support of creativity and social connection.

MASLOW'S HIERARCHY OF NEEDS

Abraham Maslow's Hierarchy of Needs is one of the most popular models in leadership theory. Developed in 1948, the Hierarchy of Needs covers many disciplines, including business, management, marketing, parenting, education and psychology. Simple, orderly, intuitively sensible, cognitively appealing and offering order out of chaos, it has only one problem: unlike the symmetry of the BBDM, it is plain, flat, and distorts reality. A fascinating article by Pamela Rutledge in *Psychology Today* entitled 'Social Networks: What Maslow Misses' (November 2011) points out that Maslow's model misses the role of social connection and this could explain why the model was represented this way.

Maslow's model, as its name suggests, organises groups of human needs into levels in a hierarchical structure, forming a pyramid (as shown on the following page). You must fulfil the requirements of one set of needs before you can rise to the next level. This progression of learning is also emphasised in the BBDM.

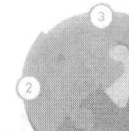

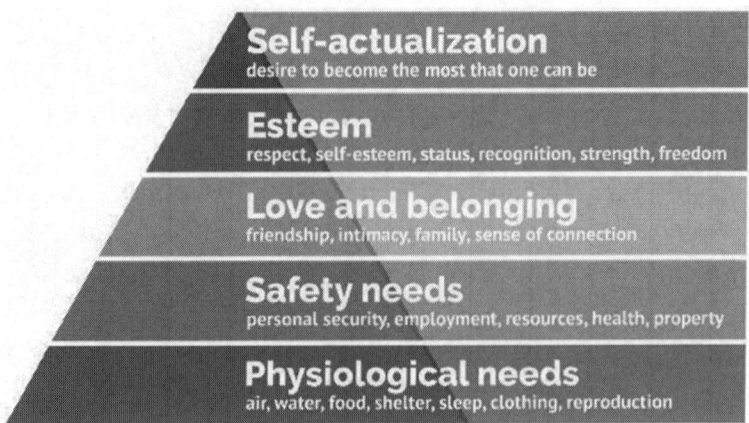

Maslow's Hierarchy of Needs[31]

Maslow's model is hierarchical. The human brain at the base is driven by a fundamental instinct to survive with food, drink and shelter. The second level is made up of safety needs. The third comprises social needs such as family, affection, relationships, work groups and community. The fourth level holds the egocentric internal needs of achievement, responsibility and reputation. Finally, at the top, are self-actualisation, personal growth and fulfilment. The four sets of classifications in the BBDM are more interconnected and are rationalised by the biological and physiological primary growth pathways and corresponding objectives. The alignment of the opposing growth objectives is supported from an evolutionary, personality (MBTi), learning (Kolbs's) and mathematical symmetrical basis.

'Here's the problem with Maslow's hierarchy,' explains Rutledge. 'None of these needs – starting with basic survival on up – are possible without social connection and collaboration … Without collaboration, there is no survival. It was not possible to defeat a woolly mammoth, build a secure structure, or care for children while hunting without a team effort. It's truer now than then. Our reliance on each other grows as societies become more complex, interconnected, and

---

31 'Maslow's Hierarchy of Needs', www.SimplyPsychology.org, Saul McLeod, 2018. Used with permission.

specialised. Connection is a prerequisite for survival, physically and emotionally.' I tend to agree, and a hierarchy does not promote the associations and relationships from one level to the next. By providing a life cyclic basis, the BBDM defines roles and responsibilities in support of other quadrants while connection is supported by association (many-to-many, many-to-one, and so on), stage (infant, child, and so on) and organisational functional relationships (administrative, sales and service, HR, and so on). Collaboration is essential to enhancing relationships, however the BBDM states collaboration is a developed quality to be honed over many years.

'Rethinking Maslow's Hierarchy:
Implications for a socially-connected world'[32]

'Needs are not hierarchical. Life is messier than that. Needs are, like most other things in nature, an interactive, dynamic system, but they are anchored in our ability to make social connections. Maslow's model needs rewiring so it matches our brains. Belongingness is the driving force of human behaviour, not a third-tier activity,' Rutledge

---

32 Pamela B. Rutledge PhD, MBA. Used with permission.

writes. 'The system of human needs from bottom to top, shelter, safety, sex, leadership, community, competence and trust, are dependent on our ability to connect with others. Belonging to a community provides the sense of security and agency that makes our brains happy and helps keep us safe.' Learning to belong and attachment (including basic human needs – food, water, shelter, and so on) influence our value system and are among the first development objectives in the BBDM, providing an essential foundation for success in other quadrants. These are described as biological objectives.

In the BBDM, I put bonding or belongingness in the first stage to balance out our fears, but in some ways life hasn't changed our fundamental human needs. Whether it's the ancient savannah or using today's Facebook and Twitter, our behaviours adapt to the environment to support that most basic of human attachment needs. Social connection is ever-present, and social media has made it much easier for 'remote' social connection to take place, so today's young people who have grown up in this interconnected world expect the workplace to reflect that. When creating dynamic workspaces, there should be plenty of opportunity for employees to connect in open environments. It's only natural for people to want to protect their personal space, but providing new and challenging ways to connect will encourage employees to confront their social inhibitions.

MASLOW'S LEGACY AND HUMANISM

Maslow does deserve credit for writing that human beings are motivated by unsatisfied needs, and that certain lower needs must be satisfied before higher needs can be fulfilled. This was revolutionary at the time, and his Hierarchy of Needs was an alternative to the determinism of Freud and Skinner. Maslow thought people were basically trustworthy, self-protecting and self-governing, and that humans tend toward growth and love. Although there is a continuous cycle of wars, murder, deceit, and so on, he believed that human nature is not meant to be savage and that violence and other evils occur when human needs are not fulfilled. In other words, people who are deprived of lower needs such as safety may defend themselves by violent means.

My take is that if people are not provided with a safe environment and have not learnt to feel safe then they will seek to protect themselves however they see fit. Maslow did not believe that humans are aggressive because they enjoy violence, or that they lie, cheat and steal because they enjoy doing so. It has even been suggested he didn't want to represent his needs in a pyramid, but the powers that endorsed his findings of the time insisted.

Maslow was also a strong supporter of the humanistic approach in psychology, developed as a rebellion against what some psychologists saw as the limitations of the behaviourist and psychodynamic psychology. The humanistic approach is thus often called the 'third force' in psychology after psychoanalysis and behaviourism (Maslow, 1968). 'Humanistic', 'humanism' and 'humanist' are terms in psychology relating to an approach that studies the whole person and the distinctness of each individual. Essentially, these terms refer to the same approach in psychology.

Sometimes the humanistic approach is called 'phenomenological'. This means that personality is studied from the point of view of the individual's subjective experience. For Rogers, the focus of psychology is not only on behaviour (Skinner), the unconscious (Freud), thinking (Wundt) or the human brain, but how individuals perceive and interpret events.[33] Rogers is therefore important because he redirected psychology towards the study of self.

IMPLICATIONS FOR MANAGEMENT

In 20th-century management, Maslow's Hierarchy of Needs was helpful in pointing out to managers why traditional management styles – hierarchical bureaucracy with managers acting as controllers – were unlikely to meet the psychological needs of employees, but it offered an unrealistic route to meeting those needs: ascension up the Hierarchy of Needs towards self-actualisation. The truth is that not everyone wants or needs or is able to be a self-actualising artist or leader.

In fact, Rutledge's rewired version and the BBDM suggest a more realistic pathway – through social connection and emotional

---

33 'Humanism', www.SimplyPsychology.org, Saul McLeod, 2015.

development – to meet our varying psychological needs. What they imply – and the experience of emerging management styles confirms – is that people working together in self-organising, agile teams can meet most psychological needs without positing unrealistic goals of self-actualisation as the be-all and end-all of life. As more of a leadership objective, self-actualisation may be a difficult personal endeavour without the environment to support the learnings. Creating the right environments at each development stage focuses the individual or team on the objectives at hand before having to contemplate the next hurdle.

Adapting the leadership styles of self-actualisation takes substantial effort, self-analysis and a lot of motivation. Not everyone is driven to achieve this level of capability, but for those who seek recognition and to express their purpose, having a meaningful roadmap as provided by the BBDM will deliver huge rewards and wellbeing.

20. WHY CHANGE INITIATIVES OFTEN FAIL

AN INDIVIDUAL MUST APPRECIATE THE NEED FOR CHANGE

The biggest challenge to organisational growth is resistance to change.

Change based on unidirectional, rational and traditional app-roaches has very definite limitations. If the leader makes all the decisions and expects subordinates to simply follow, there is no requirement for employees to grow, and they will not feel invested in the outcome. The command–control approach disrespects capability, limits an important avenue for employee development and growth, and is likely to influence future job security negatively. Regardless of how well these top-level decisions are made, successful change is inhibited because this approach ignores so much of the organisation's ability to optimise change. People tend initially to resist forced change, especially top-down approaches to change.

With a top-down approach to change management, decision-making is centralised at higher levels of the organisation, excluding lower-level employees in the change process, even though they are directly affected and will have to help implement the changes. This is why top-down approaches to change management increase resistance. Top-down change is about making changes quickly and dealing with problems only when necessary.

There is, however, a place for top-down approaches when far-reaching, transformative change is required and employees cannot contribute in the necessary timeframe. Leadership and communications should set out the objectives of such far-reaching change, and be prepared for resistance. Top-down approaches should only be contemplated as a last resort when an organisation has limited options. Implanting change champions in the business to work as a conduit between management and staff is one way of limiting the fallout. The change champions have to be open and honest to build the trust of the employees. Change champions identify and coach resistors as a priority. This approach has worked for me when working on red projects, so named when a project or business is at risk of failure. It takes strong leadership, excellent communications and supportive management to ensure the change endures and the objectives are met. Employees must be fully aware of the risks and consequences to cooperate and not obstruct the project.

RESPECTING AN INDIVIDUAL'S RIGHT TO BE INVOLVED IN CHANGE DECISIONS

It is rare to leave employees completely out of change decisions. As a matter of respect, it's better to be open and honest when presenting change strategies, even if the change is transformational. You can lose some of your best staff if you don't respect what they may perceive as their right to know and be involved. And leaders unwilling to listen to junior employees' ideas, suggestions or feedback generate poor employee motivation and performance.

Decision-making when limited to the top of the organisation can lack depth of information, and inhibit suggestions and ideas from the coalface. With limited delegation in the change process, lower-level employees may feel ignored, incompetent and underqualified. If you want your organisation to step up and have a high-performing culture, you need to be inclusive and listen to your staff. Top-down change is too often a symptom of leaders clinging to the belief that power, privilege and success lie in their core group.

Change initiatives need to focus on the individual while appreciating their level of development. With reference to the BBDM, dealing with one's insecurities and vulnerabilities is a natural requirement to transform to a positive, change-tolerant, independent mind. However, denying the need to personally develop and begin the journey to self-awareness may delay or even prevent this transformation, especially in men. Peer pressure in friendships or among colleagues may further prevent the transition as change involves adopting independent thought. The stage 3 emotional transformation will only occur if acknowledged and challenged by the individual.

Communicating to peers a readiness to change plays a crucial dual role:

- it awakens peers to the desire for change and admits a readiness to enter adulthood

- it reinforces the individual's willingness to step up and assume responsibility for adapting a more selfless, caring attitude towards others.

Open communication is central to directing change, while keeping the change process to the upper level of the organisation breeds scepticism. Misunderstandings arise from communication problems and inadequate information. Differing assessments of a situation can occur. Employees not given the chance to participate in and be abreast of change objectives do not know the exact circumstances underlying the change and therefore resist it.

Of the many change and transformation projects I have worked on, the most successful have been where I have implanted myself in the organisation to coach and facilitate change, acting as an independent soundboard to gauge resistance and strategically bringing minds together to lift confidence and talk through change scenarios and to agree actions to move forward. Preparation, planning, simulations, role playing and practice are the tools HR professionals, managers and change managers can call on to alleviate change resistance. Open communication and respect are key to enabling this level of engagement. A can-do attitude is also essential to exploring the most viable solutions.

TIPS FOR COACHES TO SUPPORT A GROWTH MINDSET

In revisiting the key findings of Carol Dweck's research from chapter 9:

- Encourage employees to be comfortable with setbacks and confusion.

- Don't praise talent, praise the process and the team effort. Dweck's research revealed that praising individuals leads to fixed mindsets. Praising the process includes acknowledgement, resilience, effort, collaboration and the experience of defining deeper solutions.

Be comfortable with confusion for your employees and yourself, and don't worry about not finding the answer right away.

* * *

Approaching learning with an individual development bias to encourage a growth mindset allows employees and teams to expand, grow and engage fully in the process without the constraints of individual performance outcomes. Following the growth approach Dweck describes requires a conscious effort and the right mindset and skillset, as well as self-confidence. And it's a perspective that educators can model and foster themselves by making learning challenging, acknowledging and allowing for failure, and emphasising the process of learning rather than the outcome.

21.
ESTABLISHING YOUR BUSINESS'S VALUES FOUNDATION FROM THE 'BOTTOM UP'

'Trust the vibes you get, energy doesn't lie.'

Genereux Philip

WORKING WITH YOUR EMPLOYEES TO ESTABLISH BUSINESS VALUES

Life throws a fair share of problems at us, but working through these challenges moves us forward. **The main point to remember is that we are personally responsible for our actions.**

A solid foundation of trust enables us to live our values and build awareness so that we know and understand who we are. Do not be persuaded that someone else is responsible for your problems, or that you can in any way control another person. This deceives only ourselves, reduces our effectiveness, and is one of the main deceptions in the world today: muddled values and motivations foster division and adversity where there are none, only to increase stress, distress, resistance and associated health problems by perpetuating the confusion in our lives. Balancing a strong left-hemisphere value foundation with a big-picture right hemisphere supports wellbeing and purpose.

In chapter 9 I explained that every experience, decision and action is determined by our perceived priority of values. Every decision is based upon what we feel will provide advantage over disadvantage and reward over risk to live our highest values. The more managers understand their own and their employees' priorities and values, the more they can communicate, educate and empower themselves and their employees. Therefore, it is vital to ensure employee values are not only aligned to their role, but also to the organisation's.

Determining individual employee values

Avoid forcing value systems on employees. Use an open-source development approach. Employees' values change as they develop the skills and knowledge to balance them, so it's important to revisit them regularly. A manager may choose to review an individual's values during the annual performance review and goal setting. Available motivational tests may not be necessary if the employee has a firm understanding of their own motivational drivers.

When an employee is revisiting or determining their values, suggest they present them using the following Eduard Spranger framework, where they prioritise the six motivational groupings from the one that most resonates to the least. Cross out the ones at the bottom that don't resonate or have no association, and then ask the employee to list in their own words their values that resonate most under each motivational grouping – what they feel they need to get a handle on. The motivations should be personal, but may include some career motivators if that helps them clarify their drivers.

Talk through the values selected with your employees and how they influence their strengths, and help them to prioritise so the manager understands them better and can ensure their development plans address their needs and ability to achieve their strengths and goals.

MOTIVATOR	DESCRIPTION	EMPLOYEE VALUES (PRIORITISED)
Theoretical	A passion to discover truth. The chief objective in life is to order and assimilate knowledge and the meaning behind that knowledge.	
Utilitarian/ Economic	A practical interest in money and a passion for what is useful. Time and resources are considered with an eye to efficiency and future economic gain.	
Aesthetic	Interest in form and harmony. Life is a series of episodic events, each enjoyed for its own sake. Has a heightened sense of beauty and inner vision.	
Social	Inherent love of people. Seeks to eliminate hate and conflict. Other persons are ends in themselves, not means. Altruistic, kind, empathetic and generous, even to their own detriment.	
Individualistic/ Political	The primary interest in this value is power – not necessarily politics in the traditional sense. Research indicates that leaders in most fields have a high power value; other people may be seen and used as simply a means to an end.	
Traditional/ Regulatory	Unity and order. The need to be regulated or the need for structure from an outside source. Seeks to comprehend the universe and to relate to a global totality. Dislikes change and chaos. Inflexible regarding convictions.	

The six basic personal interests, attitudes and value motivators

Getting the team on board

Once all employees have determined their values, have a group session with your team to openly discuss motivations, strengths and goals. This will help team members understand what their colleagues want to achieve. Use the session to try to align individual preferences, keeping in mind the organisation's aims and milestones. Let the team agree on the values and goals for the period and how they support the organisation.

Talk about key performance metrics (KPM) for both team targets and individual targets, and make sure such metrics are **S**pecific, **M**easurable, **A**ttainable, **R**elevant, and **T**ime-bound (SMART), as well as meaningful to the employee and greater community. Use a balanced scorecard approach to ensure you attribute KPMs to both financial and non-financial perspectives (internal processes, customer and community, and learning and growth).

* * *

Ensure your employee values and performance metrics align to the overall strategy of the business. If you wish, and if it's appropriate for your department, set out a vision and a mission statement in support of all individual and organisational objectives to ensure relevance at functional or team level.

22. BRINGING MEANING TO YOUR ORGANISATION'S CULTURE

If civilisations drove the huge increase in our intellectual capacity, then don't we just have to replicate the characteristics that brought about this expansion in the workplace? There was a reason why the earliest civilisations were established in sub-tropical regions, where abundance developed intelligence and delivered social rewards. Even if we'd had to subsist in a dry climate, Ice Age or natural disaster, we would have valued cooperating to find solutions. The sum of the parts is vastly more valuable than individual contributions. Securing future growth creatively by diversifying skills and advancing capability underlies our desire to cooperate and connect to explore shared rewards and social purpose.

THE IMPORTANCE OF DEVELOPING MEANING IN YOUR WORKPLACE

While perks such as free food and games in the office may be a draw-card for new employees, Teresa Amabile, a business administration professor at Harvard Business School, says 'none of this matters unless people feel they have meaningful work and are making progress at it.'[34] She goes on to say: 'In over 30 years of research, I've found that people do their most creative work when they're motivated by the work itself.' So the first thing to look at when trying to build a positive, productive culture is the work itself.

Not surprisingly, increased stress or struggle tends to reduce happiness levels, but also often contributes to feelings of meaning. Doing things that are demanding and difficult, such as raising children or working on big projects, can be more rewarding and add sense to our lives despite simultaneously reducing our levels of happiness. Meaning is also tied closely to personal values and self-awareness. When we spend time thinking about and acting within a larger community, we're more likely to feel a strong sense of accomplishment, whereas happiness is more closely aligned to simply seeking out the satisfaction of our personal needs. Meaning is not necessarily tied to happiness.

Consider the latest survey findings from The Energy Project, which found employees who derive meaning from their work are more than three times as likely to stay with their organisations – the highest single impact of any survey variable they tested.[35] Here meaning trumps learning and growth, connection to a company's mission and even work–life balance. So what does this say? Add life meaning to your company mission statement and ensure that employee development plans and wellbeing programs define worthwhile objectives, adding significance to people's lives.

---

34 'How to Develop a Meaningful Company Culture', Belle Beth Cooper, Focus: the creativity and productivity blog.

35 'Why You Hate Work', Tony Schwartz, The Energy Project.

PURPOSE AND SOCIAL RESPONSIBILITY

What is meaning in relation to human psychology? Is it the security of having a purposeful role that gives back? Is it sharing the fruits of your labour with your community, knowing you are contributing? Is it connecting socially and sharing the difference you make to people's lives?

One study indicated that organisations perceived as purpose-driven and particularly socially responsible improved a sense of meaningfulness for employees' work.[36] Civilisations were founded on a desire to participate in the qualities of life and create shared benefits from diverse niches. Cooperating creatively to broaden skills and to collectively identify, appreciate and diversify rewards increases our future security. Flourishing environmental diversity and creative pursuits provided the means to define new opportunities and develop specialist roles. In just over 5,000 years of adapting specialist roles through sharing responsibility, civilisations and the proliferation of niches have created an explosive expansion in human intelligence and capability.

Creativity, resilience, passion, self-awareness, independence and hope are just some of the rewards of Ei. Emotional intelligence is a product of being socially connected, and has developed alongside the rise of civilisations. As cities have expanded, the establishment of communities has further diversified our collective purpose by creating an array of services above subsistence and primary activities. The expansion of Ei and community has increased innovation and created a proliferation of capability.

OUR PASSION FUELS OUR AWARENESS

You will be insensitive to your environment if you do not acknowledge or admire your surroundings. This admiration can take on many forms. Those who engage and are passionate about their environment will more likely develop an acute awareness aligned to their motivations. Understanding what your employees are passionate about should define a business's community development programs. For social enterprises, this should be reasonably simple to determine. For other

---

36 'The Power of Purpose: How organizations are making work more meaningful',
   Alison Alexander, Northwestern University.

companies, what motivates the majority may take some investigation. Where I live in Sydney, seemingly unregulated population growth continues to influence the quality of life. In the future, families will be forced to inhabit apartment buildings where there are limited facilities for children, and schools will be built in high-rise blocks. The land required to sustain us is being sold to developers, and in 20 years food will have to be imported. How will children identify what life attributes sustain them when living in structured environments? The population is increasingly stressed and heavily in debt, and transport is at capacity. No strategy or policy exists to deal with the consequences of the imbalance that is occurring.

Allowing value and creativity to flourish

Generally, government institutions tend to invite more risk-averse, insular recruits, who would tend to regulate our experiences rather than promoting open environments. Protective, command–control, 'boss' styles often prefer solitude over actively engaging in experiences. A population is more easily controlled and more likely to contract dependencies in controlled environments. Self-motivated governments seem unaware of the damage they cause by structuring our environments, regulating our freedoms and restricting our experiences. People need freedom to experience, to associate and grow. **Bureaucratic command–control styles can inhibit growth and influence dependency.**

We need to breathe life back into the community so that value and creativity can flourish and balance can be restored. We must support our community businesses in their struggle to compete with large business concerns that through size alone achieve favoured investment status and volume efficiencies. Globalisation, standardisation and competitive advantage have confused the essential role the community plays in defining a distinct identity, developing behavioural attributes such as social esteem, relationship trust and self-awareness, and defining a collective purpose. **It takes a village to define an identity and raise a child.**

What does this mean for your business?

The extent of today's social problems may be attributed to community severance and the inability to collaborate to secure the future and quality of life. Organisations should encourage communities to define their own identity, maximising the value of the collective to guide a future of flourishing, meaningful organisations. Organisations should take the lead in independently developing and implementing different cultural models based on trust, diversity of capability, ethical value objectives and social responsibility to support working communities.

It is evident in today's uncaring, consumerist nation states – such as the US, China and, increasingly, Australia – that the product of a diminished, underrated identity is detachment and depression. Individuals, families and communities are increasingly victims of failed marriages, family violence and the stress of unresolved vulnerabilities. Mental disorders are common. An estimated 22.1 per cent of Americans aged 18 and above, about one in five adults, suffer from a diagnosable mental disorder.[37]

Insecurities and stress are indicators of life's imbalances and the failure to grow. Behavioural disorders are expressed as bullying, discrimination and hate crimes. Lack of care and meaningful work opportunities for the disadvantaged result in low self-esteem in the population and increasing obesity, and drug and alcohol abuse in the US and Australia causes problems: gambling to excess, and serious crimes. These are all products of detachment and the mythical search for happiness. Organisations need to lead by example and help support flourishing, functional, meaningful communities.

COOPERATION FOR MUTUAL BENEFIT AND GROWTH

Imagine if, in a balanced community, services, professionals and organisations – both government and private – cooperated for mutual benefit. If the definition of 'sustainable production and consumption' were the use of goods and services responding to basic needs and bringing

---

37 'The De Facto Mental and Addictive Disorders Service System', D.A. Regier, W.E. Narrow, D.S. Rae, et al.

a better quality of life while minimising the use of natural resources, toxic materials and emissions of waste and pollutants[38], the needs of future generations would not be jeopardised. My own experience and observations have produced a strong appreciation of what supports sustainability in populations with strong independent identities and security.

Environmental awareness is completely dependent on developing our locus of control throughout a lifecycle. Without proper leadership, the collective will believe that environmental degradation is outside their control and deny responsibility. In failing to respect our environment, we fail to engage the emotions that support the development of our awareness and superior capability.

Imagine your community authority providing the basic infrastructure and facilities to encourage mobility, collaboration and interaction. Schools, childcare, university, retail, support groups, police, neighbourhood watch, recreational groups and all manner of services would all tap into a centralised knowledge base to plan for the future together. With the objectives of inclusion and respect for knowledge creating diversity of thought to secure future generations, and a common goal to plan and achieve quality of life, imagine the immeasurable community spirit, prosperity and intellectual diversity that would result. In applying justice and ethics to overcome the divisiveness of external competition, what if the community cooperated on patents, privacy, market research, communications and development to innovate and provide future job security?

Cooperating to encourage greater community prosperity and engagement ensures the skills and knowledge of all individuals are valued. In Sydney I am a member of several organisations that do not include member, business or community development as part of their charter. If available, personal and emotional development would influence members' lives positively. This is slowly changing. The Returned and Services League now offers support in finding work for ex-servicemen and assisting with post-traumatic stress. A balance of social support and development programs would support a community's distinctive culture and capability growth.

---

38 As defined by the Oslo Symposium in 1994, sustainable consumption and production (SCP).

THE IMPACT OF IMBALANCE

Businesses and communities must support our creative, intuitive ability to promote social integration. Organisations that have distanced themselves from the environment and deny accountability are the most resistant to change. Our childhood behaviours of envy, greed and mistrust have dominated the recent phase of our evolution to deliver an imbalance in our environment and a reason for the underdevelopment of humanitarian awareness.

We are part of an evolutionary experiment that has succeeded in delivering a substantial increase in life and divergent cultures across our planet. Successful adaptation had increased populations in every corner of the world long before the colonialists took to the seas to plunder wealth. An extended period of climatic stability has allowed life to flourish, increased diversity and improved our intellectual capability, but whether this has been influenced by humanity's growing ability to influence balance in the environment has yet to be fully understood. IQ scores have been steadily falling for the past few decades, and environmental factors are to blame, a new study says.[39] Looking at populous cities, it is very obvious that overtly structured, standardised environments have a detrimental impact on our awareness.

---

39 'Flynn Effect and its Reversal Are Both Environmentally Caused', Bernt Bratsberg and Ole Rogeberg, June 2018.

23. THE POWER OF BEHAVIOUR AND POSITIVITY TO INFLUENCE GROWTH

POSITIVE ENERGY = GROWTH

Until now there has been no accepted theory as to why we experience positive emotions. From the standpoint of physics, electrons are negatively charged, attracted to the positive and repelled by the negative. If energy were represented in humans as the purest indicator of emotion, wouldn't energy or emotions or natural inclination go from negative to positive? Does the natural energy sequence from negative to positive indicate our natural propensity for growth? **Do instincts and intuition guide our preferred development path?**

The following figure shows our emotional and cultural natural inclination and how it moves from negative to proactive.

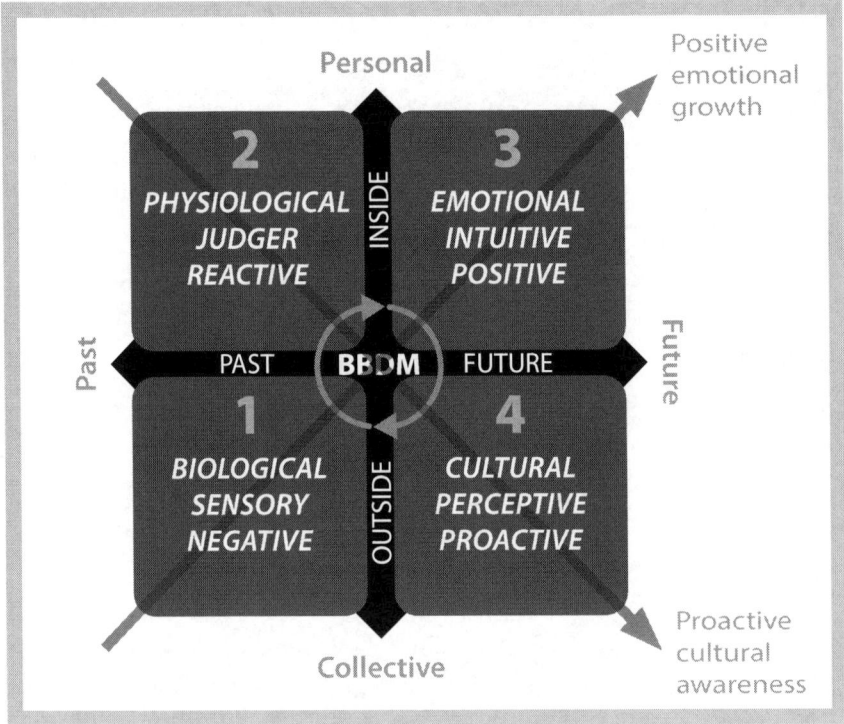

Our emotional and cultural natural inclination

THE POWER OF POSITIVITY

What does a positive mind mean for evolution and the course of life? It means absolutely everything for reproduction and nurturing. Throughout pregnancy a mother inevitably switches to a positive state of mind for nurturing. Her hormones and heightened intuitive instincts support this. While this stimulates her capacities, her brain also employs short-term memory to ensure nothing is left to chance.[40]

---

40 'What Happens to a Woman's Brain When She Becomes a Mother', Adrienne LaFrance, *The Atlantic*.

WHAT DOES THIS MEAN FOR YOUR BUSINESS?

Why are these positive, nurturing instincts so important to business? Because, like a parent, a selfless, caring manager can more readily influence the development of an employee who knows the manager has their best interests at heart. A manager must be seen to be independent of an organisation's objectives, and to genuinely care about the employees and know if they should be entrusted with development objectives.

In business I have often seen a supportive, trusting manager explaining objectives to persuade employees to challenge themselves. If an employee suffers from behavioural vulnerabilities or long-held fears, the manager needs compassion to guide the conversation. A manager who is not emotionally aware may not even appreciate the benefits of development.

Emotional maturity and a positive mind are essential to nurturing and development for responsible HR professionals and managers as well as doctors, nurses, specialists, and in fact all caregivers. An emotionally immature carer may have selfish objectives and be uninterested in basic care or look to profit from misfortune. Emotional maturity and a positive mind should be requirements for coach and carer roles.

BEHAVIOURAL LEARNING IS CRUCIAL TO OUR DEVELOPMENT

Behaviour influences our thoughts, which then influence our emotions, which then influence our behaviours in a perpetual cycle. Behaviour is how we learn. Our development after conception, our success or failure, are strongly influenced if not dependent on environmental influences. It seems easier for scientists, psychologists and the research community to discount behavioural influences rather than try to understand them.

Before isolating the causes by identifying a genetic basis for adversity, we need to understand the behavioural influences that may also contribute to imbalance. Sometimes identifying a genetic reason deflects the underlying behavioural cause, so those troubled may deny the real source, often a lack of self-belief or self-awareness. On the other hand, identifying a genetic cause may have a placebo effect, allowing the person to confront the influences more positively. It is not helpful for research to continually try to isolate a genetic basis by disregarding behavioural implications.

It is apparent in human evolution that little is left to chance and we all enter the world with similar characteristics. Our identity is undeveloped and our environment determines if we succeed or fail. Identity means everything, and understanding ourselves assists our self-awareness and allows us to address issues that might otherwise impede us. To progress, we need to know why we identify in a particular way, so we can rewire our brains by learning, unlearning and relearning.

THE CHOICES WE HAVE IN DEVELOPING MEANING

The considerable advantages of my own various perspectives have led me towards cultural competence. There are two pathways to custodianship and to making a contribution in life: biological to emotional (relationships, reproduction, nurturing, coaching and caregiving) or physiological to cultural (life purpose, causation, work contribution, philosophy, ethics and leadership) – or both.

What would life have been like had things been different? We need to relish and understand how every aspect of our lives has moulded and crafted our identity. I am fortunate in over 35 years of professional and personal exploration, development and achievement to have developed the insight, skills and competencies that have fuelled my knowledge and career.

BEHAVIOUR STARTS WITH THE INDIVIDUAL AND MUST BE RESPECTED

The insight that a lifetime brings is that behaviour must be respected in the community and in organisations, as it is everything to human beings. Knowledge should be directed at the individual, not the organisation, and individual behaviours must be nurtured and made responsible. Behaviours define us and allow us to thrive. **Don't 'accept' behaviour; understand it!**

* * *

Some of my life's most transformational turning points came from compassionate coaches who gave me permission and methods to allow me to be myself and move on – my Sexologist who convinced me I was different but special being gay, and my Psychiatrist who diagnosed and helped me to confront my Social Anxiety Disorder in as little as six months. We all know deep down that marginalised individuals and communities need respect and support. In your organisation you must recognise that inclusion, acceptance and respect can change the world, and humanity has a common genetic, emotional and development pathway. Everyone is special and needs to feel valued. It is evident that individuals who were badly treated in their youth can correct this injustice as adults. If we respect these people, many of their problems will be corrected. Diversity of capability is only as powerful as our willingness to listen and respect.

24. HOW THE WORK ENVIRONMENT INFLUENCES SELF-VALUE AND PRODUCTIVITY

EACH DEVELOPMENT STAGE HAS ITS OWN SET OF OBJECTIVES

Each of the four development stages in the BBDM provides a complementary set of objectives to guide HR professionals to develop employees in their respective stage. Knowing how the objectives influence the achievement of each stage is one thing. However, providing the right environment to encourage growth is also essential.

Providing a safe and secure environment is important for stage 1 employees to bond and feel secure. A team-based environment works for stage 2 employees to compete in dynamic ways to learn decision-making but also to moderate behaviour. Stage 3 is about challenging employees to explore deeper understanding and reasoning in one-to-one exchanges. Stage 4 is about creating opportunities to allow leaders to develop their one-to-many executive functions.

Organisational psychology has provided insight into how work environments influence self-worth and productivity. Recent trends to encourage supportive, open business environments have increased performance and innovation.[41] New, 'organic', agile organisations can be self-organising, with self-managed teams, and may sometimes be referred to as network organisations. They are modelled on start-ups as opposed to more established businesses, and are more responsive and adaptable in today's rapidly changing world. The move by some governments to make organisations accountable for stress recognises the influence of the workplace on lives.

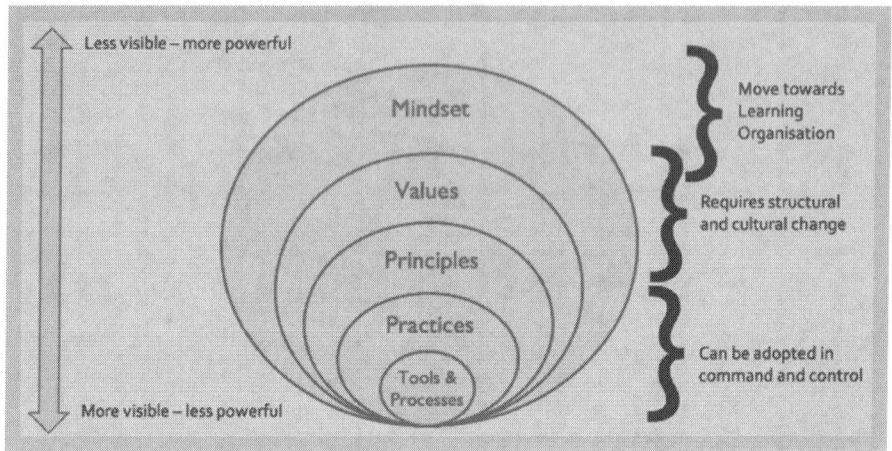

What is agile?[42]

These more 'organic' forms of organisation cultivate empowerment in employees more than the hierarchical, rigidly structured companies of the past, and also address the nature of management control. If management exists to support employees' efforts to be fully productive members of their organisations and communities, then any form of control is counterproductive.

Agile work practices are not only for IT projects, they can work in any organisation. One approach I use to pilot the methodology is to dedicate a half day a week for employees to work on business improvement projects. Using the stop/start/pause change approach, an initial project would free up time by reviewing work practices to

---

41 'Leadership and Innovation', Joanna Barsh, Marla M. Capozzi, and Jonathan Davidson, *McKinsey Quarterly*, January 2008.

42 Adventures with Agile, Simon Powers. Used with permission.

understand if they add value. If they don't, the task can be stopped or paused so the employee's time can be reallocated to work on business improvements. Employees agree and prioritise the projects based on their biggest challenges faced in performing their day-to-day responsibilities. The project's members can cross a number of functional streams. Employees are encouraged to join projects that promote their strengths and interest. A scrum master is appointed from the team based on their ability to coordinate the project through to conclusion.

Simple project tools help the team to scope the project, build a roadmap, and assign accountabilities and timeframes. A project sponsor or leader facilitates and coaches the team, ensuring there are enough resources and time allowances to successfully complete the project. The self-supporting team members are encouraged to be open, responsible, show genuine commitment, respect all contributions, avoid groupthink by being allowed to be imperfect, be positive and have fun.

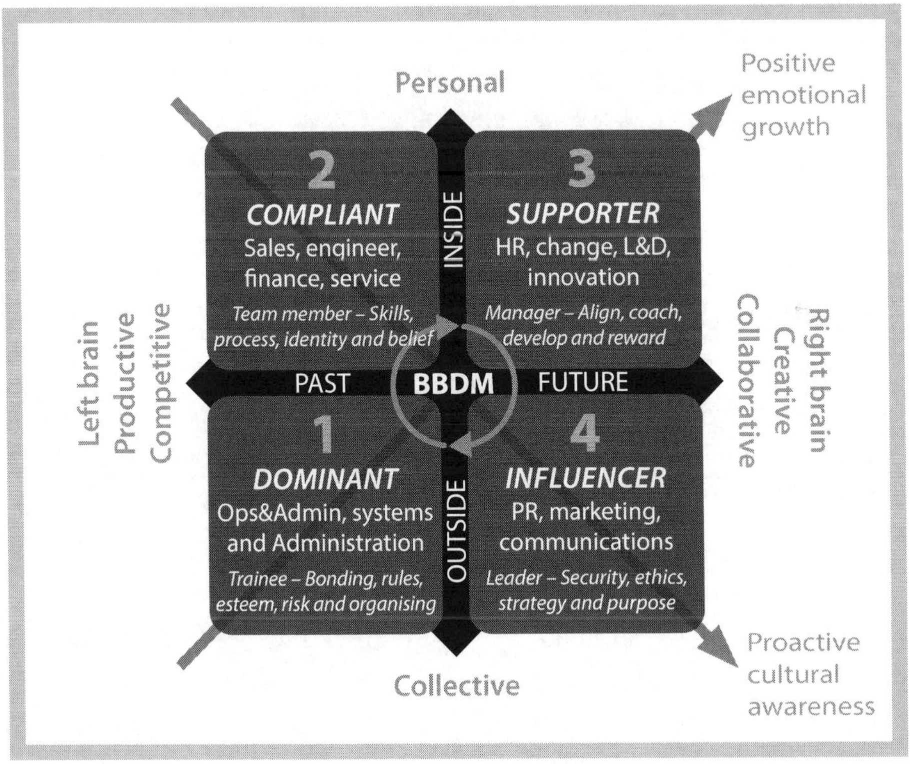

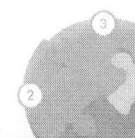

Personal

Positive emotional growth

Left brain
Productive
Competitive

INSIDE

2
COMPLIANT
Sales, engineer, finance, service
Team member – Skills, process, identity and belief

3
SUPPORTER
HR, change, L&D, innovation
Manager – Align, coach, develop and reward

Right brain
Creative
Collaborative

PAST **BBDM** FUTURE

1
DOMINANT
Ops&Admin, systems and Administration
Trainee – Bonding, rules, esteem, risk and organising

OUTSIDE

4
INFLUENCER
PR, marketing, communications
Leader – Security, ethics, strategy and purpose

Proactive cultural awareness

Collective

The BBDM organisation design model

This approach breaks down functional silos and encourages employees to play to their strengths but also provides an environment for aspiring managers to selectively address their weaknesses. This initiates an open, supportive, positive culture and over time employees are encouraged to align to the functional role where they feel they can contribute most. Motivations do change as we grow in confidence and it's important to provide a fluid environment where people can move onto bigger stage challenges or revisit stages when they feel the need to.

The decision of the employee to align to a particular quadrant will largely be based on the particular behaviours each quadrant promotes. As suggested earlier, it's up to the organisation based on community expectations to define the divergent behaviours associated with each of the quadrants. Each community is different and, for a culture to have meaning, behaviours should be selected and aligned to support the organisation and the community it serves. When aligned purposely, behaviours drive growth, so it is important employees understand what behaviours are expected from each quadrant they align to. The previous framework provides the start point for discussions and ensures behavioural development objectives are balanced around the divergent capabilities.

DEVISING EFFECTIVE DEVELOPMENT PROGRAMS

Ei-enabled HR coaches support functional managers who determine the most appropriate role and needs of each employee. Functional managers work with team members to devise development programs aligned to the capabilities in their quadrant.

Stage 1

In stage 1, trainees develop their sense of belonging, learn about safety and to feel they are valued, and may also be involved in assessing and mitigating risk to develop their sense of security. A graduate program should introduce a diversity of capabilities, inducting an employee in an operational or administrative role until they learn about the operating environment. Learning to be more assertive may be a reason an employee elects this stage as an avenue for improvement.

Appoint a mentor to help the trainee assimilate, encourage their active participation in social programs, and explain the organisation's values and operations. Employees can be encouraged to take calculated risks and talk through mitigation strategies with their manager or mentor. Above all, new employees should be encouraged to take responsibility for their actions. The environment should be non-threatening to allow an employee to speak up, experiment and dare to be different.

Organisations should not only respect diversity but also encourage employees to voice their different points of view without fear of being judged. Constructive feedback should always be the objective of a mentor or coach, and also enhances their own leadership traits.

The family plays a key role in providing a sense of personal security, particularly in times of uncertainty and mistrust, and an organisation must provide this same level of security to encourage their employees.

Stage 2

Whereas stage 1 is about operating successfully within the family or organisation, stage 2 develops team dynamics to build strong employee identities and self-belief. Encouraging interaction in the workplace and the community builds a healthy, competitive team spirit. Employees should be encouraged to try different approaches and decide on their best course of action as a team. Their growing ability to make sound judgements will give them confidence. An inclusive team involves every member and builds up a healthy camaraderie by sharing in success and failure, and moderating insensitive emotions.

To broaden an employee's identity outside the organisation, competing against other teams can be of benefit in diversifying cultural understanding. Any activity can drive team spirit, shared goals and achievement. Which skills to focus on depend on the industry you are in. Sales targets, customer renewals, service rankings and industry rankings may all provide a basis for team-based competitions, and a lot can be learnt from comparing high-performing teams in different

locations by identifying what motivates their winning attitude and beliefs. Meaningful storytelling from community leaders is also a powerful means of learning and establishing proud identities.

Promoting a high achiever to team leader or scrum master will develop interpersonal skills and increase their self-confidence. Mentoring team members in their sales or service targets supports this development. The team leader identifies and encourages desired behaviours and agrees on rewards as a team. The team should also agree on appropriate penalties for undesirable behaviours – a reprimand or even a warning. Self-managed teams encourage members to be considerate, objective and controlled, and promote accountability. Team involvement is as much about exploring problems as presenting solutions. Teams need to identify issues and draw their own conclusions. Team decisions can then be pitched to the facilitator or coach.

Stage 2 team leaders and mature-minded employees confident in their roles may elect to transition to stage 3 self-discovery.

Stage 3

Stage 3 strengthens characteristics and resilience. Whereas the development of our left brain in stage 2 was all about developing skills and knowledge, the emergence of right-brain characteristics in stage 3 is about action and application. An Ei coach helps an employee understand what is involved and assists them through the process if the candidate chooses.

Knowing how Ei contributes to growth and wellbeing, how does an employee initiate the journey to emotional maturity? Having already amassed skills, knowledge and confidence, we are likely to sense when we are ready to graduate to a right-brain prevalence.

Chapter 22 sets out how to develop maturity and independence. Challenging new things make us happy – living in a rut and dealing with the mundane doesn't. Extend yourself. The rewards come over long periods of time; don't expect them overnight.

An Ei coach should be:

1   trusting, and acknowledge development benefits

2   supporting and empathetic to employees' needs

3   an active listener

4   able to encourage and empower

5   respectful when an employee wishes to improve

6   able to plan and structure interaction

7   clear on the purpose and goals of an interaction

8   positive about the employee's development potential

9   ethical and moral.

Mindfulness may assist at this stage to encourage an employee to relax, reflect and be authentic and curious. Thus begins the journey to self-awareness and trusting their own instincts that prepares an employee for a management role in stage 3. During this period of reflection and transition, analysing and emotionally associating long-held concerns, worries and stresses raises self-awareness. Searching deep into the past, deconstructing limiting beliefs and resolving vulnerabilities and understanding motivations may reveal life skills to discover a new job role.

Developing an independent, mature mindset is inextricably linked to discovering a role in society. Role insecurity may come from controlling or subservient characteristics in adulthood. An appreciation for compassion, kindness and guardianship manifests a right-brain preference. Our passion builds when we appreciate life's beauty both inside and outside, personally and collectively.

By challenging employees to initiate meaningful conversations, explain what motivates them and talk about the merits of organisational objectives and distinctions between problems and solutions, reasoning skills emerge when challenging participation, social skills and higher achievement. Trust and self-awareness promote authenticity, understanding and individual points of view.

Stage 3 is about exploring value in relationships and creative activities. Design training programs to encourage employees to participate in meaningful and creative conversations.

Stage 4

What does it mean to develop a cultural competence in stage 4? Cultural competence is our fully adapted ability to apply all our learnt behaviours in an automatic, multidimensional capacity to exploit an opportunity or niche in our environment. The advantage of humans over other life forms is that we can adapt to most – if not all – circumstances and can, as guardians, influence and create life in an almost limitless array of shapes and forms. We can invent our own niche and define our habitat, and even successfully inhabit some of the most adverse locations on the planet.

Our entire lifecycle is a progression of learning, designed to expose us to all capabilities and varying perspectives so that at the peak of our development we can selectively employ any one of those behaviours or capabilities to deliver on an objective or implement a strategy. **Our objective is to grow and diversify our capability.**

Big-picture, future-focused cultural awareness represents the apogee of our learning and development. This cultural leadership empowers the individual to love life in all its many forms, thus realising personal fulfilment. A custodian cultural capability is only accessible to humanists who respect life. Those who disrespect the fragility of life may not evolve beyond our primitive animal instincts and may just have to accept a life more ordinary.

LIKELY CHARACTERISTICS OF EACH DEVELOPMENT STAGE

Outlined in the following BBDM is a summary of characteristics of each development stage. These are likely to vary across organisations, communities and industries, so I suggest reviewing, supplementing or extending them to match your cultural and business objectives. Aligning objectives to roles within each stage will help. Motivating an employee with the characteristics of each stage may help the HR practitioner or manager cast them in a particular role. An industry may fall into any one quadrant or across multiple quadrants, and an organisation can use the associated characteristics to appeal to their customers.

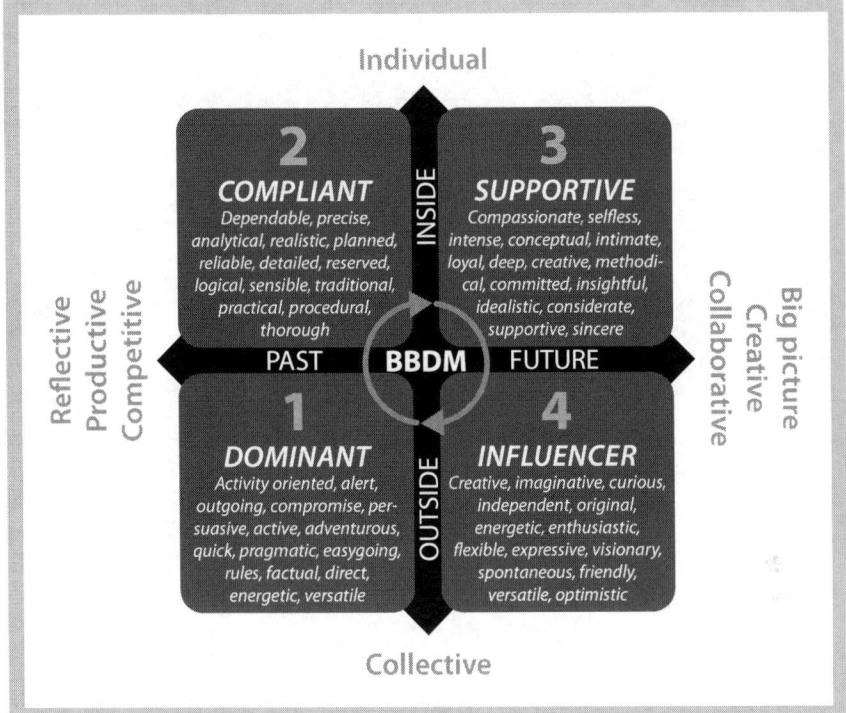

Insights to characteristics of each development stage

25. PREPARING EMPLOYEES FOR RAPID CHANGE

'Culture eats strategy for breakfast.'

Peter Drucker

INSTILLING A HIGH-PERFORMANCE CULTURE

Leaders without the positive attributes of Ei may have a limited concept of how visionary strategy works and how social connection supports it. Hopefully by now you believe all behaviours can be adapted and there is an optimal cycle of development. The BBDM approach to transformational change centres on fostering employee capability and innovation by understanding the divergent functions within an organisation that define and motivate different behaviours. By understanding an employee's progress and how divergent attributes assist or detract from their engagement, work environments can be designed and training programs targeted to maximise performance in each functional area.

For example, HR can create positive workplaces by being seen to act independently, promoting trusting, collaborative relationships and encouraging individuality. Building the future-directed, big-picture attributes of intuition and perception in the workplace is a product of these objectives. When combined with Ei programs and directed for purpose, these right-brain characteristics will support innovation. HR's primary role in encouraging behaviours is to promote trusting relationships throughout the organisation, allowing the freedom to experiment.

25. Preparing employees for rapid change

Finance, admin, IT, sales, customer service, engineering, marketing and the leadership team have different roles and objectives as represented in the BBDM. Aligning these divergent roles and objectives is essential to increasing workplace capability and innovation. A new recruit or graduate begins work experience in a stage 1 role. For a fledgling accountant this may be bookkeeping or even data entry. After learning the foundations of the business, their roles will rise to stage 2 attributes, building skills in analysis, process improvement, customer service and team dynamics, allowing them to acquire knowledge and build up their identity and self-belief. Every organisation is different, and these career pathways and role distinctions should be encouraged by managers and HR learning and development. The following figure shows some functional objectives of each stage.

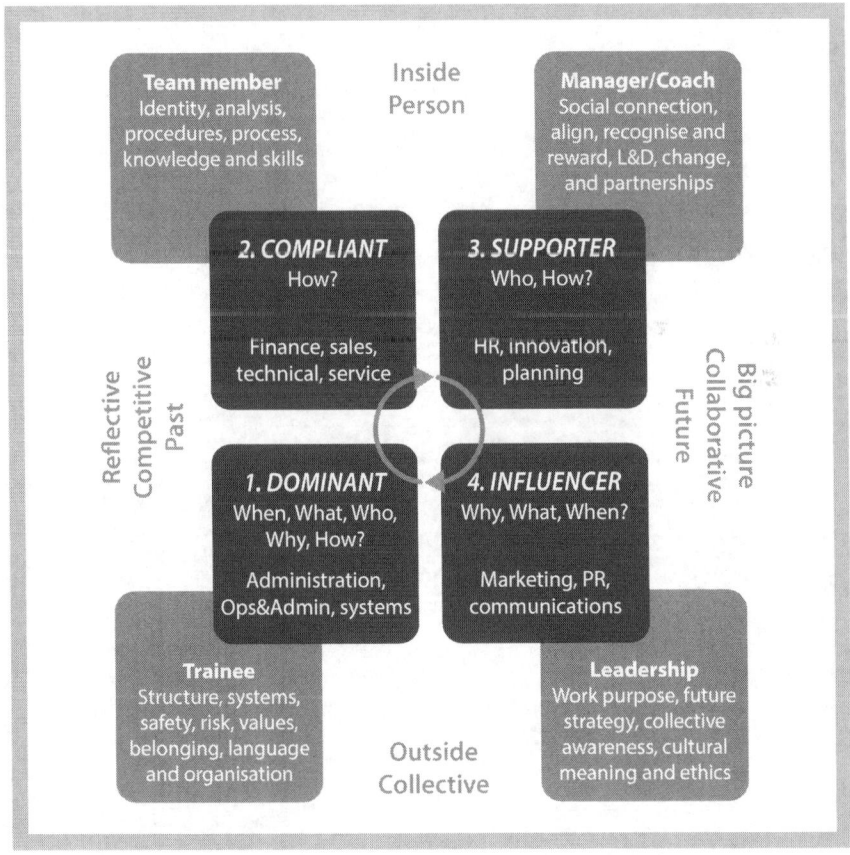

The BBDM: balancing functional objectives

There are four progressive stages of professional development needs, as shown in the following table.

DEVELOPMENT STAGE	STYLE	LEARNING AND DEVELOPMENT CHARACTERISTICS
1. Trainee	Dominant	Promote an inclusive, safe workplace; assign a mentor; educate in core values, systems, safety, rules.
Balance fears	Who, what, when, where, how?	Requires proof/evidence; factual; considers consequences; mitigates risk, cautious.
		Needs to be correct.
		Orderly and conformist.
		Avoids criticism.
2. Team member	Compliant	Seeks validation, recognition, team involvement; accommodating; competes for identity; respects authority; knows the customer; calculating; plans; can be selfish; answers a question with a question.
Balance insecurity	How?	Needs harmony, stability, security.
		Avoids conflict and saying no.
		Can be reserved and quiet.
3. Manager	Supportive	Respects individual views; social; independent thoughts; rewards diversity; inclusive; creative; in the moment; tells stories; open and honest; motivational; natural; easily distracted.
Balance trust	Who, how?	Needs to be liked, connected.
		Avoids detail, accountability, rejection.
4. Leader	Influencer	Results orientated; urgent; dynamic; opportunistic; outcome driven; has goals and milestones; values efficiency.
Balance security	Why, what, when?	Will say no.
		Adaptable, authoritative and independent.
		Needs results and outcomes, and truth.
		Time-bound.
		Avoids failure, indecision, sympathy, carelessness.

Understanding development characteristics for each quadrant

By applying a behavioural approach to business transformation, the BBDM increases engagement and motivates a change-ready workplace in support of strategic growth. Considering and aligning behaviours for growth is a very different approach to how most organisations currently direct business performance and change, which is primarily focused on financial outcomes. This is a new avenue for accelerating business performance.

SEVEN STEPS TO OPTIMISE BUSINESS GROWTH AND CULTURAL TRANSFORMATION

As a leader and a change agent, are you ready to implement an evolving, adaptive, proactive culture built on purposeful objectives to empower growth strategies? If so, you are ready to implement the BBDM development approach that automatically adjusts to community expectations and market opportunities. Below I overview an approach to rapidly transform your business and culture to achieve this objective. Ensuring you have the right environment for change is essential.

1. Ei programs for leaders and managers to empower change and growth

In the words of Steve Jobs, promote 'an incredibly collaborative company'. It's important to ensure the HR department and management team have the resilience and preparation to administer the change head on when embarking on a business transformation, system upgrade or to improve business performance. Successful companies prove that an employee-centric approach sets them apart from their competitors, who may be plagued with employee apathy and turnover. Empowered employees are more productive, engaged and loyal, and contribute positively to a company's financial goals, which assists future growth.

Ei expresses personal qualities, trust and individualism. Those proficient in Ei engage easily with others whom they intuitively perceive to be emotionally intelligent. Social rehearsal is one way to lift emotional awareness, but this can be difficult if you are surrounded by socially reclusive people. People who are emotionally centred tend to be more respectful of others and happier, as they use their individual perspectives and senses to develop greater security and meaning.

Ei is the key to adapting a growth mindset, and ensures managers are well equipped to guide employees through change objectives.[43] Identify leaders and managers who need Ei coaching.

2. Creating a powerful story to implement strategy

Ensure there is a compelling reason for change and the communications department is equipped to deliver it. A revised company vision, strategy and values should support employee growth and community development. Better still, it should be built bottom up to encourage employee ownership. The communications department is responsible for telling the story, reinforcing the strategy and ensuring everyone is abreast of developments. Regular newsletters should highlight community events and achievements, and feature how the organisation works in support of the community. They should also keep people abreast of change initiatives and corporate results. Employees love this level of information – it is meaningful reality at work, and builds a strong corporate identity as well as employee pride and self-belief.

3. Intelligent dashboards

All employees should be aware of and understand how changes may reinvigorate each function. A compelling strategy translates into results when complemented by intelligent dashboards. An intelligent dashboard is a data visualisation tool that displays the status of business analytics metrics, key performance indicators (KPIs) and important data points for an organisation, department, team or process. A balanced scorecard links customer and community outcomes, people development and processes and systems. Use the BBDM to bring in pertinent behavioural objectives, including emotional development. Ensure optimal value drivers are articulated and the right behaviours exhibited. These also need to be included in employee development plans. Behavioural objectives should not be forced on employees – it

---

43   Further reading on this topic: *An Everyone Culture: Becoming a deliberately developmental organisation*, Robert Kegan and Lisa Laskow Lahey.

should be their decision to adapt. Ensure the business is in tune with the psychology of dashboarding to avoid the high failure rates common in dashboard implementations. The best approach is to develop the dashboard bottom-up.

It's important to put a performance framework in place to encourage the behaviours necessary to challenge employees to develop and foster the associated characteristics of an open, innovative organisation.

An effective dashboard is an asset for any organisation to feedback progress and – when implemented properly – the organisation should see a rapid return on investment.

4. Systems alignment

One outcome of the Ei programs, agile teams and BBDM framework is that coaching and deeper investigative analysis may show a need for process and systems alignment, improvement or upgrade. Implementing an Ei program and realigning behaviours is recommended prior to any technology modification as it prepares the organisation for change and allows it to gauge process and systems enhancements. If the implementation of the technology platform is likely to disrupt the organisation, inhibit creativity or undermine cross-functional collaboration then it should be reconsidered.

Ensure the HR-managed performance framework and the financial planning and analysis (FP&A) management reporting structure are complementary and aligned to encourage behavioural change and business growth.

5. People focus

Every employee needs to be involved in a change process. The transformational team working with HR, finance and functional heads should ensure that every department supports organisational growth. High-performing organisations employ similar value objectives. It is important to work with management to identify your particular values and competitive advantages in each community to help motivate employee performance. The transformation objectives should be relevant and meaningful to employees and their community. Most importantly, HR coaches should work with managers to ensure each employee is motivated to optimise performance methods and embrace change.

Encouraging flatter structures and agile teams simplifies the environment and is more effective, making business improvement more about personal growth while ensuring the appropriate feedback of information to the management team. Managers act as facilitators and coaches to build trust and respect by focusing on relationships.

Organising employees into self-supporting teams will also prepare them for change. These self-supporting teams should assist members who are not convinced of the benefits. Teams need to be open, respectful, supportive and inclusive, from the executive through to administration, so as to explore how their development can be woven into the fabric of the organisation and how to promote their own and other teams' growth.

Studies of classroom environments indicate interaction at a micro level creates group identities that affect the perception of peers and facilitators. Facilitators create and impose identities on employees, influencing their ability and motivation to learn. Employees networking with their peers have an equally important role in the learning environments. Identities are generated at different levels:

- facilitators create and develop identities for employees
- employees create and develop identities for facilitators
- employees create and develop identities for each other.

Thus, a 'community of practice' (Walters, 1996) is created that is not fixed, but that is important in learning the language. These group learning and language inference dynamics are important when coaching a team.

Teams develop strong capabilities and identities. Many forward-looking companies are already on board. Here is some text from the ANZ bank's website, expressing their intention to move to agile teams:

> ANZ is scaling agile across parts of the company to enable us
> to respond more quickly to changing customer expectations,

engage and empower staff, and continue to improve efficiency. This transformation is starting in our Australia Division. Agile at scale is a proven approach for running businesses based on small, autonomous, multi-disciplinary teams. It is used by leading digital companies such as Spotify and Google and in large financial services companies such as ING and ABN AMRO. ANZ already uses agile to deliver around 20% of our technology and digital projects, including initiatives such as Apple Pay.

Whether a bank, an accounting firm or a function within an organisation, multidisciplinary agile teams broaden capability and support a strong, outcome-driven, solutions-focused unit empowering business improvement.

6. A simplified, customised approach

No two companies are the same, so each business performance transformation and approach will be different. Business environments may be complex, but they don't have to be. A central objective of a business performance transformation should be to get back to basics and explore ways to engage and challenge employees to grow in support of strategy. One way is to canvass employee improvements in given areas by asking them to identify their biggest challenges and roadblocks on post-it notes under key headings on a whiteboard. All suggestions should be analysed and prioritised for their growth potential.

7. An open-source change approach

Encouraging the individual to change, trust the process and adapt should be inherent in the process. The primary objective of any change management program is to build understanding and a strong association between the individual and the organisation in defining roles, responsibilities and expectations to support their purpose and willingness to change. Once established, the organisation and individual can work together for their mutual benefit. The organisation can now actively involve the individual in defining, supporting and executing strategy and continuously improving and innovating.

In highlighting the key attributes above, the change approach for success promotes:

1   Individual contributions make sense when accompanied by a compelling change story.

2   Successful change programs take a bottom-up, inside-out approach.

3   Change happens when individuals alter their thinking, beliefs and behaviour to align with a business's objectives.

4   Transformation involves changing minds in the organisation.

5   Admired senior managers should be role models for the desired behaviours.

6   Individuals must embrace change – they will be more committed when they choose for themselves.

7   IT, processes and rewards must align to the new behaviours.

* * *

An employee's requirement for purpose and growth influences their choice of role within an organisation in a particular location. Management must respect that the potential of the individual may be largely unrealised. A supportive manager and HR department – together with leading technology and processes designed around change management principles – will ensure a smooth, positive learning experience. The underlying requirement in achieving this equilibrium is trust.

The following Boston Consulting Group table provides an alternative insight into the characteristics of high-performing organisations. Leadership, organisation design, people, change management, culture and engagement are key determinants of high-performing, successful organisations.

EXHIBIT 1 | Highly Effective Companies Manifest 14 Characteristics

LEADERSHIP	• High-performance teams of individual leaders drive urgency and direction • The pipeline is stocked with future leaders whose skills are matched to future needs • Middle managers embrace and translate strategy
DESIGN	• Structure and resource allocation reflect strategic tradeoffs • Few layers separate the CEO and the frontline, and spans of control are wide • Accountabilities, decision rights, and collaboration are constructed with thoughtful consideration • Individual capabilities are matched to role requirements
PEOPLE	• The employer brand is a core asset • Critical roles and key talents are clearly identified and treated with care • HR is a strategic partner and an enabler of the business
CHANGE MANAGEMENT	• Change is a disciplined cascade • The organization is evolutionary
CULTURE AND ENGAGEMENT	• Culture accelerates strategic objectives • Engagement is measured and cultivated to generate discretionary effort from employees

Source: BCG analysis.

BCG: Highly Effective Companies Manifest 14 Characteristics[44]

A holistic, development-based approach is necessary to transform your organisation into a proactive, strategically aligned, high-performance growth culture built on desirable growth behaviours and bottom-up, meaningful objectives. When a strategy and vision are presented this way and the responsibilities are aligned to the stage objectives in the organisation, the outcome is powerful – all employees are challenged to grow to secure their futures for the benefit of the organisation and the community.

---

44 'High-Performance Organisations', Vikram Bhalla, Jean-Michel Caye, Andrew Dyer, Lisa Dymond, Yves Morieux and Paul Orlander, Boston Consulting Group (BCG), September 2011.

26. UNDERSTANDING DIFFERENT LEARNING STYLES

HOW OUR LEARNING IS INFLUENCED BY OUR EXPERIENCES

Our learning styles evolve over our lifetime as we develop skills, experiences and associations to enable us to view the world from more mature perspectives. In 1984 David Kolb published his learning styles model, from which he developed his learning style inventory. Kolb's adult Experiential Learning Theory is the process of learning through experience, and is specifically defined as 'learning through reflection on doing'. The theory works on two levels: a four-stage cycle of learning, and four separate learning styles, as shown in the following figure.

It is worth noting that Kolb originally released his learning inventory when management styles were very different from today. Even though his theory is still relevant, when applying his theory to the BBDM I have added references from associated frameworks and change management. Much of Kolb's theory is concerned with the learner's internal cognitive processes and shares some similar observations to the BBDM. Like the BBDM's development approach, effective adult learning is seen when a person progresses through a cycle of four stages: (1) having concrete experience, followed by (2) observation of and reflection on that experience, which leads to (3) the formation of abstract concepts (analysis) and generalisations (conclusions), which are then (4) used to test hypotheses in future situations, resulting in new experiences.

Concrete Experience
(doing / having an experience)

Active Experimentation
(planning / trying out what you have learned)

Reflective Observation
(reviewing / reflecting on the experience)

Abstract Conceptualisation
(concluding / learning from the experience)

1. Concrete Experience - (a new experience or situation is encountered, or a reinterpretation of existing experience).

2. Reflective Observation of the New Experience - (of particular importance are any inconsistencies between experience and understanding).

3. Abstract Conceptualization (reflection gives rise to a new idea, or a modification of an existing abstract concept).

4. Active Experimentation (the learner applies their idea(s) to the world around them to see the results).

Kolb's learning cycle[45]

---

45 www.SimplyPsychology.org, Saul McLeod, 2017.

Kolb views learning as an integrated process, with each stage supporting and progressing into the next. A fully developed adult can enter the cycle at any stage and follow it through its logical sequence. Kolb suggests effective learning only occurs when a learner can execute all four stages of the model; therefore, no one stage of the cycle is effective as a learning procedure on its own. This is very similar to the BBDM, although the BBDM emphasises an evolutionary basis, which means that people develop the four levels of competence only after mastering and maturing through each stage. The BBDM also outlines the desired behaviours necessary to enter at any stage. Only a mature, fully developed adult can execute all four stages effectively. People who have not developed a right-brained, big-picture, active-experimentation capability may have difficulty in applying the mature adult, futurist Ei/Ci attributes. To synchronise Kolb's styles to the BBDM, the bold, italic references ('global' and 'intuitive') were moved to balance the model and ensure the BBDM cycle remains true.

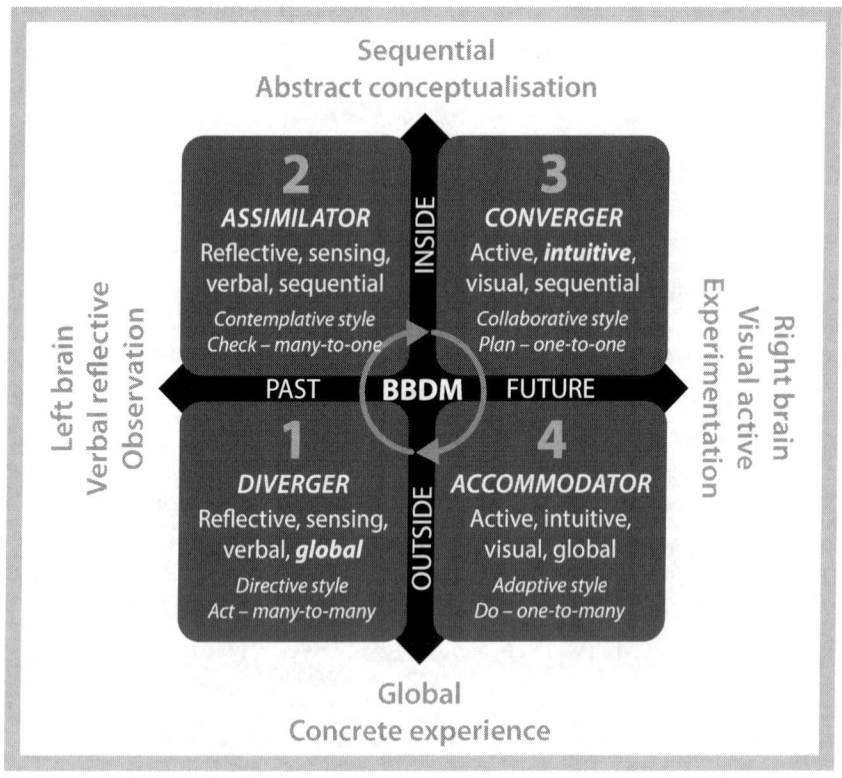

Evolving learning styles (adapted from Kolb's LSI)

26. Understanding different learning styles

According to Kolb, experiential learning for a fully developed adult can take place without instruction, and is indicative of the individual's direct experience in discovering meaning. As a complete learning cycle, experiential learning is said to be more efficient than passive learning such as reading or listening. Though gaining knowledge occurs naturally, a genuine learning experience requires certain elements, and – according to Kolb – knowledge is continuously gained through both personal and environmental experiences. Kolb states that to gain genuine knowledge from an experience:

1   the learner must be actively involved in the experience (stages 1 and 4)

2   the learner must be able to reflect on the experience (stages 1 and 2)

3   the learner must possess and use analytical skills to conceptualise the experience (stages 2 and 3)

4   the learner must have the decision-making and problem-solving skills to use the new ideas gained from the experience (stages 3 and 4).

According to Kolb, Concrete Experience (CE) emphasises active involvement, relating to other people, and learning by experience. Learners in the CE phase are open-minded and adaptable, sensitive to their own and other people's feelings.

Reflective Observation (RO) is the stage in which the learner watches and listens, and looks at issues from various points of view to develop their understanding of the learning material through self-talk.

Abstract Conceptualisation (AC) is the application of reasoning and logic to the learning situation. Planning, creating theories and scenarios, respecting capabilities, and reasoned analysis between the positives and negatives are part of this stage. Although Kolb excludes feelings, a measure of Ei is required to ensure the best people are selected to implement the preferred approach.

The last stage is Active Experimentation (AE), which involves testing and applying the scenarios, carrying out plans, and influencing people and events through activity.

Kolb believes that a complete cycle of learning involves each of these stages, and specifically identifies implementing plans as part of the AC stage, and the adaptive attributes of the AE stage as better able to put learning into practice and to predict what happens next by formulating strategic plans.

FOUR LEARNING STYLES

Since students often use all four stages, Kolb combined scores to determine which of the four learning styles an individual preferred. He encouraged students to become familiar with their own learning style and its strengths and weaknesses to get more out of each learning experience. Let's have a look …

1. Divergers (inductee/trainee – concrete experiencer/reflective observer)

Functions: operations, administration, systems, risk, shop floor, data entry, clerical

Divergers (many-to-many associations) are best at using the experience and observation steps to learn. They can view situations from different perspectives, and take experiences and think about them, thus allowing multiple possibilities in terms of what they may mean. They:

- are adept at gathering information
- tend to have broad interests
- prefer to involve themselves in an experience and generate ideas
- like to ask 'why'
- start from detail to systematically work up to a conclusion
- enjoy participating and working with others, but like a calm ship and fret over conflict
- are generally influenced by other people
- like constructive feedback and to learn via logical instruction or hands-on exploration with conversations that lead to discovery.

Instructional methods that suit Divergers include:

- lecture method – focusing on specifics such as the strengths, weaknesses and uses of a system

- hands-on exploration of a system

- the instructor interacting with students, answering questions and making suggestions.

Ready reference guides and cheat sheets provide handy, organised summaries for this kind of student.

The BBDM perspective

Trainees and junior employees new to the organisation are able to assume any number of the functional roles outlined above. An inductee should be encouraged to undertake a variety of roles during their first one to three years, to help them bond, learn the language and acronyms, and understand the systems, operations, health and safety, policies, values, and how to act among their peers. This also allows them to determine which function they would prefer to specialise in at the next stage. A prospective recruit usually selects an organisation with similar values and motivations. Consider if they will fit in prior to employing them. Appoint an Assimilator/Compliant as a mentor for a Diverger.

2. Assimilators (team member/leader – abstract conceptualiser/reflective observer)

Functions: finance, IT, sales, service, engineering, supply chain

Assimilators have the most cognitive approach, preferring to observe and think rather than act. They ask, 'What is there I can know?', and, 'How?', and they prefer organised, structured understanding. They can create theoretical models, identify ideas that predict outcomes, and describe how different factors interact. They tend to respect expert knowledge, and prefer lectures for learning with demonstrations where possible, but are not comfortable randomly exploring a system. They

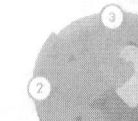

like to get the right answer to a problem and use inductive reasoning, and can usually come up with logical explanations.

Instructional methods to suit Assimilators include:

- lecture method (or video/audio presentation) followed by a demonstration

- exploration of a subject in a lab, following a prepared tutorial (which they will probably stick to quite closely) for which answers should be provided.

These students may need less intensive instruction, as they will follow prepared exercises carefully.

The BBDM perspective

This stage is all about encouraging the development of individual identities, strengths and specialisations to build confidence and self-belief. Team involvement helps students to differentiate themselves from their peers in a healthy, competitive way. Once a student has selected a functional specialisation, they are introduced to a functional team. Team members should be encouraged to be active and to contribute. Members should agree on their strengths and which roles they are best placed to undertake, and their capabilities will broaden over time. Scrum sprints, agile teams and huddles are great ways to build a spirit of contribution and define specialist roles to complete tasks. Roles may be fluid and assigned to challenge individuals.

Decisions may be agreed by the team and then rationalised to the manager, who may either agree or provide alternatives. Teams should be encouraged to compete against each other across the organisation, across similar organisations and in the community. Insecurity is a natural response to not having developed the skills, processes or knowledge to address our limitations. Teamwork ensures everyone has an opportunity to practise, experiment, rehearse, and act out as many different situations and simulations as necessary to build capability. Situational analysis (SWOT analysis) and service design are good ways for students to gain experience and learn to understand the customer, also supplementing their identity and helping them to confirm their career choice. They may then add vocational learning to a role they are passionate about and make a valuable contribution to the company.

An Influencer (Kolb: Accommodator) should be appointed to mentor an Assimilator team; for example, marketing director to mentor the sales team, and communications to support the service team.

3. Convergers (manager – abstract conceptualisation/active experimenter)

Functions: planning, innovation, change, human resources, learning and development

Convergers like to conceptualise, but they also favour the application of concepts. They may draw on their instincts, reason around alternatives, and then try out their ideas to see if they work in practice. They like to ask 'who' and 'how', can provide independent – sometimes creative – perspectives, and seek to improve efficiency by making small, careful changes. Although they are good collaborators, they may prefer to work one-on-one or by themselves, thinking carefully and acting independently. They learn through interaction, so intuitive, computer-based learning may be more effective with them.

Instructional methods that suit Convergers include:

- interactive not passive instruction

- possibly computer-assisted instruction

- problem sets or workbooks.

The BBDM perspective
Since much of a Converger's role is coaching, emotional development should be front and centre of their training if it is not already sufficiently developed. Assuming an Ei capability, I have provided a different perspective on a Converger stage to that used by Kolb. HR can coordinate innovation, development and planning groups consisting of managers from all departments to discuss various scenarios and agree department objectives. On-the-job and community training are the most effective methods, and should be the primary development

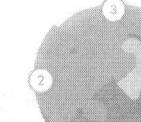

approach for all employees. Objectives and outcomes should be meaningful to the organisation's employees and their community.

The following diagram is used in change management to understand learning processes and delivery. It is similar to the 'OODA loop' (observe–orient–decide–act) developed by US military strategist John Boyd. It also mirrors Kolb's learning cycle and can be used by Convergers to plan for learning and development.

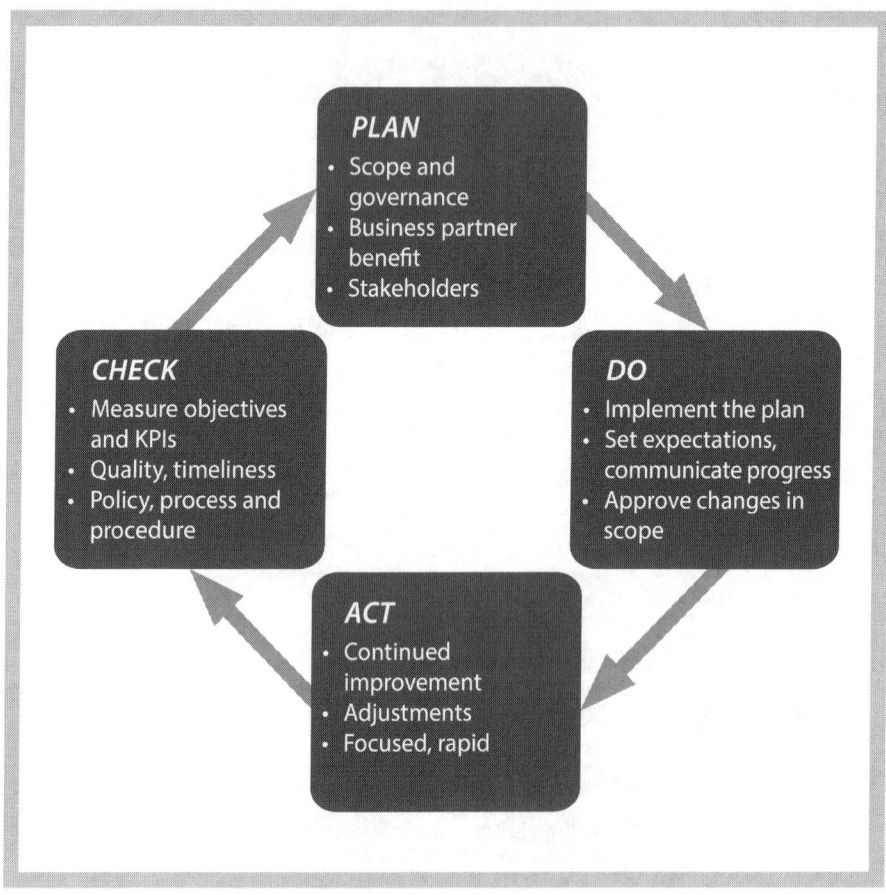

PLAN
- Scope and governance
- Business partner benefit
- Stakeholders

DO
- Implement the plan
- Set expectations, communicate progress
- Approve changes in scope

CHECK
- Measure objectives and KPIs
- Quality, timeliness
- Policy, process and procedure

ACT
- Continued improvement
- Adjustments
- Focused, rapid

Adjusted PDCA management cycle

Team leaders, scrum masters or their delegates may be invited to present to the manager groups to provide updates and explain the success of different programs. Constructive feedback may be filtered to the teams, and managers can agree on further investment where skills are lacking. As well as coaching Assimilators, Convergers should provide support and present to the executive team (Accommodators) on organisational effectiveness and the outcomes of key programs. A balanced scorecard is an excellent tool to focus attention across all requirements, both financial and non-financial, while a project status report is effective for project or program progress reporting.

4. Accommodators (leader – concrete experiencer/active experimenter)

Functions: marketing, public relations, communications, strategy, organisational development

Although I prefer the term Influencer or Inspirer, Accommodators have the most hands-on approach, with a strong preference for doing rather than thinking. They like to question to support their action-first approach, do not like routine, and will take creative risks to see what happens. They understand complexity and can see relationships in the aspects of a system. As might be expected, they like hands-on and practical learning rather than lectures, and seek the meaning in the learning experience. They consider what they can do as well as what others have done previously, often act on intuition rather than careful analysis, and are quick to discard more thoughtful approaches in favour of improvisation. Instructors should expect devil's advocate–type questions, such as 'What if … ?' and 'Why not?'

These teaching methods work well for an Accommodator:

- encouraging independent discovery
- active participation in learning.

The BBDM perspective
Kolb's Accommodator label for this quadrant may indicate his research base were not confident leaders or they were unable to perform in their environment. The alternative Influencer (DiSC) reference is more

attuned to the emotionally developed, charismatic, goal-orientated leader. As highlighted above, the fully developed, culturally competent leader needs little developmental input and can meet their needs on the job, setting out strategy, selling a meaningful vision, defining stretch targets and innovative milestones while governing ethics and intellectual freedoms.

* * *

Although Kolb's Experiential Learning Theory was initially researched and released over 50 years ago, his findings are still highly relevant. His observations were ground-breaking and, being principally based on experience, fully support the BBDM cycle of learning. Every teacher or trainer needs to understand the significance of behavioural and emotional experience as the source of learning and development. *Experiential Learning* by David A. Kolb is a must-read for learning and development coaches. Our positive intuitive core records our experiential learning. Our emotions are used to associate and recall these experiences.

27. PROMOTING DYNAMIC, VISIONARY LEADERSHIP

LEADERS WHO EXPRESS PURPOSEFUL FUTURE STRATEGIES UNDERPIN GROWTH

'In business … what distinguishes leaders from laggards, and greatness from mediocrity, is the ability to uniquely imagine what could be. To get to the future first, top management must either see opportunities not seen by others or must be able to exploit opportunities that others can't … As much as anything, foresight comes from really wanting to make a difference to people's lives.'

Gary Hamel and CK Prahalad, 1994

We engage in life, so we influence life; we are responsible for life inasmuch as we are accountable; what we take from life we are indebted to replace. If we influence life we are morally accountable; in appreciating the rewards of life we are therefore respectful of life. In broadening these ideals outside our realm to support balance in the community, we cooperate to improve the quality and value of life. Expressed in legal terms, we share 'joint and several' liability with every other human being who engages in the continuum of life.

Many people only develop to the extent the environment allows. Cultural leaders who employ visionary strategy and purposeful goals fill our minds with possibilities. We need to appreciate the influence of the creative mind in delivering rewards associated with making a purposeful contribution and guiding us through life. True transformational leaders respect our right to be an individual and our freedom of choice.

As a leadership coach, I appreciate compassion inspires mental toughness and raises awareness. Emotional strength will define the successful leaders of the future, who are selfless in their intentions, can deploy big-picture strategies (spatial awareness), and use critical reasoning to offer balanced perspectives. These leaders are actively working in our businesses and communities today and making a real difference. They don't seek recognition – they earn it.

Command–control leadership styles need to be left in the past. We have all experienced the competitive, 'boss-style' mindsets – people who rely heavily on plotting and short-term tactical plays. These conservative mindsets often introduce skewed values, and may hold the organisation and community back by regulating experiences in response to problems. These conventional, often apathetic boss styles are not equipped to represent long-term visionary strategy, and may be leading us down the wrong path to overpopulation, insecurity and, unless addressed, eventual environmental failure. The truth is, the protected environments they often inhabit limit the development of their big-picture awareness. Bureaucratic policies extinguish creativity and enforce barriers to entry to those inspired to make change. These aspiring leaders need to invest in their emotional development to represent hope and strong, secure direction. Paradoxically, they usually express their insecurities externally rather than dealing with them internally. In overtly adversarial environments, many leaders and politicians appear to have only a limited idea of how to promote community development and longer-term security. Indicative of their underdevelopment, they are more likely to be consumed by personal agendas and will preach fear and insecurity. Conventional and conservative leaders are typically ruled by insecurity and present in command–control styles.

CULTURAL LEADERS MUST TAKE ACTION

Leadership needs to be focused back to the community, where life holds meaning and where people can influence sustainability and future security. Life – and all its rewards – must respond to the environment's ability to sustain it. It's within our natures to preserve and create abundance. This book is a call for leaders to take action. People are not developing to their full capability because their environment does not allow them to. Leaders must represent diverse growth environments, not just productivity and jobs growth. Almost everyone understands this, although many deny it. The organisation's values and governing ethics should be publicly available and display how it supports community development, diversity, equality and social purpose. Every organisation needs to be a social enterprise – they will be the true winners in a world built on social ethics.

Strength in Ei, or self-awareness, supports the strategic power of the humanitarian mind and can be misunderstood when not present in leadership. This is a real issue at a time when emotion and behaviour are too easily discounted by science and academic communities in search of complexity. Without a strong identity and social interaction, the human mind does not develop beyond the child phase to structure a matrix of skills and knowledge around fears and insecurity.

Pure capitalism (left brain) in isolation is no more sustainable than communism (right brain), and will fail if the imbalance is not managed. Far from being a conspiracy, this is reality and truth. The mistrust in our youth and population is an indication that life is more than competitive instincts and materialism: it is about cooperation for emotional growth and mutual respect. This is the only way jobs can be secured, relationships can develop trust, and quality of life can be realised in the future.

Up to now, insecure left-brain thinkers have dominated Western civilisation. The huge imbalance of paternal attributes should not flourish in a balanced world. Many of today's social problems can be traced to these obstructive old-world views. Future conclusions will be drawn from the 'boss' ego and why it inhabits artificial environments, measures life materially and labour as a unit, and aligns itself to hierarchies – and, most importantly, why it disregards emotional development. Without developing emotions and self-awareness, these styles will present in competitive bureaucratic environments. The failure of these industrial age 'boss' styles is we have created a society where weakness is supported and is taken advantage of.

We've probably all experienced or been witness to workplace bullying and reactive cultures. Jim Huse, Director of workplace psychology consultants Huse Hill Associates, says gossip can be symptomatic of a dominating, hierarchical work environment or the lack of understanding between individuals. Gossip thrives in dominating work environments where a pecking order separates the manager from individuals and responsibilities are not clearly defined. Individuals may gossip about the way the organisation is run, about the management, or about each other in a bid to survive and climb the ladder. Employers need to develop a business culture that values and understands its staff and encourages mutual respect. In some instances, no amount of mutual understanding will prevent dislike or insecurity through differences in religion, looks or status. It is easier to confront or ignore gossip if you know you have the support of the organisation.

A strong belief in a leader's ability anchors workforce security. An employee's creative aptitude depends on attaining a level of self-confidence and trust to freely explore their emotional awareness. Organisations can cultivate innovative environments by creating an independent HR function tasked with developing trust and purposeful relationships. By reporting to the board, and with a remit to represent all employees equally, HR leaders will be better placed to cultivate supportive environments, allowing employees to hone their strengths and challenge their limitations. Employee capability is maximised by aligning core competencies and strengths to divergent functional quadrants as represented in the BBDM. Professional development is supported by coaching and networking capability to encourage creative solutions and innovation around perceived market opportunities. In aligning capabilities and needs in a balanced model, an organisation builds an evolving diversity of intelligence and characteristics to adapt skills dynamically to strategic initiatives. Organisations, communities and governments should actively encourage social purpose and connection. Following the example of the Nordic countries, governments and leaders should assume responsibility for social development with a safety net for a more independent, secure and inclusive population. They should focus on community, and emotional and cultural development by making people aware of the need to challenge themselves to emotionally develop. Countries that understand this will be the most progressive and attract the best talent.

Growth is hindered if emotional development is not nurtured and challenged. A culture may develop or deteriorate over time. A rise in insecurity can be seen in the US, Australia, Myanmar, the Philippines, and many other places around the world. The measure of the success or cohesiveness of a community is whether it can pull together in response to opportunities. Isolated communities are an opportunity cost. Strong, purposeful communities fuel emotional connection and growth.

How does our inability to mature express itself? How does ignoring our elevated caretaker responsibility and the stresses of underdevelopment, fixed mindsets, overpopulation and conformity influence our health? Stress shows in many unhealthy ways, and is also a subconscious reaction to boredom and, no doubt, an indicator of controlled growth or decline. On Earth, balance ensures life advances through a natural continuum to increase cultural diversity and knowledge transfer. Diverse environments promote growth by broadening our experiences to increase intelligence and have to be respected.

THE ATTRIBUTES OF INCLUSIVE LEADERSHIP

A leader should embody the human need to develop trusting relationships and purpose. In balancing complex skills with creative attributes, a leader confirms a common belief in identity through cultural purpose. Strategic principles motivate a proactive work environment and raise awareness for sustainable growth. The vision is clear and inspires. Supporting professional development, aligning core capabilities, and promoting behavioural growth create a business environment that adapts to market opportunities and evolves dynamically.

The following table shows how to balance personal and community perspectives.

EXTERNAL REALITY (COMMUNITY)	INTERNAL REALITY (PERSONAL)
Inspired story telling	Sense of higher purpose
Collective goals	Personal goals
Respect individuals	Respect diversity
Ethics – moral principles	Learnt characteristics
Cultural values	Personal values
Environmental adaptation	Behavioural acclimatisation
Collective behaviours	Behavioural mastery
Collective awareness	Cultural intelligence
Inspiration/charisma	Self expression

Balancing personal and community perspectives

Knowing that emotional associations and experiences broaden our emotional bandwidth and build our capability, leaders of the future must ensure their visions and strategies promote functioning communities and an environment with plenty of room to roam and play, where communities promote inclusion and allow the young freedom to explore, experiment, associate and identify. Companies that support the development of our communities will be the first choice for top talent. First and foremost, we need to focus on our own communities to correct the imbalances. For those who seek to limit our freedoms, to protect, regulate and control, please respect our need to experience and grow to realise wellbeing.

To make their dreams a reality versus the many who just talk, a leader requires clarity on what specific results to accomplish. What's your Why? Reasons come first, solutions come second. How will you do it? What tools, strategies or resources do you need to make it happen? Whose guidance or help will speed up your results? Those who stick to their values and goals have an understanding of why they are doing what they are doing. They have a purpose and meaning that's a selfless motivating driver towards the goal. When you set your goals, be sure they truly excite and inspire you.

Take for example billionaire tech entrepreneur Elon Musk, who is CEO of both Tesla and SpaceX. He gets a lot done in part because he has a strong Why and has a solid belief in his ability. 'The thing that drives me is that I want to be able to think about the future and feel good about that,' says Musk, speaking to a group of governors gathered in July. 'We are doing what we can to have the future be as good as possible, to be inspired by what is likely to happen and to look forward to the next day.'

Once you have an understanding of why your vision is important, the next step is to create a strategy and to identify the tools that will help you manifest what you want. Without a plan, your vision will remain a dream and a prayer.

Every community on this planet has the power to make their environment sustainable and liveable. People need to cooperate, experiment and learn. We are accountable and responsible for our own environment, and we have the creative power to bring sustainability and environmental diversity to secure our communities. The massive wealth accumulated by the advantaged few cannot be maintained. They carry a huge burden in amassing such wealth when communities are suffering. This includes global corporations and individuals who offshore their tax liabilities. Capital should be spent on supporting communities, with access not determined by size or advantage alone. Economic growth stalls when wealth is not distributed, and increasing youth poverty proves the failure of trickle-down economics. Strategy and future objectives need to account for the collective, not personal agendas. The security of the planet and life must be our first priority – a selfless consideration.

Cooperating for security has allowed human beings to broaden our emotional bandwidth, supporting greater intelligence for developing and adapting to different environments. Our quest for the meaning of life is driven by our inherent appreciation of its beauty as a social unit within a community. A strong sense of contribution and connection gives heightened purpose, empowerment and understanding.

4

CONCLUSION: WE ALL HAVE WORK TO DO

Best Behaviour explores how 200 million years of human behavioural evolution mirrors a person's development lifecycle. Like Maslow's Hierarchy of Needs, a framework of stage objectives is presented for progressive intellectual and capability development.

The book's underlying assumption is behaviour guides our capability; we are all born into the world with very similar behaviour characteristics, essentially a blank canvas. We evolve and adapt over time according to our environment following a progression of intellectual programming and behavioural development. As we complete the encoding of each intellectual stage, we then adjust our behaviour to focus on the next level of capability.

Whereas IQ is lateral and analytical, Ei is an automatic multidimensional capability delivering an authentic, independent perspective. Being a spatial intelligence, mastering Ei requires a solid foundation of knowledge and self-confidence to help position a person's awareness in the present. It is boosted by trusting your intuition (emotional associations tag our experiences) and developing a strong sense of self-awareness to expose a powerful ability to leverage relationships for purpose. The BBDM framework allows individuals and businesses to align behaviours and support this difficult stage of development, for mutual benefit. The critical reasoning skills Ei promotes substantially increase our capability.

Ei supports social skills and connection, and organisations need to take responsibility for developing the skills as a public responsibility or social good. The benefits to an organisation are substantial as people are better able to engage and share ideas. Many of today's social problems relate to people being disconnected and unable to appreciate the benefits and ease of relating to other people. The major expansion of our human intelligence happened during the rise of civilisations, with social interaction being the major driver. This evolutionary hurdle is still being tested, as evident in our outdated hierarchical organisations and divisive political systems that are more likely to impede connection and collaboration. We need to breathe life and energy into these outdated structures. As individuals, if we fail to engage this expansive intellectual capacity then we fail to evolve. Inasmuch as energy or light is a constant, so is evolution. If we are not challenging and expanding our capability then we fail to appreciate life's rewards. We easily become bored and unhappy if we are not challenged to grow or if our environment does not allow.

We humans develop our humanitarian hemisphere through honing our emotional awareness (Ei) and cultural awareness (Ci) by showing empathy and being passionate guardians of our community. From early childhood we are programmed to identify security as we develop skills to balance our insecurities. Immersing ourselves in life and caring for the environment both productively and sustainably fuels our passion. This allows us to realise our spatial awareness to plan for future security by engaging our executive functions for big-picture understanding. When directed purposefully and proactively, emotions help to address our weaknesses and empower our cultural competence, allowing us to engage a full spectrum of behaviours for adaptation. Our strengthening emotions improve the way we work, increase collaboration and support a powerful radar in search of growth opportunities. This fully developed leadership capability is 64 (4^3) times more powerful than our baseline conditioning intelligence, known as the monkey brain to some, to others a productive unit of labour.

More than a realisation, accepting the challenge to emotionally mature involves a complete reversal of direction. Trauma or a life challenge may reveal the need to change and drive your growth. However, our over-structured environments can easily create a barrier to confronting our emotional growth, limiting our personal search for purpose in marriage, relationships or cultural identity. Rather than promoting a productivity mindset fixated on cost control and its divisiveness, social connection should be encouraged in the workplace and community to support emotional strength and meaning. We are made for growth. We need to let it happen.

The key to balancing the mind and using its full potential is to unlock our creative free spirit and allow our humanitarian awareness to work unhindered. You need to unclutter and free the mind to realise its true capability and be aware of the potential around you. It takes an understanding that the duality of behavioural opposites are in fact pathways to growth, from fear to trust, insecurity to security. HR and managers can and must lead the way with emotional development. Having adopted a coaching mindset, they can begin to selectively realign employees in their organisation for growth and, if necessary, to assist employees who are ready to take on the challenge to grow emotionally. The environment must be inclusive and respectful for people to grow.

Motivations guide us and give rise to our strengths and purpose – 'the Why' is what defines us. We need to move beyond face value and instant gratification to find deeper meaning to engage this powerful capability. There are however many obstacles to achieving this level of awareness. The more we understand about how we got here, the more we can define the future to lead a life of fulfilment and passion. So why is this so important to managers and HR leaders? If you are not feeling or searching for deeper meaning, then you may be engaging only a fraction of your potential. If too focused on compliance, you may be neglecting the growth of your organisation. Compliance is important but can be delegated to those who need to learn the skills. Leaders need to focus on relationships, strategy and securing the future. Strategy empowers growth and superior profits.

Security is built on a common belief in a future that needs peace and harmony to enjoy life's rewards. By trusting in our environment, we are able to build trust in ourselves to realise our own Ei. As we do that, we gradually refocus our past protectionist instincts on our present internal locus of control, both unique and creative. We can then direct our capability to future growth.

A strong desire to cooperate in support of a vision will switch our perceptions to the future to implement creative solutions. We are all gifted with the power to create security, but only common acceptance will provide the level of truth required to pass our valuable intelligence on to future generations. We must love this internal power to harness it.

Collaboration is the key to developing and unlocking our ability to understand the extensive span of our highly adaptable, emotionally fuelled, creative minds. Imbalances in society are being questioned and may manifest as stress in the individual. Our potential as a species is being tested, and our inability to create balance may obscure our quest for growth. We can put things right and secure our environments. It will take some work, but the rewards will be substantial and benefit your business and our society as a whole. The focus just needs to be directed back to our communities, where people derive meaning and can discover their purpose.

Growth is supported by a strong will to survive and a will to understand life's meaning. It is an expression of our relationship with our environment and represents our superior ability to adapt and succeed. Experiences and associations are an important enabler of our capability, and our environmental connection is a measure of our success. Anyone can be developed into a leader if the environment allows. HR professionals and leaders have a responsibility to create safe environments where people can engage, experiment and challenge themselves to grow. The most successful periods in history looked to the future and applied knowledge to promote security and guardianship to advance life.

Nelson Mandela, Mahatma Gandhi, Martin Luther King: our most respected leaders stood symbolically against life's inequalities to present their own truths in rallying the population behind a common belief in humanity. These self-assured leaders had security of purpose and a selfless collaborative spirit. They employed big-picture strategy rather than competitive personality politicking that only confounds strategy. Organisations and politics must change to remove this element of behaviour as it feeds on insecurity. Leaders must promote inclusive, connected communities and a vision of the future. Jacinda Ardern, Oprah Winfrey, Michelle Obama and Justin Trudeau are indicative of the positive, secure leadership styles of the future. These leaders are not about self-promotion but are driven by a deep sense of purpose and fairness.

The creative mind is essential to support understanding, inspiration and humour in an independent, healthy human being. Leaders who symbolise the importance of identity and value the contribution of individuals are in short supply in a world in need of direction. Failure to recognise this value driver disadvantages countries and organisations in an evolving new world as creative intelligence is used for substantial change, progression and innovation.

This book presents a very unique view on organisational development. The framework has been crafted acknowledging the search for security, mathematical symmetry, balance in the duality of opposites, and is based on several underlying hypotheses. It is not for the faint-hearted. It is pitched to the top quartile of HR leaders and managers who know who they are, value their capability, and respect human potential. To those charismatic leaders who have developed compassionate hearts, the BBDM provides a holistic, complete, inclusive, balanced organisational development tool to coach the diversity of capability and promote the relationships required to motivate employee growth, connect strategy, to innovate and supercharge output.

Humanity is being tested. If we are to succeed, our elementary survival instincts need to be relegated. Our political system, economic theory and banking and monetary systems are built on basic competitive instincts. We need to broaden their objectives to support and connect communities. Our higher humanitarian capabilities are

Ei (Creative) and cultural (Environmental) intelligence. By encouraging a cultural belief in the community, social connection anchors our highest human need to interact and establish meaningful relationships in support of a life purpose. A cultural leader expresses purposeful goals to help our youth to develop skills to sustain life in the future. Culture is not about the past: it is about building a belief in the future to bring trust and truth to social interaction for prolonged sustainability. What we don't have today we will create very quickly when balance is represented and intelligence is purposely engaged and directed.

It's time to get serious about behaviour, because our insensitivity and disconnection are having a perverse impact on how we live and interact in our environment.

We can't expect to be true guardians of our environment until we understand and are aware of its diversity and beauty. The evolution of our Ei and cultural intelligence is closely aligned to our custodian acceptance of the planet we live in. The framework to bring balance to secure our world is outlined in this book.

TESTIMONIALS

'Highly recommended. Tony Holmwood has written a challenging and transformative book that firmly puts HR and people development back into the mainstream of corporate strategy. In drawing from sources as diverse as Maslow, Dweck, Myers–Briggs, Kolb and others to inform and create his Balanced Behavioural Development Model (BBDM), Tony has developed a well-rounded and ultimately new way of looking at the role of personal development in the corporate space – and how to implement it. *Best Behaviour* is a book that is destined to be viewed as a game changer in years to come.'

Geoff Hetherington – The Profitability Coach
(www.geoffhetherington.com)

'Tony presents some thought-provoking and ground-breaking insights that will enable HR managers to coach their employees, thereby helping them discover their intrinsically driven purpose and engaging and empowering them to more productively develop and grow.'

Dr John Demartini – International best-selling author of
The Values Factor

'Tony presents a practical and innovative coaching framework that helps HR and line managers build more emotionally intelligent employees – for better business outcomes.'

Siobhan McHale – EGM HR at Dulux Group

'Tony in his book *Best Behaviour* eloquently captures the real and lasting impact of emotional intelligence as a critical leadership skill impacting not only employee engagement and creativity but sustainable business results.

'Emotional intelligence is the critical leadership factor differentiating a "Great Leader" from a "Good Leader" in the workplace!

'As Tony has identified in his book, leaders with high levels of emotional intelligence understand that when employees feel "safe" in the workplace, they are not only happier and perform better, they are more likely to contribute their ideas freely and develop better solutions through tapping into their creative potential.'

Sonia Motum, Executive Coaching and Development (www.energycoaching.net.au)

'A book so needed in our corporate world. Emotional wellbeing and emotional intelligence, while talked about, often lack in practice. Tony's insights bridge the gaps. He ties the mind–body connections with practical and pragmatic frameworks.'

Arishma Singh, Founder, Thrive With EFT (www.thrivewitheft.com)

'With exponential technology changing the face of business and corporate life, most leaders forget the first exponential technology is people. Tony's book *Best Behaviour* is a definitive guide on how to lead, manage and coach people. *Best Behaviour* is a comprehensive, research-driven road map that should be on every business owner's and corporate leader's bookshelf. Implementing the information in this book will give the reader an almost unfair advantage in their ability to harness people power.'

David Dugan, Business Coach and Mentor, Abundance Global (www.abundance.global)

'This book challenges business and HR leaders to rethink three culturally-defining fundamentals: organisational purpose, performance and people development. Tony links his BBDM model to existing theories and practice, providing ample evidence in support of his ultimate assertion – that through developing emotional intelligence to genuinely empower our people, our workplaces will become more socially and environmentally connected. With disruption, constant change and a blurring of work–life boundaries now the norm, I wholeheartedly agree that the future of organisational success depends on this authentic approach.'

Helen D'Arcy, Principal Consultant, The Learning Pyramid

'The thing I love about *Best Behaviour* is that Tony gives a methodology that to the employer and their HR team feels scalable, but to the individual would feel very tailored and personal. Surely this is the dream HR process.'

Marty Wilson, Resilience Through Change Expert, TED Speaker (www.martinwilson.com)

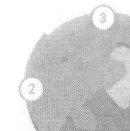

'Positive energy = Growth

'Tony has hit the nail on the head here and it is this and many considered a-ha moments throughout his book that make this such an invaluable resource for those in people management and leadership support. It is rare that we effectively see the marriage of harnessed personal experience and corporate insight as effectively as Tony so embodies. He is 100 per cent on message and as such brings his framework to life. Here's to a seismic business shift triggered by *Best Behaviour!*'

Rhys Parry Badkin, Chief Enthusiast and Transformational Coach, Get A Quick Word

'Tony brings novel ideas to the forefront of people dynamics in change and the role of the organisation in getting the most of their talent. Human resources (HR) is often viewed as a compliance activity, more focused on getting information boxes ticked than on ensuring a good fit with strategy and strong employee engagement, development and performance. Bringing the talent management back into business strategy, highlighting that the human capital plan must fit hand-in-glove with the strategic plan, this book will deliver exponential value to the business and the aspirations of individuals.'

Irene Vervliet, Organisational Change Thought Leader, Author of *Take Action*

WWW.OUTPERF4M.COM